Understanding Records

Understanding Records

A Field Guide To Recording Practice

Jay Hodgson

continuum

2010

The Continuum International Publishing Group Inc
80 Maiden Lane, New York, NY 10038

The Continuum International Publishing Group Ltd
The Tower Building, 11 York Road, London SE1 7NX

www.continuumbooks.com

Library of Congress Cataloging-in-Publication Data
Hodgson, Jay.
Understanding records : a field guide to recording practice / by Jay Hodgson.
    p. cm.
    Includes bibliographical references.
    ISBN-13: 978-1-4411-6950-1 (hardcover: alk. paper)
    ISBN-10: 1-4411-6950-4 (hardcover: alk. paper)
    ISBN-13: 978-1-4411-5607-5 (pbk.: alk. paper)
    ISBN-10: 1-4411-5607-0 (pbk.: alk. paper) 1. Popular music—Production
and direction. 2. Popular music—Analysis, appreciation. 3. Sound recordings—
Production and direction. I. Title.

    ML3470.H64 2010
    781.49—dc22   2010004157

ISBN: 978-1-4411-6950-1 (Hardback)
ISBN: 978-1-4411-5607-5 (Paperback)

Typeset by Pindar NZ, Auckland, New Zealand
Printed and bound in the United States of America by Sheridan Books, Inc

Contents

Introduction

It is generally agreed that what people do to make and hear a record — which I call "Recording Practice" — is different than what they do to make and hear a live musical performance.[1] However, almost nothing has been written about Recording Practice which treats it as a totally unique way of musically communicating. Besides a few notable exceptions, analysts and historians have considered Recording Practice nothing more unique than a technological adaptation of live performance practices. Not surprisingly, then, even the most fundamental of record-making techniques — say, compressing and equalizing an incoming audio signal — remains conspicuously absent from the lion's share of published research on music. This leaves researchers and practitioners a very limited collection of writings to consult should they want to understand what people actually hear when they listen to recorded music.

The current dearth of professional research on specific record-making techniques used on commercially available records likely has much to

---

1 I use the term "record" throughout this field guide to designate a complete production, regardless of format. Thus The Beatles' *Sgt. Pepper's Lonely Hearts Club Band* is a record, as is the track "Sgt. Pepper's Lonely Hearts Club Band (reprise)," regardless of format, that is, if distributed on vinyl LP, audio cassette, compact disc, mp3, et cetera.

do with the technical nature of Recording Practice. Musicians and fans often describe record-making as a process which is as equally mystifying and compelling as, say, building a bilge pump. A kind of defensive snobbery has consequently tended to dominate critical, historical and academic commentary on Recording Practice, the vast majority of which treats Recording Practice as only a technical support, something like building scaffolds, for the "true art" of music making. My first goal in composing this field guide was to change that attitude. Recording Practice is a technical affair, to be sure. But it is also immensely artistic. Dave 'Hard Drive' Pensado (in Droney 2003: 145) explains:

> [Recording Practice] is unique, in that you have to be technical, and creative, at the same time. It's hard to imagine [Pablo] Picasso designing the first computer. It's also hard to imagine Bill Gates painting "Guernica." And as a recordist, you have to be Bill Gates for thirty seconds, then Picasso for thirty seconds. You're constantly shifting back and forth.

Recording Practice is a complete, self-sufficient musical language. The likes of Glen Gould and The Beatles said as much when they retired from concert performance altogether in the mid-1950s and mid-1960s, respectively. Their controversial absences from the concert stage loudly proclaimed that, unlike before, success in musical communications could be had just by making records. The technical and aesthetic considerations which guided musical communications for centuries before should no longer apply, these musicians maintained. Most crucially, performability should no longer play a guiding role in record-making. According to Virgil Moorfield (2005: 29), The Beatles' *Revolver* marks the dramatic turning point in this historical development:

> From this album [read: *Revolver*] on . . . The Beatles would experiment with abandon. They dispensed with the concept of 'realism', or what could be called "figurative" recording, often constructing

instead a virtual or imaginary space unconfined by what is possible in the "real" world of live performance on conventional instruments. For [producer George] Martin and The Beatles, the performability of *Revolver* and the groundbreaking records that followed it was not a concern, not only because The Beatles were not obliged to perform live (they retired from touring in 1966), but because the records themselves succeeded in shifting the audience's expectations from a replicated concert experience to something more.

Recording Practice is now the dominant musical language of popular music communications. However, that language remains a total mystery to most listeners. This field guide is designed to rectify this state of affairs. Working their way through this field guide, any interested reader can learn to recognize and reproduce the most fundamental musical terms that recordists use to communicate now. Drawing on records that shaped the postwar pop soundscape, and ensuring that each cited track is available from a reputable online distributor like iTunes, Bleep or Beatport, this field guide:

(i)   explains the fundamental terms of Recording Practice, presented in chronological record-making sequence, that is, in the order they typically arise during a conventional record production;

(ii) explains and elucidates the techniques that recordists use to create those terms;

(iii) provides original audio examples designed to clarify the musical techniques and procedures which those terms operationalize;

(iv) describes, and locates on a number of hit records, common musical uses for those terms; and, finally,

(v)   situates them within the broader record-making process at large.

This field guide is by no means exhaustive. Recording Practice is an immense, and immensely complicated, topic which requires volumes of encyclopedic exposition to comprehensively elucidate. The musical techniques I survey in this field guide are simply those that recur most often on modern pop records. In so doing, they comprise a fundamental musical lexicon, or a basic musical vocabulary. Aside from a few pioneering exceptions, though, this lexicon remains notably absent from professional research on popular music history and practice. Surprisingly, these musical terms are also absent from the vast majority of audio-engineering textbooks currently on the market, which usually only sketch the technical details of Recording Practice without explicitly referencing any of the aesthetic programs that recordists deploy their musical practice to service.

Gaps in knowledge are to be expected in a field as young and diffuse as popular music studies.[2] Numerous insightful and challenging analyses of record-making have indeed emerged in the last two decades.[3] But these studies typically address the analytic priorities and concerns of disciplines which are not primarily interested in musical technique *per se*, like cultural studies, sociology, media studies, cultural anthropology and political-economics. As such, Recording Practice usually fails to register in these disciplines as a fundamentally musical affair. A straightforwardly technical perspective on Recording Practice has only very recently begun to emerge, as the taboo on studying popular musics (and, thus, pop recording practices) that once gripped university music departments gradually slackens.

However, even as musicologists and music theorists turn their analytic attentions to pop records, they remain largely fixated on musical

---

2 To be clear, a number of articles and books consider Recording Practice (i.e., Jones 1992; Moore 1993; Chanan 1995; Théberge 1995 and 1997; Gracyk 1996; Toynbee 2000; Zak 2001; Taylor 2001; Warner 2003; Schmidt-Horning 2004; Bartlett and Bartlett 2005; Doyle 2005; Greene and Porcello 2005; Moorefield 2005; Lacasse 2007). However, few go very far beyond a simple description of what common recording technologies can do, to explain specific musical uses which recordists devise for them.

3 A brief sample would have to include, among many others: Eisenberg 1987; Chanan 1995; Théberge 1995 and 1997; Toynbee 2000; Zak 2001; Taylor 2001; Coleman 2003; Schmidt-Horning 2004; Doyle 2005; Millard 2005; Moorefield 2005; Zagorski-Thomas 2005; Lacasse 2007; Williams 2007; and Milner 2009.

details that can be notated — formal contour, harmonic design, pitch relations, metered rhythms and so on — even though many of these authors reject notation as an analytic tool. No matter how *avant-garde* their methods, in other words, many commentators still typically fixate on the very same musical details that musicologists and music theorists traditionally analyze. They simply disagree over how best to interpret those details. Recording Practice itself only registers in a small, albeit growing, collection of articles and books.

It is within this growing collection that the following field guide should be situated. This field guide is designed to: (i) demonstrate, (ii) describe and (iii) elucidate the fundamentally musical nature of Recording Practice, which traditional analytic modes have only heretofore described as an extra-musical technologization of live performance practices. At the same time, the book provides a broader aesthetic orientation for the technical procedures that audio-engineering textbooks detail. The primary inspiration for this field guide was pioneering studies produced by practicing and retired recordists, and analysts of record production, like Albin Zak (2001), Alexander Case (2007), Roey Izhaki (2008), Paul Théberge (1997), Virgil Moorefield (2005), William Moylan (2007), Michael Chanan (1995), Simon Zagorski-Thomas (2005) and Bobby Owsinski (2006). It is my ultimate hope that this field guide will add some more musical insights to the crucial information that these scholars present in their pioneering studies and, at the same time, that it provide future recordists with a useful aesthetic and technical orientation to the immensely complicated craft they are determined to learn.

A QUICK NOTE ON ORGANIZATION

This field guide was designed to introduce the particulars of Recording Practice to a general (albeit research-minded) readership. Analysts, historians and practitioners alike should find information in this field guide to help them in their endeavors. I adopted the organizational approach of sequential entries, each of which is concerned with some technique or sub-technique of the broader record-making process at large. I divide record-making into four roughly chronological phases: (i) tracking, (ii) signal processing, (iii) mixing and (iv) mastering. I then divide each of these four phases into a series of component, constitutive "meta-techniques" and "sub-techniques". For instance, I divide the tracking phase into three meta-techniques, namely, "transduction", "direct-injection" and "sequencing". However, embedded within each of these broader meta-techniques is a galaxy of constitutive sub-techniques, each of which requires analytic attention as both singular procedure and a component of Recording Practice.

From a practical perspective, such divisions will always be artificial. Each time recordists select a particular microphone to record a particular sound source, for instance, they filter the frequency content of that sound source in particular ways; in so doing, they equalize and mix their records, even at this very early stage. Recording Practice is an entirely holistic procedure, after all. Tracking, signal processing, mixing and mastering cannot be separated — not in practice, at least. They are easily excised in theory, though, because each procedure is tailored to produce a different result. During the tracking phase, for example, recordists capture raw audio signals which they later massage into final form using a variety of signal processing, mixing and mastering techniques. During the signal processing phase, recordists filter and refine the "raw audio signals" they collect during tracking; and, moreover, we will see that many kinds of signal processing are done during tracking. Mixing is done to spatially organize the component tracks in a multi-track production into well-proportioned shapes, and during mastering recordists apply a finishing layer of audio varnish to their mixes, to ensure that they sound at their optimal best on a variety of playback machines and in a variety of different formats.

I saw no reason whatsoever to dumb down the explanations for the procedures offered in this field guide. Though I have done my absolute best to provide simple, easy-to-understand explanations for each of the concepts and techniques surveyed in the following pages, I also struggled to ensure that I did not over-simplify anything in so doing. Recording Practice is an artistic *and* technical affair. Readers interested in learning anything about Recording Practice should thus prepare to consider a number of unambiguously technical concepts and procedures, which inhere in every recorded musical communication. As Dave 'Hard Drive' Pensado so aptly put it, the most successful recordists are equal parts Bill Gates and Pablo Picasso — neither the technical nor the artistic disposition should dominate.

I should also note the three-fold selection criterion used to choose the musical examples cited throughout this field guide. First, whenever possible I sought verification (in print) that the tracks cited feature the musical techniques I say they feature. Then I considered whether they provide the clearest possible illustration of those techniques. Finally, I verified that the tracks are readily available for purchase from a reputable online distributor, such as iTunes, Bleep and Beatport. I also intentionally culled examples from as random a sample set as I could muster, to emphasize the fact that all of the musical terms in this field guide are, unless otherwise noted, deployed by recordists working in any musical genre.

A FINAL NOTE ON HOW TO USE THIS FIELD GUIDE

This field guide is designed to be a multi-sensory learning experience, useful for practitioners, historians and analysts alike. As such, while they work their way through the guide, readers should do their very best to listen as much as they read. A website (www.fieldguidetorecordingpractice.com) has been constructed to house accompanying audio files. Readers who navigate to this website will find numerous original audio examples to download, each designed to illustrate the audible character of a musical concept or procedure surveyed in this book.

Prompts are given in the body of the text when musical examples are available, and information is provided about which musical features readers should focus on while they listen.

The accompanying website also contains a number of multi-track audio "stems" that readers can download. Those who have access to workstation software are encouraged to import these stems into an open multi-track session. Each stem has been "bounced" to align, when positioned at the very beginning of a multi-track session (i.e., starting at 0:00). Created by Rion C (www.myspace.com/rionc) and Mark Collins — two recordists with considerable experience and exceptional skill — these stems provide readers with materials for testing out the techniques they read about and will allow them to hear, first hand, how working recordists use the musical concepts and procedures surveyed in this field guide to create coherent, aggregate musical statements. Stems and audio examples will be uploaded to this website on a regular basis. Readers without access to workstations can download demonstration versions from company websites onto their computers. Ableton, for instance, has a "light" version of its celebrated Ableton Live workstation available for download on their site (www.ableton.com); and demonstration versions of Steinberg Cubase and ProTools M-Powered are available, free of charge, with the purchase of entry-level interfaces and keystations from manufacturers like M-Audio and Alesis.

Readers who nevertheless find themselves unable or unwilling to attempt the practical component of this study should at the very least endeavor to listen carefully to the commercial tracks and original audio examples cited throughout, and precisely when they are cited. Again, it is crucial that readers listen as much as they read while working through this field guide. "The most important music of our time is recorded music," notes Alexander Case (2007: xix), whose *Sound FX: Unlocking The Creative Potential Of Recording Studio Effects* was a primary inspiration for this book. "While the talented, persistent, self-taught engineer can create sound recordings of artistic merit, more productive use of the studio is achieved through study, experience and collaboration." I would simply add that listening, too, is a useful and instructive tool. To make records, and to understand the musical language of Recording Practice, recordists and analysts alike should first learn to *hear* Recording Practice. It is my ultimate hope that this field guide will help readers from all disciplinary backgrounds, and levels of expertise, do just that.

ACKNOWLEDGMENTS

I owe many people my heartfelt gratitude for their help with this project. First and foremost, thanks are due to David Barker at Continuum, who provided me with the opportunity to create this field guide, and, relatedly, to Jonathan Sterne, who offered helpful suggestions during the proposal stage for this project. I would also like to thank my colleagues in the popular music studies department at the University of Western Ontario, but especially Bob Toft, who has been indispensable to my academic survival. Thanks are also due to Rion C and Mark Collins, who generously donated tracks and multi-track files. Both went above and beyond the call of duty in donating their considerable talents and time to this project — I simply cannot thank them enough for their input. Thanks also to Ryan Chynces, who has patiently and brilliantly taught me the ins and outs of the new "glitch" and "tech" paradigms. Ryan also edited and offered substantial insights on early drafts of this text, both as an interested friend and copy editor. I cannot overemphasize his contributions, and I am ever grateful for his encouragement, friendship and support (my "tele-rhetorical handshake" still stands!).

I dedicate this book to Ryan Sackrider, who taught me the proverbial "everything I know" about Recording Practice while we were both enrolled as students at the Berklee College of Music in the mid- and late 1990s. Ryan handled production duties for most of the records I made at Berklee, and he formulated and taught me an astonishingly comprehensive philosophy of record-making in the few short years we had together. His insights into the unique musical language of Recording Practice thoroughly re-shaped the way I think about and make music. Moreover, Ryan's decision to allow me to join him, and musical co-conspirator Michael Preis, in designing and building RP Major Studio One — a short-lived but no less legendary "underground" recording studio in Brooklyn — was one of the most crucial and shaping moments in my life, let alone as a musician and analyst. I am grateful that I was able to bend your ear, Ryan, even if only for such a short period of time.

Berklee was a truly magical place. I was fortunate enough, while I was there, to meet and work with musicians and recordists who have since gone on to earn Grammy nominations, number one Top 40 hits, and other professional accolades and successes. I have always maintained that I learned more from working with these future stars, while they were still students, than I did from any particular class. I have done my very best, in this field guide, to distill the immense insights these musicians and recordists were gracious enough to offer me, into a viable aesthetic orientation towards the practice of record-making.

I also want to thank Bruno Canale and Tobias Enhus, two more friends from Berklee, for their excellent production work. Both handled production duties for tracks I include with this field guide. Bruno oversaw production for "Stains" and "A Harlequin Romance," while Tobias oversaw production for "Devil Take A Bow." Though Tobias and I rarely saw eye-to-eye on extra-musical topics, we rarely disagreed about music. Tobias taught me enough about Recording Practice to fill multiple books, in fact. In particular, Tobias was an early champion of the digital-audio paradigm, and he provided me with my earliest glimpses of that emerging world in the mid- and late 1990s. I'm indebted for that early glimpse, obviously. Thanks are also due to the musicians who contributed their immense talents to many of the tracks which I include with this field guide: Ludvig Girdland, Rohin Khemani, Craig Bryant, Dave Palan, Jordan Holt, Mike Preis and Jason Getzel. I owe you all a great deal more thanks than I was able to muster while we were still a band. And I owe gratitude to my current musical "fellow travelers": Brent Rodger, Brendan Glauser, Ed Elyahky, Marc Collins, Ryan Chynces, Rion C, Jonny Kwong, Ashley Stanton, Cameron Metcalfe, Adam Aimers and John Barrett. Thanks are also due to a number of students who brought information to my attention which I consider in this field guide: Brendan Glauser, Ted Peacock, Daniel Crystal, Daniel Shore, Daniel Rosen, Matthew Shelvock, Peter Murphy, Scott Way, Emily Gale, Amanda Lewis, Myron Gray, Alexa Woloshyn, Kara-Lis Coverdale and Anthony Cushing.

Finally, thanks to my wife, Eva, without whose support I would have crumpled long ago. I worked very hard on this field guide, spending the better part of each day, for more than 16 months, toiling away on it. Eva was ever patient and understanding throughout. And, of course, thanks go to our two beautiful boys: James Georg and Alec Alan. Besides being the strongest little boys in the world, which is a godsend when there's a house that needs lifting, my sons have inspired me to rediscover the unconditional love for records that, in the first instance, prompted me to risk everything for a career in music. Having played for them almost every record I own, it is The Beatles' *Help* which never fails to please them. As I submit an electronic draft of this manuscript, right now, The Beatles' "You've Got To Hide Your Love Away" plays; the volume is set to an earth-shaking level, and my wife and our two sons are "happy dancing" behind me.

Chapter 1

Tracking

Making Audio Signals

W hen recordists track a record, they create the raw audio signals which they later shape into a so-called "master cut", ready for duplication and release, using a range of signal processing, mixing and mastering techniques. The material form this raw audio signal takes depends completely on the technology recordists use to create and store it. If they use an Edison cylinder-phonograph, for instance, recordists create raw audio signal in the form of bumps and pits on a wax cylinder. If they use a computer, on the other hand, the raw audio signal they make takes shape as a digital sequence of binary code.

The number of separate audio signals, called "tracks", which can be combined into a master cut also depends upon technology. Early acoustic devices, like the phonograph and gramophone, had only one track available for recording. Tape machines, which are electromagnetic devices, expanded that number from two to, eventually, sixty-four (and more) available tracks. And now, with the advent of digital-audio (computer-based) recording technology, recordists can create and combine a theoretically unlimited number of tracks. Regardless of the technology they use, though, recordists have only three fundamental techniques at their disposal for tracking records, namely: (i) transduction, (ii) direct-injection and (iii) sequencing. Transduction remains the most common of these techniques and, as such, warrants immediate attention. A brief explanation of direct-injection and sequencing techniques follows.

1. TRANSDUCTION

Transduction, that is, conversion of one kind of energy into another kind of energy, is the technical basis of tracking. The three most iconic recording technologies — microphones, headphones and speakers — are, in fact, transducers. Microphones transduce (convert) acoustic energy into electrical energy, while headphones and amplifiers transduce electrical energy back into acoustic energy. As Jonathan Sterne (2003: 22) explains, to make and hear recorded musical communications, recordists and listeners use

> devices called transducers, which turn sound into something else and that something else back into sound . . . Telephones turn your voice into electricity, sending it down a phone line and turning it back into sound at the other end. Radio works on a similar principle, but uses waves instead of wires. The diaphragm and stylus of a cylinder phonograph change sound through a process of inscription in tinfoil, wax, or any number of other surfaces. On playback, the stylus and diaphragm transduce the inscriptions back into sound. Digital sound reproduction technologies all use transducers; they simply add another level of transformation, converting electric current into ones and zeros.

A number of variables mediate every transduction. First among these mediating variables are microphones. Each microphone has a biased way of hearing sound which recordists call its "frequency response".

Some microphones exaggerate, while others attenuate, certain frequencies, for instance; while still other microphones only transduce sounds coming from particular directions. Variations in frequency response are vast, and seemingly endless. Given the crucial role that microphones play in the tracking process, it should come as no surprise to discover that these variations guide microphone selection and placement processes in their entirety. As William Moylan (2007: 280) writes:

> The sound qualities of instruments and voices are shaped, and can be significantly transformed, when captured by a microphone. The selection of a particular microphone, placing the microphone at a particular location (within the particular recording environment), and how these complement the characteristics of the particular sound source will determine the final sound quality of a recorded sound. The recordist needs a clear idea of the sound quality sought. With this [in mind], the recordist will determine which microphone is most appropriate by comparing the characteristics of the sound quality of the sound source and the performance characteristics of the microphone, to their vision of the final sound quality sought. Perhaps no other decision shapes sound quality more than microphone selection and placement.

To understand the almost total influence frequency response exerts over the tracking process — and, in turn, to understand the crucial role that microphone selection plays in determining the final audible character of tracks on a record — readers must first understand what it is that frequency response shapes, namely, a sound source. I will thus explain the concept of a sound source before I elucidate the microphone selection process. Readers who are already familiar with the physics of sound should feel free to skip ahead to the following section of this field guide, 1.1 Microphone Selection I.

SOUND SOURCE

A sound source is a vibrating physical object — no more, no less. As objects vibrate, their back-and-forth motions displace the air molecules surrounding them, forcing them to compress (bunch together) and rarefy (thin apart) in recurring patterns called "soundwaves". The vibrational energy of a sound source is rapidly conveyed from air molecule to adjacent air molecule in the form of a soundwave until it reaches, for my purposes, human ears or a microphone. The tympanic membrane in the human ear vibrates in sympathy with soundwaves, which is to say, the membrane moves back-and-forth at a rate which is directly proportional to the vibrations of the sound source itself; and, through a complex electrochemical process, this sympathetic back-and-forth motion creates a sequence of electrical impulses, which, in turn, the brain interprets as sound. With microphones, a diaphragm rather than a tympanic membrane sways sympathetically with the changes in air pressure that a soundwave creates. This sympathetic motion is then translated into electrical current and conveyed by cables through routing technology (i.e., mixing consoles), processing technology (i.e., signal processors) and, ultimately, to storage technology (e.g., tape machines and computers).

Recordists visualize soundwaves as waveforms (see **Figure 1.1** and **Figure 1.2**). Waveforms are graphs that show the changes in air pressure that characterize a soundwave. The horizontal axis of a waveform represents time while the vertical axis represents changes in air pressure. The pushing-and-pulling energy of a soundwave is thus flipped onto its side in a waveform graph, and is represented as an up-and-down motion along the vertical axis. Upward motion along the vertical axis of a waveform represents compressions of air molecules, while downward motion represents rarefactions. The horizontal axis delineates the time it takes for each successive compression and rarefaction to occur.

The vertical expanse of a waveform, which recordists call "amplitude", delineates the total displacement of air molecules a soundwave

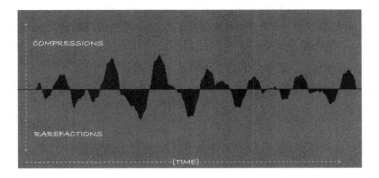

Figure 1.1 A waveform representation of the changes in air pressure produced by plucking the bottom string of an acoustic guitar.

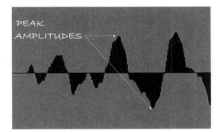

Figure 1.2 A close-up of the waveform from Figure 1.1, with peak compression and rarefaction amplitudes noted.

generates. As such, amplitude represents the total displacement power of a soundwave. This displacement power is usually measured in deci-bels (dB):

> Literally, one tenth of a "bel". The "bel" is named after Alexander Graham Bell, and the number of bels is defined as the common logarithm of two powers. Thus, two powers, one of which is ten times the other, will differ by 1 bel; 10 watts are 1 bel higher in level than 1 watt. A 360-horsepower car is 1 bel more powerful than a 36-horsepower motorcycle. Any power ratio may be expressed in bels, and it is important to note that only power ratios are allowed ... Decibels have caused untold confusion among audio people,

and most of this is due to the failure to realize that decibels are not quantities of anything and can represent only power ratios. (White and Louie, 2005: 99–100)

Contrary to popular belief, amplitude doesn't measure volume. Amplitude and volume reference two very different sonic phenomena. To judge volume, the human ear uses both the peak amplitude reached by a soundwave and the amount of time it spends at, or near, that peak amplitude. As Daniel Thompson (2005: 109–10) puts it:

> Perhaps the simplest type of amplitude measurement, called peak amplitude, is found by measuring the highest point above zero reached by the wave in a given cycle. The peak-to-peak amplitude of the wave is found by measuring the difference between the highest and lowest points in a given cycle, which will be equal to twice the peak amplitude for any periodic wave . . . Given two similar soundwaves, the one with the greater peak amplitude will sound louder. However, given two different waveforms, the correlation between peak amplitude and actual loudness becomes less obvious. The square wave will sound significantly louder than the sine wave because it spends virtually all of its time at its maximum or peak amplitude. The same is true of musical signals. Transient signals, which don't spend much time at peak level (such as acoustic piano), sound less loud than similar signals of equal peak value but greater sustained level (distorted guitar).

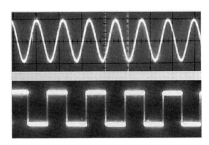

Figure 1.3   A "sine wave" (above) and a "square wave" (below).

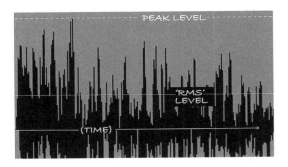

Figure 1.4   Crest factor refers to the distance between a waveform's peak amplitude and its average amplitude (RMS [Root Mean Square] level). The
waveform shown is of a single snare hit.

Recordists call the difference between the peak amplitude of a soundwave and its average amplitude "crest factor" (see **Figure 1.4**). As Daniel
Thompson (2005) noted, transient (percussive) sounds usually exhibit
a greater crest factor, that is, they exhibit a greater difference between
their peak and base amplitudes, than do sustained pitches. Waveforms
which spend all or most of their time at peak amplitude, on the other
hand, like the "square wave" in **Figure 1.3**, exhibit practically no crest
factor at all.

FREQUENCY

Frequency measures the number of times per second that the changes
in air pressure which define a soundwave recur, and it is usually
expressed in Hertz (Hz) and kiloHertz (kHz). A soundwave which
repeats 20 times per second is said to have a frequency of 20 Hz, while
a soundwave which recurs 20,000 times per second is said to have a
frequency of 20 kHz. Humans are only equipped to hear frequencies
more or less within this range. Barring variations in biology, frequencies below 20 Hz and above 20 kHz are actively rejected by the human
ear. Moreover, as Alexander Case (2007: 73–4) explains:

Human sensitivity to sound is strongly governed by the frequency content of that sound. Human hearing is never flat in frequency response. Uniform loudness comes from a range of sound pressure levels across the frequency axis. Similarly, uniform sound pressure level across the frequency axis would lead to a broad range of perceived loudnesses . . . Human hearing is less sensitive to low and high frequencies and most sensitive to middle frequencies. This trend is shown to exist at a range of amplitudes. Human hearing consistently remains most sensitive to [the] upper-middle frequency range near about 3500 Hz, across a range of amplitudes — from quiet, just-audible sound pressure levels (0 dBSPL) up to painfully loud, and possibly unhealthy, sound pressure levels (100 dBSPL).

The human ear interprets frequency as pitch. Soundwaves which recur with greater rapidity than other soundwaves sound like they have a higher pitch. In fact, pitch is directly related to the vibrational motion of a sound source. For instance, if a motor idles at a rate of 1,200 rotations per minute (rpm), which translates into a rate of 20 rotations per second, it generates a soundwave with a frequency of 20 Hz (Thompson 2005: 97). Compared to the soundwave created by a motor which idles at a rate of, say, 2,400 rpm, the motor which idles at 1,200 rpm produces a lower sounding pitch. **Figure 1.5** below provides the specific frequencies for certain keys on a standard acoustic piano keyboard, running from middle-C to just over an octave above.

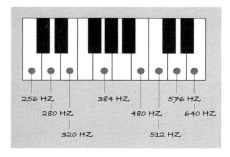

Figure 1.5   Keys on a standard acoustic piano keyboard as frequencies, spanning slightly more than an octave above middle-C.

> **Example 1.1   Frequency And Pitch**
>
> Example 1.1 sweeps through the audible spectrum, from 20 Hz up to 20 kHz (0:00–0:30) and back down (0:30–1:00). Then six frequencies sound in succession, each for a duration of roughly 30 seconds, at the same volume (−20 dBFS [decibels Full Scale {digital weighting}]): (i) 20 Hz; (ii) 200 Hz; (iii) 500 Hz; (iv) 1 kHz; (v) 12 kHz; and (vi) 20 kHz. Readers may not hear the 20 Hz and 20 kHz frequencies, as both fall outside the usual hearing range for adults. A simple sine wave was used to create this track. The sweep readers hear during the initial minute, and any subsequent differences in pitch, are all wholly the product of quickening and slowing the cycle rate of the original 20 Hz soundwave. Readers should lower the volume on their playback devices to hear this example, since the difference in perceived loudness is immense.

WAVELENGTH

Soundwaves occur — or, better yet, they recur — in both time and space. The physical distance a soundwave must travel to complete one cycle of compressions and rarefactions (its wavelength) is directly related to its frequency. Higher more rapidly recurring frequencies require smaller wavelengths, while lower less rapidly recurring frequencies require longer wavelengths. **Table 1.1** below lists the wavelengths of common musical sounds, expressed in feet. Even just a cursory glance through this table should convince the most stubborn of skeptics that a massive variance in wavelength inheres across the audible spectrum.

Table 1.1   Frequency (in Hertz) and wavelength (in feet) for common musical sounds.

Sound	Approx. frequency	Wavelength (ft)
Lowest audible frequency	20 Hz	56.5 ft
Lowest note on a piano	28 Hz	40.4 ft
Kick drum fundamental	60 Hz	19.0 ft
Concert tuning note (A440)	440 Hz	2.57 ft
Highest note on a piano	4.18 kHz	0.27 ft
Vocal sibilance(s)	5 kHz	0.23 ft

(continued)

Sound	Approx. frequency	Wavelength (ft)
Cymbal sizzle	16 kHz	0.07 ft
Highest audible frequency	20 kHz	0.05 ft

Though the concept of wavelength may seem completely academic, it actually plays an important and thoroughly practical role in the tracking process. Wavelength is a core player in the creation of standing waves and room modes, for instance, which acoustically bias a room into exaggerating the amplitude of only certain frequencies, usually at the lower-end of the frequency spectrum. When recordists track in a room that acoustically exaggerates, say, 384 Hz, each time an electric bassist plucks that frequency it registers at a higher volume than other frequencies from the electric bass. This presents myriad problems during mixing and mastering. Faced with a spiking volume each time the bassist plucks 384 Hz, recordists have no choice but to somehow minimize that frequency each time it sounds without disfiguring the broader dynamic and frequency balance of the track. I examine this phenomenon, and some common strategies recordists use to combat it, in greater detail during the final chapter of this field guide, Mastering: The Final Say.

PHASE INTERFERENCE AND COMB-FILTERING

When a soundwave recurs exactly for an extended period of time it is called a "periodic soundwave". The period of a periodic soundwave is the amount of time it takes to complete one cycle, which is to say, one time through the pattern of compressions and rarefactions which defines it. Only rarely do recordists transduce a sound at the very beginning of its cycle, however. Soundwaves are typically transduced at some point in their "phase" after zero degrees. Daniel Thompson (2005: 99) explains:

> The "phase" of a periodic wave refers to its current position with respect to the completion of a full cycle, and is measured in degrees.

A full cycle would represent 360°, as with one full rotation of a circle. One half-cycle would measure 180°, and so on. Thus, the term "in phase" implies occupying the same relative position in time with a given cycle.

The concept of phase underwrites many tracking procedures. When recordists transduce the same sound source using more than one microphone, they risk inducing phase interferences, which are tonal distortions created by combining multiple copies of the same sound-wave transduced at different points in its phase. As Mitch Gallagher (2007: 9–10) notes:

> Phase is extremely important in . . . recording in general because waves that are "out of phase" [that is, which are recorded at different points in their cycles] by even a small amount can cancel each other, resulting in tonal changes. Likewise, waves that are "in phase" [that is, which are recorded at (roughly) the same points in their cycles] reinforce each other, making the signal stronger. Phase problems occur when sound bounces around within a room, for instance; the reflecting waves interfere with each other destructively, causing all sorts of problems.

In extreme cases, phase interference can produce a peculiar kind of tonal distortion called "comb-filtering" (see **Figure 1.6**):

> Combining a musical waveform with a delayed version of itself radi-cally modifies the frequency content of the signal. Some frequencies are cancelled, and others are doubled. The intermediate frequencies experience something in between outright cancellation and full-on doubling . . . Taking a complex sound like guitar, which has sound energy at a range of different frequencies, and mixing in a delayed version of itself at the same amplitude, will cut certain frequencies and boost others. This is called comb filtering, because the alteration in the frequency content of the signal looks like teeth on a comb. (Case 2007: 232)

Example 1.2   Phase And Comb-Filtering

Example 1.2 demonstrates the audible character of comb-filtering. A virtual synthesizer repeats a rapid five-pitch sequence. After 6 seconds, the sequence is doubled (copied) and the double is offset by 20 milliseconds (ms). The onset of the peculiar tonal distortion called comb-filtering is immediately apparent. After another 6 seconds, the double track is offset by another 20 ms, so it sounds 40 ms "out of phase" with the original sequence. Six seconds later, the double track is offset by 80 ms; and, then, after another 6 seconds, it is set out of phase by 160 ms. The comb-filter strengthens as the amount of delay between the original and double tracks increases.

Far from purely academic considerations, the related concepts of phase, phase interference and comb-filtering direct recordists while they track, especially when they use more than one microphone to do so. Returning once more to Daniel Thompson's (2005: 99) explanation:

Phase has significant implications, particularly when recording using more than one microphone. The phase of the signal captured by each microphone will depend on the position of the microphones with respect to the source. When out-of-phase signals are combined, frequency cancellations occur that may distort the sound of the source signal, causing audible loss of high, mid, or low frequencies. Thus, special care in the placement of multiple microphones and in monitoring the resultant sound (checking it in both stereo and

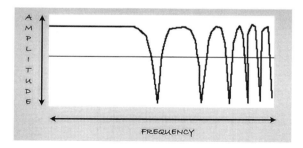

Figure 1.6   A comb-filter, so-named for its resemblance to the teeth on a comb. Each dip in the comb-filter, which recordists call "notches", represents a silent band of the input spectrum.

mono) is crucial. This allows us to take advantage of constructive summations (full sound) and avoid unpleasant destructive cancellations (thin or unnatural sound).

In fact, recordists have devised a number of tracking techniques specifically built on the concept of phase interference. Bob Ezrin (in Pedersen 2007) offers a good example:

> On an emotional level, it's difficult to get vocalists to deliver exciting performances if they feel uncomfortable wearing headphones. I'd typically have them sing without headphones and let them monitor the tracks through some huge speakers. To diminish leakage from the rhythm tracks into the vocal mic, I'd use the old trick of putting the speakers out of phase. Somewhere between those two speakers will be a point at which the sound-pressure level is close to zero. All you have to do is have someone move the mic around while you listen in the control room for the spot where there's almost no leakage. Leave your mic in that spot. Now your vocalist can stand in front of this great big PA system and feel the music surround them, just as if they were singing onstage.

1.1 Microphone Selection 1

When recordists transduce a sound source, they use one or more microphones to represent its vibrational energy as an audio signal. Understanding how microphones "hear" is thus a crucial step in understanding how recordists create the sounds on any given record. "The study of microphones is a lifelong quest," notes Bill Gibson (2002b: 5):

> Each mic offers a creative tonal color for your audio palette. Whereas you might struggle to get the perfect sound using one specific mic, simply changing to a different mic could yield excellent results . . . There's much more to mic choice than finding a trusted

manufacturer that you can stick with. There's much more to mic placement than simply putting the mic close to the sound source. The difference between mediocre audio recordings and exemplary audio recordings is quite often defined by the choice and placement of microphones.

Microphone selection is one of the most important techniques in all of Recording Practice. As Albin Zak (2001: 119) writes:

> The first step in the signal path is the microphone. In many ways microphones are the technological soul of any recording project; the effectiveness of all other tools and techniques depends upon the quality of the image that the microphone is able to deliver . . . The microphone serves as an alchemic doorway between performance and text. Sound enters the doorway as fleeting vibrations in air pressure and is instantly transformed — or, more precisely, transduced — into a corresponding electrical signal that can be printed on some form of recording medium. But the process originally changes the sound in some way. The coloring effects of the microphone itself, along with those of its placement, must be appropriately matched with both the source material and the stylistic expressive intentions of the project — a task requiring aesthetic judgment and technical expertise. Decisions about microphone choice . . . depend on a feel for the affective character of the sound in question and a sense of its role in the track.

Experienced recordists do not randomly select microphones and hope it all turns out well. They select a microphone and place it in relation to a sound source using a multifaceted and highly nuanced musical reasoning. Microphone selection is usually an extremely personalized technique, in fact. Despite the proscriptions of audio-engineering textbooks there is no single correct way to select, let alone use, a microphone. "Choosing the right microphone to capture a great sound is an art in itself," writes David Franz (2004: 89). However, Franz (2004: 89) continues:

there are no recipes for doing this and many times you have to improvise or compromise, depending on your mic selection and available space . . . There is an infinite number of ways to mic instruments. Everyone has their own techniques . . . None of them should be considered the [correct] one.

To make appropriate microphone selections — to choose the microphone which best relates a sound source to the peculiar needs of a particular musical project — recordists educate themselves about the unique frequency response characteristics of each microphone in their arsenal. Over the course of their careers, recordists will usually develop a short list of "go to" microphones they regularly use to track certain sound sources. Bruce Swedien (2009: 120–1), whose production and engineering credits include records by top-tier Top 40 pop vocalists — like Michael Jackson (*Off The Wall, Thriller, Bad, Dangerous*), Donna Summer (*Donna Summer*), Roberta Flack (*I'm The One*) and Jennifer Lopez (*Rebirth*) — starts the microphone selection process with the short list in **Table 1.2** below as his guide.

Table 1.2 Bruce Swedien's (2009) "go to" list of microphones, related to vocal timbres.

Vocal characteristics	Microphones
Well-rounded, naturally good-sounding voice	Neumann U47; Neumann U87; Neumann U67; Telefunken 251; AKG C12; Sony C800G.
Thin, weak voice	RCA 44BX
Loud, brassy voice with good projection	Shure SM7; AKG 414 EB; RCA 44BX
Good voice, but too sibilant	Neumann U47; Neumann U67; RCA 44BX; Shure SM7

Regardless of the sound source, or of the specific models of microphone in their "go to" list, modern recordists chiefly use only one of three different kinds of microphone to transduce: (i) dynamic (or, moving coil) microphones; (ii) condenser (or, capacitor) microphones; and

(iii) ribbon microphones. Each of these microphones has an unique "operations principle", that is, each transduces sound using unique materials configured to function in particular ways. Though, as noted, recordists can use microphones however they see fit — including as drum sticks, billy clubs and chopsticks — most microphones are manufactured to transduce sound in very specific ways which recommend them for only a limited set of uses (a vintage ribbon microphone, for instance, will often break if presented with an overabundance of sound pressure; its specifications thus recommend uses other than transducing a heavy-hitting drummer like The Who's Keith Moon, Tool's Danny Carey, Led Zeppelin's John Bonham or Mountain's Corky Laing from a close proximity). To make the best microphone selection, recordists have only one technique at their disposal, namely, to arm themselves with as much information as they can muster about the unique operations principle of each microphone in their toolbox. To understand microphone selection, then, we will have to do the same.

DYNAMIC (OR, MOVING COIL) MICROPHONES

Dynamic microphones function like miniature speakers put in reverse (Ryan and Kehew 2008: 164). Inside every dynamic microphone is a magnet, and suspended inside its magnetic field is a coil of wire, called a "voice coil", with a diaphragm attached to its end. Soundwaves vibrate the diaphragm, which pushes the coiled wire back-and-forth inside the microphone's magnetic field. This back-and-forth motion, in turn, generates an electrical current that is eventually converted into an audio signal.

One of the most celebrated frequency response profiles in the pop world belongs to the Shure SM57 dynamic microphone. This microphone follows the operations principle detailed in **Figure 1.7**. **Figure 1.8** reproduces frequency response specifications for the SM57, which Shure provides with each unit in its packaging. Distinguishing traits of the SM57's frequency response contour include a sharp bass

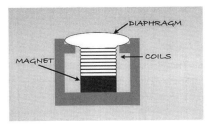

Figure 1.7   The operations principle of a common dynamic (or, moving coil) microphone.

roll-off beginning at roughly 200 Hz and an upper-mid-range peak centered at about 6 kHz. Just as human ears tend to exaggerate the upper-midrange (1–5 kHz) of what they hear, and reject frequencies roughly below 20 Hz and above 20 kHz, so the Shure SM57: (i) sharply attenuates all incoming sound below 200 Hz and above about 12 kHz; (ii) exaggerates frequencies between roughly 2 kHz and 7 kHz; and (iii) rejects everything under 40 Hz and above about 15 kHz.

The SM57 shares the basic shape of its frequency response with most other dynamic microphones. Because they are typically manufactured to withstand especially high sound-pressure levels (SPLs) and rugged uses, which could easily destroy the delicate internal circuitry of, say, a vintage RCA 44 ribbon microphone, dynamic microphones remain industry standard for a number of live and close-mic applications. The bass roll-off which characterizes its frequency response is a

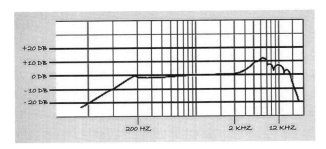

Figure 1.8   Frequency response specifications for the Shure SM57 dynamic microphone, provided by Shure with each unit in its packaging (c. 2007).

manufactured bias, designed to attenuate "proximity effect" exaggerations of bass frequencies which every kind of directional microphone generates when placed in close proximity to a sound source. At the same time, the SM57's exaggerated peak between about 3 and 12 kHz emphasizes the attack transients of most rhythm and lead instruments in a pop arrangement, thus enhancing their clarity on record.

CONDENSER (OR, CAPACITOR) MICROPHONES

Condenser microphones use two conducting plates to transduce the vibrational energy of a soundwave into electrical current (see **Figure 1.9**). These conducting plates comprise a capacitor, that is, an electronic mechanism designed to store energy in the form an electrostatic field. One of the plates in the capacitor, known as the "backplate", never moves. The other plate, called the "front-plate", functions like a diaphragm, vibrating sympathetically with changes in air pressure around it. When excited by a soundwave, the distance between the backplate and the front-plate changes, which in turn modifies the capacitance of the capacitor. When the front-plate moves toward the backplate the microphone's capacitance increases and a charge current registers; when the front-plate moves away from the backplate the capacitance decreases and a discharge current registers.

Recordists typically prize condenser microphones for their neutral and expansive frequency response. Bill Gibson (2002b: 7) explains:

> Condenser microphones are the most accurate. They respond to fast attacks and transients more precisely than other types, and they typically add the least amount of tonal coloration . . . Condenser microphones typically capture a broader range of frequencies from a greater distance than the other mic types. In other words, you don't need to be as close to the sound source to get a full sound. This trait of condenser microphones is a great advantage in the recording studio because it enables us to record a full sound while still including some of the natural ambience in a room.

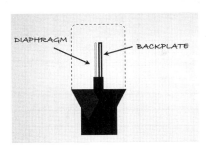

DIAPHRAGM

BACKPLATE

Figure 1.9 The operations principle of a common condenser (or, capacitor) microphone.

Of course, condenser microphones aren't completely neutral. No microphone transduces sound in an entirely neutral way across the audible spectrum. Condenser microphones are simply the most neutral of all the microphones which recordists presently use. **Figure 1.10** reproduces frequency response specifications for Neumann U47 and U48 condenser microphones set for a variety of directional response patterns. I use these two microphones as examples because they are among the most celebrated of condenser microphones in use today. A quick scan of their frequency response contours demonstrates that any deviation from 0 dB remains minimal, rather than neutral, across the audible spectrum. Two steep +10 dB roll-offs, beginning at 250 Hz and again at 12 kHz, characterize the U48's frequency response; and multiple +/−6 dB variances obtain between about 2 kHz and 15 kHz with both the U47 and the U48.

Most condenser microphones have a frequency response contour which closely resembles that of the U47 and U48. Manufacturers use extremely light and thin materials for the diaphragms in these microphones. The operations principle of a condenser microphone is thus far less prone to inertia (stasis, or, lack of movement) than are the coiled wires in a dynamic microphone, even if those coiled wires can handle much higher SPLs without distorting. Not surprisingly then, condenser microphones transduce a much more expansive array of

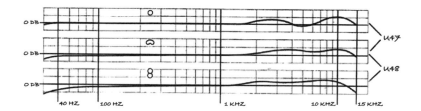

Figure 1.10   Frequency responses of Neumann U47 and U48 large-diaphragm
condenser microphones, set for three directional responses (top to
bottom: omni-, uni- and bi-directional).

frequencies, and with greater accuracy and efficiency, than dynamic
microphones transduce; and they maintain that accuracy from greater
distances, too. This makes condenser microphones an ideal choice for
tracking: (i) sound sources comprised of energy spanning the audible
spectrum; (ii) sound sources which require tracking from a distance;
and (iii) reverberations.

The size of the diaphragm in a condenser microphone plays a crucial
role in determining its frequency response (see **Figure 1.11**). Small-
diaphragm condenser microphones, that is, condenser microphones
with a front-plate diameter of less than about two and a half inches,
do not respond to lower frequencies with the same level of detail as
do large-diaphragm condenser microphones; however, they respond
faster, and with greater accuracy, to frequencies above roughly 3 kHz
(they also tend to produce a slight bump in their frequency response
between 4 and 6 kHz). Recordists thus tend to use small-diaphragm
condenser microphones to track sound sources which contain highly
detailed high-frequency content like cymbals, hi-hats and steel-string
acoustic guitars. They use large-diaphragm condenser microphones
to transduce sound sources comprised of an obviously expansive
array of frequencies like lead vocals, classical guitars, drum kits and
reverberations.

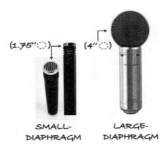

(1.75" ⭕)→   (4" ⭕)

SMALL-   LARGE-
DIAPHRAGM   DIAPHRAGM

Figure 1.11   A matched pair of small-diaphragm condenser microphones, and
one large-diaphragm condenser microphone (left to right: M-Audio's
Pulsar and Sputnik models).

RIBBON MICROPHONES

Ribbon microphones are actually a class of dynamic microphone.
However, as Kevin Ryan and Brian Kehew (2008: 164) explain, the
"dynamic" label has become so associated with moving coil microphones that the two have become synonymous. In fact, the operations
principles for dynamic and ribbon microphones are remarkably similar.
Both use magnets, magnetic fields and metallic elements to generate
electrical current, which is to say, both transduce based on the principle
of electromagnetism. With ribbon microphones, however, it is a thin
piece of corrugated metal, called the "ribbon", which hangs suspended
inside the microphone's magnetic field (see **Figure 1.12**). Soundwaves
push against the ribbon, prodding it to vibrate sympathetically with
their vibrational energy. This mechanical energy — the vibrational
energy of the ribbon — is then converted into magnetic energy and in
turn into electrical current.

The metallic ribbon element in a ribbon microphone is thinner and
lighter than the diaphragm and coiled wire used to make a dynamic
microphone. Ribbon microphones thus tend to register high-frequency
content with greater efficiency and accuracy than do dynamic microphones. That said, the ribbon in a ribbon microphone is still much

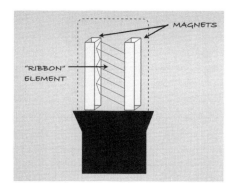

Figure 1.12 The operations principle of a common ribbon microphone.

thicker than the ultra-thin diaphragm used in most condenser microphones. The frequency response of a typical ribbon microphone is thus expansive only compared with the frequency response of most moving coil microphones. Ribbon microphones remain notably "dark", or, insensitive to high frequencies, relative to both small-diaphragm and large-diaphragm condenser microphones.

Ribbon microphones are the most fragile microphone type. As such, they remain exceedingly rare in project recording environments, which is to say, mobile recording environments constructed by amateur

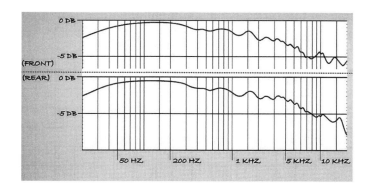

Figure 1.13 Front and rear frequency responses for the bi-directional AEA R84 ribbon microphone. Readers should compare the contour to those in Figures 1.8 and 1.10.

recordists. Aside from robust models manufactured during the last two decades by the likes of Royer and Coles, all ribbon microphones, like the RCA models 44 and 77, are extremely fragile — they even need to be stored in an upright position in order not to damage them, as Bruce Swedien (2009: 116–17) explains. It is also generally not a good idea to:

> place a ribbon in front of a loud sound source that generates high SPLs, such as an electric guitar amp or a kick drum, although newer ribbon mics are more rugged and better able to handle high SPLs. In addition, because of their construction, ribbon mics must NOT receive any external power. The thin ribbon element is likely to overheat and burn up. While moving coil mics also do not need external power, under most circumstances, they will be unaffected by it. (Thompson 2005: 16)

1.2 Microphone Selection II

Though it would be reasonable to assume that a jagged frequency response contour is somehow deficient — that a neutral contour is more desirable — no frequency response is inherently better than another except given a particular application. The fact that ribbon microphones transduce a stunted range of frequencies while condenser microphones transduce an expansive range, for instance, simply recommends both microphones for a distinct gamut of uses. Bruce Swedien (2009: 22–3) provides an exceedingly clear example:

> I learned long ago that using ribbon mics in the initial recording of percussion tracks definitely makes life easier when it comes to mastering a recording. Listen carefully to Michael [Jackson] and his brothers playing glass bottles on "Don't Stop 'Til You Get Enough" . . . I used all ribbon microphones [—] RCA DX77s and RCA 44BXs. The heavy mass of the ribbon element, suspended in the magnetic field of a ribbon mic, makes it impossible for a ribbon mic to trace

the complete transient peak of a percussive sound such as a glass bottle. If I had used condenser microphones, with the condenser mic's ability to transduce the entire transient peak of the bottles, the bottle would have sounded great, played back from tape in the control room, but when it came time to master such an incredible transient peak would have minimized the overall level (on disc, cassette or CD) of the entire piece of music. In other words, condenser mics would have compromised the dynamic impact of the sonic image of the entire piece of music.

Bob Ezrin's microphone selection for Alice Cooper's vocals on "I'm Eighteen" provides another good example of this principle. When Ezrin (cited in Pedersen 2007) selected the Shure SM57 dynamic microphone to record Cooper's lead-vocals, the young Canadian producer was fully aware that, in his words, all the rules about recording vocals "the correct way" said that he should have selected a large-diaphragm condenser microphone instead. However, the condenser microphone's neutral frequency response wound up being, ironically, entirely too neutral for Cooper's voice: the evenness of the frequency response refused to yield the compelling, gut wrenching rock vocal sound that Ezrin and Cooper agreed was needed. The SM57's jagged frequency response, made all the more jagged through compression and equalization, simply related Cooper's vocals to the particular needs of "I'm Eighteen" better than any other microphone they tried. "When I listened to the tracks," recalls Ezrin (in Pedersen 2007):

> they didn't sound real to me. I went reaching for whatever I could find to give [Cooper's] vocals some sense of power and space. The only things available were EMT plate reverbs and tape echo . . . [So I] used a Shure SM57 to record Alice [Cooper's] voice. The trick to using the SM57 on vocals is compressing it to even the sound out and getting gross with the equalization. I would dial in some real tough-ass mid-range and a lot of top end.

Conventional microphone selections for tracking a drum kit belies a slightly more complicated dynamic at work in the selection process. While recordists still base their microphone selections on the frequency response they think will best relate the drum kit's component parts to the broader needs of the project at hand, the physical properties of the sound source itself obviously plays a determining role. Snare drums, kick drums, floor toms and mounted toms present extremely high SPLs which can easily damage the transducing mechanisms on ribbon and condenser microphones, especially when placed in close proximity. Recordists thus have little choice but to select dynamic microphones for these components. When it comes time to track cymbals and reverberations, however, their low SPL-demands allow recordists to select whichever frequency response they desire. And, in fact, small-diaphragm and large-diaphragm condenser microphones, and ribbon microphones, remain industry standard for tracking cymbals and reverberations now (see **Table 1.3** below).

Table 1.3   Microphone selections for drum tracks on celebrated records. Readers unfamiliar with the brands listed below should simply note the overlap between microphone selections.

Band, track (producer)	Kick	Snare	Hi-hats/ toms	Overheads
Brian Adams, "Cuts Like A Knife" (producer: Bob Clearmountain)	AKG D12	Top: Shure SM57/bottom: AKG 451	Hi-hats: AR 6451	Neumann U87
Kate Bush, "Wuthering Heights" (producer: Jon Kelly)	AKG D12	AKG D19	Toms: AKG D19	Coles 4038
Derek & The Dominoes, "Layla" (producer: Tom Dowd)	Altec 633	Neumann KM 84	Hi-hats: SONY ECM51	Neumann U47

(continued)

Band, track (producer)	Kick	Snare	Hi-hats/ toms	Overheads
Devo, "Whip It" (producer: Robert Margouleff)	Electro RE20	Shure SM57 (top) and SM58 (bottom)	Hi-hats: Neumann KM84	AKG 414
Dire Straits, "Money For Nothin'" (producer: Mark Knopfler)	AKG D12	Shure SM57	Toms: Sennheiser 421	Neumann U87
The Knack, "My Sharona" (producer: Peter Coleman)	Neumann FET 47	Shure SM57	Hi-hats: Nuemann KM84	Neumann KM84
Madness, "Our House" (producers: Clive Langler, Alan Winstanley)	AKG D12	Shure SM 57	Toms: Sennheiser 421	Neumann U87
Madonna, "Like A Virgin" (producers: Nile Rodgers, Madonna, Stephen Bray)	Neumann FET 47	Sennheiser 421	Toms: Sennheiser 421	Neumann U47
The Pixies, "Monkey Goes To Heaven" (producer: Gil Norton)	AKG D12	Shure SM 57	Toms: Sennheiser 421/ Hi-hats Neumann KM 84	Neumann U87 and U47
The Police, "Every Breath You Take" (producer: Hugh Padgham)	AKG D20	Shure SM57	Toms: Sennheiser 421	Coles 4038
Sex Pistols, "Anarchy In The UK" (producer: Chris Thomas)	AKG D12	Shure SM 57	Toms: Neumann U67	Neumann U87

(*continued*)

Band, track (producer)	Kick	Snare	Hi-hats/ toms	Overheads
The Smiths, "The Queen Is Dead" (producers: Morrisey, Johnny Marr)	AKG D12	Shure SM57	Toms: Sennheiser 421	Neumann U87
The Staple Singers, "I'll Take You Higher" (producer: Terry Manning)	Neumann FET 47	Shure 545	Hi-hats: Neumann KM84	Neumann U87
The Stone Roses, "Fool's Gold" (producer: John Leckie)	AKG D12	Shure SM57	Toms: Sennheiser 421	Neumann U87 and AKG 414
The Strokes, "Is This It?" (producer: Gordon Raphael)	Shure Beta 58	Shure SM57	Hi-hats: Shure SM57	Audio Technica 4033A
The Who, "Who Are You?" (producers: Jon Astley, Glyn Johns)	AKG D30	Shure SM57	Toms: Sennheiser 421	Neumann U87

1.3 Directional Response

Another important component of a microphone's operations principle, which plays a crucial (if often overlooked) role in the microphone selection process, is directional response. Every microphone is manufactured to "hear" sound in only certain directions, and "directional response" describes how they do so. There are three basic directional responses: (i) omni-directional microphones, which hear equally well in all directions; (ii) bi-directional microphones, which hear only in front and behind; and (iii) uni-directional microphones, which hear in front, and to their sides, but only very slightly behind (given the heart-like shape of their directional response, uni-directional microphones are often called "cardioid" microphones). Hyper-cardioid and super-cardioid microphones simply extend the basic cardioid directional response further behind (see **Figure 1.14** below).

Recordists have devised a number of practical applications for the concept of directional response. Norman Smith, for example, devised an interesting use for the bi-directional response, in particular to over-dub vocal parts for The Beatles in the early 1960s. The Beatles continued to record their vocal and instrumental parts live in the studio after they adopted four-track technology in 1964, but producer George Martin took to reserving an extra track for overdubs. As Ringo Starr (in Ryan and Kehew 2008: 376) remembers:

> Most of our early recordings were on three tracks, because we kept one for overdubs. [This] kept us together as a band — we played and played and played. If one of them could sing it, the four of us could play it until the cows came home. There was none of this, "Well, we'll put the bass on later, or the guitars." We put most of it on then and there [in the studio "live" room], including the vocals.

Amazingly, The Beatles didn't use headphones to track until they recorded *Revolver* in 1966. To overdub vocal parts, band members had to stand in front of a massive RLS10 "White Elephant" speaker which output reference tracks to sing along with. This setup could easily have

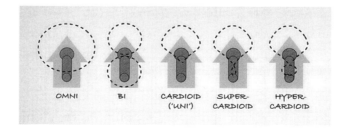

Figure 1.14 Common directional response profiles. From left to right: omni-, bi-, uni- (cardioid), hyper-cardioid and super-cardioid.

induced any number of phase interference issues. The microphone used to capture John Lennon's and Paul McCartney's vocal overdubs for "Money," for instance, might also have captured the reference tracks which Lennon and McCartney sang along with, but delayed by a few milliseconds and, thus, slightly out of phase with the original recording. To guard against this possibility, Norman Smith selected Neumann U47 and U48 large-diaphragm condenser microphones set for a bi-directional response; and he placed the microphones directly between both singers, and directly perpendicular to the White Elephant speaker (see **Figure 1.15** below), knowing that their bi-directional response would actively reject the speaker output. In this case, the bi-directional response also provided the added benefit of allowing the band to record two distinct vocal parts onto the same track, at a time when track space was at a premium.

Sound doesn't just travel in a straight line, however — it spreads in numerous directions at once. Smith's microphone selection and placement simply could not reject all the White Elephant speaker output. Some of the reference tracks from the speaker inevitably leaked onto the overdubbed tracks. Those overdubbed tracks thus introduced a slightly delayed version of the reference tracks, which, combined with the originals, produced subtle tonal distortions in the form of comb-filtering. As Kevin Ryan and Brian Kehew (2009: 377) explain:

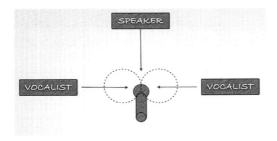

Figure 1.15   Diagram of Norman Smith's placement scheme. Set for a bi-directional response, the microphone (usually a Neumann U47 or U48) captured two distinct vocal performances onto the same track, and actively rejected reference tracks output by the White Elephant speaker.

The amount was very small, but if multiple overdubs took place, the leakage "stacked up" and was accentuated. It could also sometimes reveal itself as a very subtle phasing effect. This was the result of multiple "copies" of the same sound playing back simultaneously. The rhythm track, for instance, was recorded onto Track 1 of the tape. If a vocal was then overdubbed onto Track 3, a small amount of rhythm track leakage from the White Elephant speaker was recorded on Track 3 along with the vocals. If yet another vocal was overdubbed on top of that onto Track 4, the leakage was recorded once more . . . Upon mixing, these recordings of the leakage could interact with each other, as well as the original rhythm track. Whenever multiple occurrences of the same sound are played back in near-perfect alignment, a subtle "swishing", phasing effect can result. The effect is subtle, but headphone listening can reveal it to be quite audible in a number of tracks.

The "swishing" effect which Ryan and Kehew (2008) describe in the passage above is clearly audible on the stereo mix for "I Wanna Be Your Man" from The Beatles' *With The Beatles*. Readers can isolate the overdubbed vocal tracks by listening to only their left speaker or headphone: the band's overdubbed vocals were switched to the left side of the stereo plane while the bed tracks were switched to the right. Listening to just the left side of the mix for "I Wanna Be Your Man" reveals Ringo Starr's lead vocals, John Lennon's and Paul McCartney's backing vocal tracks, and the reference tracks coming from the White Elephant; and at 0:20 into the track, an unmistakably clear example of leakage-phasing is audible on the cymbal crash which sounds then. Paul McCartney's vocal overdubs for "Little Child," also on the stereo release for *With The Beatles*, reveal similar leakage-phasing throughout, as do vocal overdubs for "It Won't Be Long," "All My Loving" and "Devil In Her Heart."

1.4 Microphone Placement

Directional response provides a conceptual bridge between micro-phone selection and microphone placement. When recordists select a microphone, they do so with a basic concept of how they will place that microphone already in mind; and they generally follow that concept through to success or failure. If the initial placement fails to yield a desirable sound, as is often the case, recordists adjust the placement incrementally until they find a distance from the sound source that works. They may also deploy different directional responses to empha-size different aspects of the sound source. Placed in close proximity to a sound source, the uni-directional response, for instance, will exag-gerate its bass content (the proximity effect) while an omni-directional response will provide a more even response. Similarly, the bi-directional and omni-directional responses capture more reverberations than the uni-directional response. Recordists can thus deploy microphone placement and directional response in tandem to refine the frequency response of selected microphones, which in turn significantly alters the audible character of tracks on a record. Albin Zak (2001: 110) explains this best:

> The subtle art of microphone placement is nearly as important a factor in the rendering of the sonic image as microphone design, and recordists continually refine and expand their technique through experimentation. The placement determines the degree and type of coloration and defines the relationship between sound source and room sound. Considerations include not only the microphone's orientation to the sound source — as defined by distance and angle — and the acoustic characteristics of the room, but also the microphone's sound gathering properties . . . A microphone's polar pattern, frequency response characteristics, and placement, are all factors in its timbral effect.

CLOSE-MIC PLACEMENTS

Through microphone placement, recordists refine the sonic image that any given frequency response initially presents. Close-mic placements, that is, transduction using microphones placed within roughly three to twelve inches of a sound source, produce a distinctly dry or non-reverberant sound; and again, directional microphones tend to exaggerate the low-frequency content of a sound source when placed in close proximity. Seemingly paradoxically, close-mic techniques can also add a significant amount of high-frequency "edge" to tracks, depending on how the microphone is angled, because air absorption plays a relatively negligible role in the transduction. As Scott Hunter Stark (2005: 64–5) explains:

> Attenuation of higher frequencies is a particularly important factor in large environments. The higher the frequency is, the greater the loss is, so the more difficult it becomes to effectively project over long distances. Stated simply, low frequencies carry farther than high frequencies . . . This type of loss increases in severity as frequency increases because there are more interactions between individual molecules as frequency increases.

The sound of close-mic tracking has become ubiquitous in the modern pop soundscape. Electric guitars, acoustic guitars, acoustic basses, acoustic pianos, lead vocals, percussion instruments, drum kits — the gamut of instruments used on popular music records — are now tracked using close-mic placements as a rule. This likely has as much to do with the practicalities of multi-track recording as it does with aesthetics:

> The very process of multitrack production inspires and all but requires that the multitrack arrangement be built up over time, not in a single live performance. Unable to accurately predict the reverberant quality each track will ultimately need, the recording

engineer very often wishes to record tracks with little or no reverberation within the signal. Ambience and related sound qualities are
to be added later, at mixdown, when the interaction of all tracks is
before the engineer. (Case 2007: 269–70)

Precisely how close a microphone needs to be to a sound source to
qualify as a close-mic placement remains an entirely variable measure.
In this respect, close-mic tracking remains a fuzzy science. The precise
distance between sound source and close-mic varies according to the
peculiar demands of each particular sound source and the specific
needs of the production at hand. Close-mics are usually placed within a
foot of vocalists, for instance, but within inches of drum heads. And this
variability seems likely to remain a defining characteristic. In Recording
Practice — and, especially, in pop Recording Practice — product far
outweighs process: pop recordists in particular remain almost pathologically open to breaking common practice techniques for tracking,
especially if they sense that doing so will produce an aesthetically
superior product.

Close-mic placements are easiest to hear on lead-vocal tracks. In
fact, now lead-vocals are almost uniformly tracked for pop productions
using close-mic placements. Bill Gibson (2003: 13) explains:

> Usually in commercial popular music it's best to record vocals in a
> room that's acoustically neutral (doesn't have a long reverberation
> time) and from a distance of 6 to 12 inches. This approach provides
> the most flexibility during mixdown. You maintain the freedom
> to use reverberation and other effects to artificially place the vocal
> in the space that best suits the emotion of the music. Be willing to
> experiment with different acoustic settings. However, take care that
> you don't [record from such a distance] that you include so much
> room sound that the vocal loses the close intimacy that [character-
> izes] a lot of popular music.

Of course, with close-mic placements the angle between the microphone and the sound source — in this case, the singer's mouth — plays an equally crucial role as proximity in refining frequency response:

> Where you place the mic in relation to the singer will affect the tonal quality of the vocal sound. If you place the mic directly in front of the singer's mouth (pointing directly at the singer) you'll get a pretty even and natural tonal balance. But if he or she makes much noise while singing, it will come through — loud and clear — on your recorder. These noises typically include lip smacks, nose sniffs, breaths, and sometimes even the sound of air leaking through the nose while the performance is happening. If the sound isn't good directly in front of the singer, try moving the mic up about 3 or 4 inches above the singer's mouth and pointing it down at the mouth. This usually eliminates a lot of the lip smacks and other noises, plus it cleans up the nasal sound that some singers have problems with. If you position the mic 4 to 6 inches below the vocalist's mouth and then aim the mic up at the mouth, you might fill out a thin sounding voice, but you might get more extraneous noises than you care to deal with. (Gibson 2003: 13)

Clear examples of close-mic vocal tracks abound in modern pop. **Table 1.4** below lists a number of clear examples from Elliott Smith's eponymous debut album for the Kill Rock Stars label, and from his follow-up, *Either/Or*. Smith's vocals were always produced by close-mic placements on his early folk releases; and they are rife with both the unstrained character of close-mic lead-vocal tracks and extra-musical sounds that characterize the close-mic technique (e.g., heaving breaths; lip smacks; loud plosives and exaggerated sibilance; nose sniffs; etc.). For a more conventional Top 40 close-mic vocal sound, readers should consult: Lily Allen's vocals in the verses of "The Fear", Fergie's vocals during the choruses of "Glamorous", Imogen Heap's lead-vocals on "Hide And Seek", Madonna's spoken verses on "Erotica" and, arguably, Samuel Beam's whispered vocals for Iron & Wine's cover version of The Postal Service's "From A Great Height."

Table 1.4 Close-mic vocal tracks on Elliott Smith's self-titled debut and *Either/Or*.

Record	Track
Elliott Smith, *Elliott Smith*	1. Needle In The Hay
	3. Clementine
	4. Southern Belle
	5. Single File
	7. Satellite
	8. Alphabet Town
	10. Good To Go
	11. The White Lady Loves You More
	12. The Biggest Lie
Elliott Smith, *Either/Or*	1. Speed Trials
	2. Alameda
	4. Between The Bars
	6. No Name #5
	9. Angeles
	11. 2:45 AM
	12. Say Yes

DISTANCE-MIC PLACEMENTS

Despite their ubiquity, close-mic techniques are not the only placement option open to recordists when they track. In fact, recordists regularly forego close-mic placements altogether, especially if doing so seems likely to produce an aesthetically superior product. Rather than position microphones within inches of instruments, recordists may instead opt to place them anywhere beyond about three feet from the sound source. These distance-mic placements register significant amounts of room ambience and reverberations alongside the direct sound of the sound source itself; and they also produce tracks which obviously lack the same high-frequency edge that close-mic placements produce, because air absorption plays a more obvious role in the transduction.

Aside from its ear-splitting feedback, which made the record so critically controversial in the mid-1980s, The Jesus And Mary Chain's *Psychocandy* is notable for the almost total absence of close-mic placements throughout. Every sound on the record is obviously, and completely, the product of distance-mic placements, save the Reid brothers' laconic vocal tracks (the tracks are, however, treated with reverb set for cavernously long decay rates). Other exceptions to the predominance of close-mic tracking include: Robert Plant's lead-vocal tracks on a number of cuts from Led Zeppelin's *Physical Graffiti*, including "Custard Pie," "Trampled Under Foot," "The Wanton Song," "Boogie With Stu" and "Sick Again"; Tom Waits' lead-vocals on any of his celebrated "junkyard" records (i.e., *Swordfishtrombones, Rain Dogs, Frank's Wild Years, Bone Machine* and *The Black Rider*); and, finally, Mick Jagger's lead-vocals throughout The Rolling Stones' *Exile On Main Street*, but especially on "Rip This Joint," "Sweet Virginia," "Sweet Black Angel," "Loving Cup," "Ventilator Blues," "I Just Want To See His Face," "Stop Breaking Down" and "Soul Survivor."

THE CRITICAL DISTANCE

The specific ratio of direct sound to ambient sound on distance-mic tracks depends on a number of mediating variables. Frequency response, directional response and microphone placement all play an equally important role in determining this ratio, as do the physical properties of the sound source itself, and the acoustic character of the tracking environment. That said, proximity usually plays the deciding role. As Glenn White and Gary Louie (2005: 89) explain:

> In a reverberant space, the sound perceived by a listener is a combi-
> nation of direct and reverberant sound. The ratio of direct sound is
> dependent on the distance between the source and the listener, and
> upon the reverberation time in [the room]. At a certain distance the
> two will be equal. This is called the "critical distance."

The concept of critical distance plays a significant role in microphone placement techniques. It is clearly evident in the placement technique that Bob Ezrin (in Pedersen 2007) developed for tracking David Gilmour's acoustic guitars on Pink Floyd's *The Wall*, for instance:

> Whenever I recorded an acoustic guitar, the first thing I would do is stand in front of the guitarist and listen to the performance. Then I'd plug one ear — because most microphones only hear from one pinpoint source — and move around, listening with my open ear, until I found the spot where the guitar sounded the best. In that sweet spot, I would really pay attention to the tonal contour of the guitar. Is it rich in mid-range? Does it have a big boomy sound on the bottom and very little presence? The trick, then, was not to use a microphone that had the same tonal qualities as the guitar. For example, a Neumann U47 would sound too muddy on a guitar with a boomy low end.

Bruce Swedien describes a similar practice. Rather than position the microphone in relation to the sound source, however, Swedien works the other way around, moving singers a few inches away from microphones with each successive overdubbed take. Recording choral vocals, for instance, Swedien (2009: 122) explains:

> My first mic choice would be high-quality, good condition large-[diaphragm] condenser microphones, such as the AKG 414 EB, or a matched pair of Neumann M149s. These two beautiful microphones . . . are superb for high-quality vocal recording. I would then ask the singers to step back from the mic about two feet or so and record a double of the original part. By having the singers step back from the mic during this vocal pass, in order to keep the track levels consistent, we are forced to raise the volume level of the mics on this pass, thus giving greater acoustical support for the sound. Finally, I will normally mix these four tracks in the final mix in the same proportion on the same side of the stereo panorama as they occurred in the performance.

Swedien used this technique on a number of Michael Jackson's most commercially successful records. In Swedien's (2009: 19) words:

> Michael [Jackson] is such an expert at doubling his background and other vocal parts that he even doubles his vibrato rate perfectly! . . . I'll have him double the same track at the same position at the mic. After that track, I'll have him step back two paces and record a third pass of the same melody with the gain raised to match the level of the previous two. That raises the ratio of [reverberations] to direct sound. Blended with the first two tracks, this has a wonderful effect. Finally, I might even have him step back further and record a stereo pass of the same line. You can hear this technique in action for yourself on Michael's background block-harmony-vocals on the song "Rock With You" on Michael's *Off The Wall* album, or on the choir in the song "Man In The Mirror" on Michael's *Bad* album. This technique tricks the ear into perceiving a depth field that isn't really there [through the addition of discreet "early reflections" (see under Reverberation Processing in Chapter 3)].

Example 1.3   Close-Mic And Distance-Mic Vocals

Example 1.3 juxtaposes vocal sounds produced by distance-mic and close-mic placements, in the context of an original rock mix ("Stains"). The vocals for the verses, choruses and bridge are the product of distance-mic placements: a large-diaphragm condenser microphone placed two feet from the singer's mouth. Both pre-choruses — beginning with the lyrics: "nothing ever turns out right" and "kiss me soft and get on the plane," respectively — are the product of extreme close-mic placements, the same microphone having been placed within less than an inch of the singer's mouth during transduction (the singer was asked to "kiss" the microphone through a "pop screen" as much as possible). Astute listeners may notice a fair amount of sibilance on the distance-mic vocal tracks; this was a product of harmonic excitation at 4–6 kHz which, though the sibilance is regrettable, was necessary to ensure the lead-vocal track remained coherent and present throughout the track.

ROOM-MICS

Should close-mic and distance-mic placements fail to yield a sufficiently powerful and engaging sound on their own, recordists may opt to deploy both placements in tandem. Because it captures a considerable amount of room ambience, the distance-mic in a tandem placement is usually called a "room-mic", and it is typically placed far enough past the critical distance in a room that the room's ambience and reverberations transduce at an equivalent, if not greater, volume than the sound source itself. Though this tandem technique is apparent everywhere in the modern pop soundscape, it is also now industry standard for tracking rhythm guitars in rock. As Bill Gibson (2002a: 36–7) notes:

> Powerful guitar sounds often include the sound of the immediate space (the room) that the amp is in. This can be accomplished with reverb, but natural ambience can add an unusual and distinct quality to a recording . . . We can get a great guitar sound if we put one mic within a foot of the amp and one mic back in the room several feet away from the amp. With this technique, we can blend the sound of the mic closest to the amp with ambient sound captured by the mic farther away. We can combine these two sounds to one track as we record, or if tracks permit, we can print each mic to a separate track and save the blending or panning for mixdown. The effectiveness of this approach is dependent on whether the sound of the room is musically appropriate.

Jimmy Page made extensive use of this technique throughout the late 1960s and 1970s. The rhythm guitar part on Led Zeppelin's "Communication Breakdown" provides a celebrated example. Placing a small 10-watt Supro practice amplifier in what Page (cited in Rosen 1977) once called "a little tiny vocal booth kind of thing," the guitarist-cum-producer then placed a dynamic microphone roughly six inches from the amplifier with its diaphragm pointed directly "on-axis", that is, at the center of the speaker cone, and a room-mic placed about ten feet away (on-axis placements add high-frequency edge to tracks while off-axis placements tend to produce a duller sound). He then summed (blended) both signals onto the same track, producing the distinctive electric guitar tone which permeates the record. In Page's (in Rosen 1977) words:

> There's a very old recording maxim which goes, "Distance makes depth." I've used that a hell of a lot on recording techniques with the band [Led Zeppelin] generally, not just me. You're always used to [recordists] close-miking amps, just putting the microphone in front, but I'd have a mic in the room as well, and then balance the two tracks; because really, you shouldn't have to use an EQ in the studio if the instruments sound right. It should all be done with the microphones.

Rick Rubin and Ryan Hewitt used the room-mic technique to track John Frusciante's electric guitar parts for The Red Hot Chili Peppers' *BloodSugarSexMagik*. Positioning a Shure SM57 dynamic microphone within inches of Frusciante's amplifier, and angled directly on-axis to add some high-frequency edge to the track, Hewitt then added a room-mic further back in the room, specifically, a Royer R-121 ribbon microphone placed exactly 15 feet away from the amplifier (Brown 2009: 192). The same technique was also used to track Noel Gallagher's lead-guitar on Oasis' "Champagne Supernova." Gallagher tracked the part alone in a cavernous live room, with multiple room-mics distributed throughout, some of which were spaced more than 30 feet from the amplifier. The tandem technique is also clear in Billy Corgan's distorted guitar tone on the heavier cuts off *Siamese Dream* and *Mellon Collie & The Infinite Sadness*, that is: "Cherub Rock," "Today," "Bullet With Butterfly Wings," "Zero" and "Fuck You (An Ode To No One)."

ROOM SOUND

When recordists add a room-mic to a mix, they also add the acoustic character of the tracking environment. British and American records produced throughout the 1970s often sound so different, in fact, because recordists working in both countries took entirely distinct approaches to the craft of microphone placement. As Simon Zagorski-Thomas (2005) observes:

> The studios used for popular music recording tended to have larger recording spaces with higher ceilings in the UK. Of course, there were smaller studios in Britain, like Trident, and larger studios in America, like Columbia's 30th Street studio in New York. The larger studios in the US seem to have been used more for orchestral and musical theatre recordings, though. These smaller recording spaces combined with more extensive use of close microphone placement and screening in the US would certainly account for the less ambient recordings with greater separation that I'm suggesting are character-istic of the American sound . . . Close microphone placement was less common in the UK in the early 1970s. Abbey Road engineers at the end of the 1960s had to ask for special permission to use close microphone placements as it was feared that the sound pres-sure levels would damage the microphones . . . British recordings [typically] used some combination of larger rooms and a more ambient microphone placement. American recordings had shorter and sharper attack transients because of smaller rooms, greater use of screening and closer microphone placement with a microphone on every drum in a kit.

Of course, given the recent onset of the project paradigm, room-mic placements may have become, for all intent and purposes, an endan-gered species in tracking. Restricted by the limitations of the project environment, which is usually neither "tuned" (acoustically treated) nor large enough to accommodate the distances that room-mic placements

require, project recordists often have little choice but to use signal processing to simulate the acoustic information which a room-mic adds.
David Simons (2004: 13) explains:

> Over the course of history, every so often we've managed to undo
> something that is already a proven success. Take the record busi-
> ness. By 1980, digital recording technology had emerged, bringing
> with it machinery and methods that were considered revolutionary
> compared to those of yesteryear. Yet many of the records produced
> during that time now sound thin and dated. "But then you put on
> a 1950s jazz record," remarks producer Jon Brion, "and it's still the
> closest thing we have to being in the room without actually being in
> the room. It's incredible. How did we lose that?" . . . Make no mistake:
> Sonny Rollins' *Saxophone Colossus*, Miles Davis' *Kind of Blue*, Dave
> Brubeck's *Time Out*, or any of the unsurpassed masters from New
> York's "golden age" of sound would not have been possible without
> the burst of technology that had, just a few years earlier, taken the
> business from wax to multiple tracks. But improved fidelity was just
> one part of the formula: the main ingredient was the room itself.

Table 1.5 below lists a number of celebrated tracks produced in New
York City's most famous recording studios between 1954 and 1995.
Though they did not do so to the same degree as their British coun-
terparts, as Zagorski-Thomas (2005) makes clear, recordists working
in these American studios nonetheless often placed room-mics while
they tracked. The goal was to capture as much of the studio's sonic
signature as possible, that is, as much of the unique tonal coloration
which each studio's peculiar acoustics contributed to a record, without
disfiguring the impact and presence of the broader production (Simons
2004). They then blended the signal from the room-mic with the more
present tracks derived from close-mic placements. The idiosyncratic
acoustics of each studio environment listed in Table 1.5 — what
recordists would call their "room sounds" — thus played a crucial role
in shaping the sound of records made there. In so doing, these "room

sounds" importantly helped shape the tone of the American Top 40 in the decades immediately following World War II.

Table 1.5 Celebrated pop records and the New York City studios where they were tracked.

Studio	Artist, track
A&R Studio 1	Quincy Jones, "Soul Bossa Nova" (1962); Stan Getz and Astrud Gilberto, "Girl From Ipanema" (1964); Peter Paul and Mary, "I Dig Rock And Roll Music" (1967); Van Morisson, "Brown Eyed Girl"
Allegro Sound	The 4 Seasons, "Rag Doll" (1964); The Critters, "Younger Girl" (1966); Tommy James and the Shondells, "Mony, Mony" (1968)
Atlantic Studio 1	Big Joe Turner, "Shake Rattle & Roll" (1954)
Atlantic Studio 3	Aretha Franklin, "Baby I Love You" (1967); Cream, "Sunshine Of Your Love" (1968)
Bell Sound/ Hit Factory	Dionne Warwick; "Walk On By" (1964); B. J. Thomas, "Raindrops Keep Falling On My Head" (1969); Kiss, "Rock And Roll All Nite" (1975)
Columbia Studio A	Simon & Garfunkel, "Homeward Bound" (1966); The Lovin' Spoonful, "Summer In The City" (1966)
Columbia Studio B	Big Brother & The Holding Company, "Piece Of My Heart" (1968); Simon & Garfunkel, "The Only Living Boy In New York" (1970)
Columbia 30th Street	Dave Brubeck, "Take Five" (1961); Tony Bennett, "I Left My Heart In San Francisco" (1962); Sly And The Family Stone, "Sing A Simple Song" (1969)
Electric Lady Studios	Stevie Wonder, "Superstition" (1972); David Bowie, "Fame" (1975); Weezer, "Say It Ain't So" (1995)
Power Station/ Avatar	Bruce Springsteen, "Hungry Heart" (1980); David Bowie, "Let's Dance" (1983); Madonna, "Like A Virgin" (1984)
Record Plant	Alice Cooper, "School's Out" (1972); John Lennon, "Just Like Starting Over" (1980)
Sundragon Studio	The Ramones, "Blitzkrieg Bop" (1976); Talking Heads, "Psycho Killer" (1977)
Talentmasters Studio	James Brown, "It's A Man's Man's Man's World" (1966); The Capitols, "Cool Jerk" (1966); The Who, "I Can See For Miles" (1967)

2. DIRECT-INJECTION

Recordists may forego microphones altogether when they track, and use direct-injection (DI) technologies instead. Rather than route the output of an electric instrument to an amplifier, which is then transduced, recordists simply patch the instrument directly into pre-amplifier circuits on a mixing console, into signal processing devices, or into analog-to-digital converters, depending on what resources they have at their disposal; and from there, through to storage devices. However, if the output signal of the direct instrument fails to achieve "line-level," that is, if the instrument output remains too dynamically meager to be of any practical use to recordists, or if its output impedance does not match the impedance requirements of the input device, recordists may introduce a Direct-Injection Box (DI Box) as an intervening stage (impedance, or, Z, measures the amount of resistance to the flow of electrons presented by physical media in an audio chain such as electric guitar cables and preamplifier circuits). As David Franz (2004: 12–13) explains:

> "Direct" boxes are used for converting high impedance ("Z") signals to low impedance signals, or vice versa. They are used most often for transforming the signal from an electric guitar high-Z cable into a low-Z input (preamp) . . . If you plug a high-powered, high-impedance instrument (synthesizer) into a low impedance input (preamp), the high-impedance instrument can overdrive (and distort) the input because the synth is expecting a lot of resistance to its powerful signal, but the resistance isn't there. Likewise, if you plug a low-powered, low impedance device (like a microphone) into a high-impedance input, the low-[impedance] signal from the mic might meet too much resistance, and you won't be able to get enough gain for a healthy recording level, hence the need for preamps.

Line-level instruments like samplers, sequencers and synthesizers do not require a DI Box. These instruments output a signal which is already strong enough for recordists to use. DI Boxes are nowadays commonly used to record electric guitar and electric bass tracks. Returning once more to Daniel Thompson (2005: 155–6) for an explanation:

> A peculiar situation arises with electrical instrument signals from a source such as an electric guitar or bass. While the level . . . falls within the general definition of "line-level", unlike other "line-level" signals, it is a high-impedance source signal . . . If the electric guitar is plugged directly into the line input of a console or mixer, the impedance mismatch will result in a signal that is not only quite weak but susceptible to poor frequency response. The modest guitar signal with its microwatt-range power output is incapable of driving the load effectively. Furthermore, even modestly long guitar-cable runs are impossible because of the rapidly increased loss of signal, and increased gain requirements in turn mean increased noise. To exacerbate the problem, the guitar cable is unbalanced and, thus, more vulnerable to outside noise and interference.

Whether or not they require a DI Box, direct-injection techniques produce a distinct sound. Most obviously, direct-injection techniques produce an extremely dry, or, non-reverberant, tone. They also produce

Figure 1.16   The Avalon U5 Direct-Injection Box. Note the marking "Hi-Z" under the "Input" slot, which indicates that the U5 is designed to handle high-impedance signals usually outputted by electric guitar and electric bass.

a significant amount of high-frequency edge, because air absorption plays no role in the transduction. While some recordists complain that direct-injection tracks sound too dry or too edgy, direct-injection techniques remain standard for tracking electric guitars and electric bass. The leeway that direct-injection affords recordists for processing tracks later on in the (multi-track) production process, when the requirements of the mix are more fully evolved, is simply too beneficial to ignore. Moreover, direct-injection allows recordists to track without generating leakage (bleed-through) from other instruments. This can be extremely useful for bands whose music benefits from a primarily live rather than a sequentially compartmentalized tracking process but who lack access to sufficiently large live rooms for recording.

Though they did not invent the practice, The Beatles were one of the first rock bands to regularly feature direct-injection tracks on their records. The band's seminal *Sgt. Pepper's Lonely Hearts Club Band*, for instance, was one of the first records to use direct-injection tracking techniques throughout. Following the lead of Peter Brown and Peter Vince, who used direct-injection technology to track electric bass parts for records by The Hollies and The Shadows in 1966, almost every electric bass track on *Sgt. Pepper's* was produced by direct-injection techniques. Rather than patch Paul McCartney's electric bass into an amplifier, as convention dictated, engineer Ken Townsend routed the bass through a custom made DI Box, and from there onto an open track on the mixing console. As Townsend (in Ryan and Kehew 2008: 156) himself remembers:

> One of the most difficult instruments to record was the bass guitar. The problem was that no matter which type of high quality microphone we placed in front of the bass speaker it never sounded back in the Control Room as good as in the studio. One of the problems could well have been that the Altec monitors in the Control rooms were "bass light", so no matter what you did, it made little difference

to what you heard. However, although you couldn't hear it, there was bass on the tapes, and so the records were much better than you imagined at the time . . . Most of my experimental work on bass guitars came on the Hollies and The Beatles sessions, and it is not easy to remember with which I came up with the idea of feeding the output from the bass guitar straight into the mixing console. I named this method "Direct Injection".

McCartney's direct-injection electric bass tracks are most prominent on *Sgt. Pepper's* in "Lucy In The Sky With Diamonds," "When I'm Sixty-Four," "Lovely Rita" and "A Day in The Life." McCartney would also direct-inject his electric bass tracks for "Only A Northern Song" and "I Me Mine"; George Martin would do the same to create the searing and heavily "fuzzed" lead-guitar tone which introduces The Beatles' "Revolution."

More recently, the Dave Matthews Band made compelling use of the direct-injection tone on their second major label release: *Crash* (see **Table 1.6**). Cuts like "Two Step," "Too Much" and "Tripping Billies" prominently feature a direct-injected acoustic-electric guitar throughout. The album's opening track "So Much To Say," however, offers the clearest example. The track begins with only an acoustic guitar tracked using conventional means (i.e., a small-diaphragm condenser microphone placed within a foot of the guitar's twelfth fret). At 0:46 into the track, producer Steve Lillywhite then pans a direct-injected acoustic-electric guitar track to the right side of the stereo spectrum. The transduced acoustic guitar track in turn pans hard-left, creating a clear tonal dichotomy between the ultra-dry and ultra-edgy tone of Matthews' direct-injected guitar on one side, and the ambience-infused sound of his transduced acoustic guitar on the other. R&B singer Adele's "Daydreamer," the opening track on the album *19*, provides another exceptionally clear example: the track is solely comprised of a direct-injected acoustic-electric guitar and Adele's vocals.

Table 1.6 Tracks with an obviously direct-injected acoustic-electric guitar on Dave Matthews Band's *Crash*. The direct-injected track usually sounds in the right horizontal extreme of the mix.

Record	*Track*
Dave Matthews Band, *Crash*	1. "So Much To Say" 2. "Two Step" 4. "Too Much" 7. "Drive In Drive Out" 11. "Tripping Billies" 12. "Proudest Monkey"

2.1 Di-Transduction Tandems

Some recordists find the direct-injection tone simply unacceptable. The dryness of direct-injection tracks is overly jarring, they complain; the high-frequency edge they add is ear-splitting; and, moreover, the attack transients are grossly exaggerated (compare the picking sounds on the acoustic guitar track which opens Dave Matthews Band's "So Much To Say" with those on the direct-injection track which enters at 0:46). To remedy these concerns, recordists often deploy direct-injection and transduction techniques in tandem. "The two signals (direct and transduced) are routed through the console on two separate channels, and then recorded either to two separate tracks for proper balancing during mixdown, or combined straightaway and recorded to a single track," explains Daniel Thompson (2005: 158). "The benefit of this approach is that it takes advantage of the natural warmth and fullness of sound typical of the amp signal, and adds to it the clarity of attack and edge typical of DI signals."

> **Example 1.4   Direct-Injection And Close-Mic Tandems**
>
> Example 1.4 provides a clear illustration of the sound of a DI-transduction tandem applied to an acoustic-electric guitar. A quick demo sketch of an original song, called "Drowning," the production is comprised entirely of a direct-injection guitar track in the left channel, a close-mic capture of the direct-injected guitar track (transduced simultaneously) in the right channel, a close-mic lead-vocal in the center, and some random sequence elements (i.e., synth bass) in the center region. Readers can isolate the direct-injected and close-mic guitar tracks by listening to only their right and left headphones, respectively. The prominent picking sounds, and the sound of the pick periodically brushing against the pick-guard, in the guitar track situated hard-right along the stereo-plane indicate a close-mic placement. The obvious absence of those sounds in the track situated hard-left, indicates direct-injection.

Once again, The Beatles were amongst the first to deploy a DI-transduction tandem on record. After they recorded *Sgt. Pepper's*, the band regularly direct-injected and transduced Paul McCartney's electric bass tracks (this development was no doubt inspired by the band's adoption of eight-track tape in 1968). The tandem technique was used to record electric bass parts for Beatles tracks like: "Blue Jay Way"; "Baby You're A Rich Man"; "Hello, Goodbye"; and almost every electric bass part on *The Beatles* (a.k.a. "The White Album"), *Abbey Road* and *Let It Be* (except, as noted, "I Me Mine"). And of course, once The Beatles used the technique so regularly it could not be long before it became industry standard. Nowadays, when they are not sequenced, electric bass tracks are often tracked via either direct-injection or DI-transduction tandems. Clear illustrations of the tandem tone can be heard in the electric bass on Devo's "Whip It," Dire Straits' "Money For Nothin'", Duran Duran's "The Reflex" and the Stone Roses' "Fool's Gold."

3. SEQUENCING

The final tracking procedure which I examine in this field guide is sequencing, that is, operating a sequencer to create one or more component tracks in a multi-track production. The first sequencers to achieve any kind of prominence were computerized keyboards attached to synthesizer modules produced by Moog, ARP, Roland and Buchla. These original sequencers could "control eight to sixteen events (or notes) at a time, and were used primarily to create rhythmic ostinatos," as Thomas Rudolph and Vincent Leonard (2001: 8) explain. Recordists input pitches into these sequencers and, with a few more button pushes, their sequences were: (i) looped; (ii) sped up and slowed down; and (iii) tonally processed, using a connected synthesizer module. While the sequence sounded, recordists could then "modulate" (modify) the frequency and amplitude of each "event" (pitch) simply by adjusting specific dials on the connected module.

Pink Floyd's "On The Run," track two on the band's seminal *Dark Side Of The Moon* (*DSOM*), provides a clear record of early sequencing practice in the rock genre. Roger Waters, who was responsible for the majority of sequencing work on Pink Floyd's records throughout the 1970s, used a Synthi-A to craft the sequence which courses throughout "On The Run" (the Synthi-A was a compact version of the EMS VCS3 synthesizer, but with a prototype 250-step digital sequencer attached). The sequence fades-in at 0:12 of "On The Run." For the next 4 seconds, between 0:12 and 0:16, Waters subtly modulates the sequence, adjusting the cut-off frequency in a low-pass filter on the connected module, moving it up and down the audible spectrum (low-pass filters mute all frequencies above a selected cut-off frequency). Waters then repeats the process between 0:51 and 1:04, and again between 1:25 and 1:37. From 1:10 to 1:18, Waters modulates the amplitude of the sequence, creating the rhythmic trembling known as tremolo. And then between 1:45 and 2:20, he modulates the tremolo's frequency and amplitude in turn. He modulates frequency from 1:45 to 1:50 and 2:09 to 2:15, and amplitude from 2:01 to 2:08 and 2:18 to 2:20. Waters continues to modulate the sequence until a plane crash sounds at 3:03, hurried steps cross the stereo spectrum and "On The Run" very slowly cross-fades into "Time," the third cut on *DSOM*.

Example 1.5   Sequencing And Modulation
Example 1.5 demonstrates the sound of sequencing, and frequency and amplitude modulation. The example begins with an unprocessed statement of an initial sequence. Following Waters' example in "On The Run," the frequency of the sequence in Example 1.5 is then modulated, as the "shelving" frequency on a low-pass filter slowly ascends and descends through the audible spectrum. Then the amplitude of the sequence modulates, creating tremolo. Finally, both the frequency and amplitude of the sequence modulate simultaneously, creating something like auto-wah. The sequence then fades-out.

A recent documentary film about the making of *DSOM* — titled, appropriately enough, *The Making Of The Dark Side Of The Moon* — provides footage of Roger Waters while he sequenced "On The Run" in 1973. What is surprising about the footage, from a modern perspective, is that Waters performed the Synthi-A precisely as he performed the electric bass. Tracking before the emergence of modern workstation sequencers, which allow users to program modulations using "track automation", Waters had no choice but to treat the Synthi-A as he might treat any other instrument, specifically, as a sound producing technology which, despite its sequencing capacities, required human intervention. In fact, the Synthi-A did not generate a single pitch of "On The Run." Sequencers themselves don't actually generate sounds. What a sequencer does is provide a connected sound-producing mechanism with control information, which tells that mechanism what sounds it should generate, at what volume and for how long. Viewed from this perspective, sequencing looks much less like a species of performance practice and much more like a kind of computer programming.

THE WORKSTATION PARADIGM

Early sequencers only stored and triggered sequences of pitches. Today, however, sequencers — or, as modern software sequencers are called, "digital-audio workstations" (DAWs) — store, trigger, sequence and process: (i) control information for virtual synthesizers and MIDI instruments; (ii) samples; and (iii) digital-audio tracks. Moreover, modern workstations usually feature "native" (built-in) analog-to-digital and digital-to-analog conversion capacities, which means that they can store, process and "bounce" to disc transduced and direct-injected audio information. Entire records can be made now using only a single workstation, and a number of successful pop recordists work exclusively on computers. The Streets' *Original Pirate Material, A Grand Don't Come For Free* and *The Hardest Way To Make An Easy Living* provide clear illustrations of the sounds that exclusive DAW work can create, even if Mike Skinner's vocal tracks on those albums were tracked via traditional analog means. Moreover, bands like Nine Inch Nails, Radiohead, Ben Folds Five, The Beastie Boys and The Roots have begun to court this emerging workstation market by releasing DAW multi-track files of popular tracks for fans to download and remix without charge, in lieu of more traditional release strategies.

The term "workstation" now refers to any instrument or computer software which hubs (combines) once distinct sequencing, processing, digital-audio (i.e., transduction) and MIDI capabilities into a single package. However, early workstations — like the Korg N-364, Korg Trinity, Ensoniq TS-12 and the Kurzweil K2000 — functioned more like enhanced synthesizers than anything else. As Thomas Rudolph and Vincent Leonard (2001: 14) explain,

> though a workstation may resemble a programmable keyboard from the outside, it is different inside: workstations have built in MIDI sequencer and drum sounds. Workstations usually include an effects-processing device, that allows you to add digital echo and reverb to sounds and sequences. In addition, there is typically a storage device, such as a disk drive, for storing sequences. Some keyboards even offer the option of digital recording.

Whatever their capacities, Rudolph and Leonard (2001: 14) continue:

the purpose of a workstation is to provide an all-in-one instrument: a performance keyboard, a built-in sequencer, and effects devices for creating and playing back sequences. A workstation might serve as the main component of a low-budget studio.

Modern software workstations — such as ProTools, Reason, Cubase, Live, Nuendo and LogicStudio — extend the early workstation paradigm into the realm of personal computing. As noted, these DAWs function exactly like sequencers did but with added signal processing, MIDI and synthesis capabilities. Modern software workstations also enable tracking and storage of digital-audio information created through traditional modalities, that is, through transduction and direct-injection. Not surprisingly then, many recordists have heralded the emergence of the software DAW as the simultaneous death of the analog paradigm in Recording Practice. Sequencing, these recordists claim, is the new paradigm in tracking. Whether or not this is the case — and compelling arguments have been made either way — remains to be seen. What has certainly accompanied the DAW to the musical fore are certain tracking and processing procedures that can only be achieved using a personal computer, which I call "step inputting", "real inputting" and "digital-audio" recording. Before I can survey these techniques, though, I will first explain how it is that, in the first instance, digital-audio technology "hears" sound.

DIGITAL-AUDIO: HOW COMPUTERS HEAR

Recordists call the changes in electrical current which microphones produce, and which audio-tape registers, "analog", because the changes are directly proportional, which is to say, they are directly analogous, to the changes in air pressure that produce them. However, "everything that happens in a digital device comes down to strings of 1's and 0's," as Jim Aiken (2004: 20) explains. "To represent sound digitally, it has to be translated somehow into numerical form." In most cases, this translation — from sound into numbers — is achieved via an analog-to-digital converter (A/D or ADC) which measures incoming voltages from an analog device and converts those voltages into discrete numeric values. Translation in the other direction, that is, from numbers back into sound, requires a digital-to-analog converter (D/A or DAC) which translates the discrete numeric values in a digital-audio file back into analog voltages.

Digital-audio mediations do not end at A/D or D/A conversion, however. To be of any use to a workstation, sound must pass through two more layers of data-processing, namely, sampling and quantization. Just as a movie doesn't actually consist of moving pictures, a digital record doesn't actually consist of moving sounds. Movies and digital records rely on a kind of stop-motion animation to achieve the illusion of motion. Movies are actually rapid sequences of single photos, called "frames", projected onto cinema screens at rates of roughly 24, 25 and 30 frames per second. Likewise, digital records are actually rapid sequences of sonic snapshots, called "samples", transduced in such rapid succession that listeners hear a continuous sequence of sounds, rather than a series of discrete digital-audio recordings.[1] To achieve this illusion, samples must be transduced at a staggering rate of at least 40,000 samples per second; therefore, digital-audio technology must be able to create samples with equal rapidity.

In fact, a sample rate of 44,100 samples per second — that is, a sample rate of 44.1 kHz — is now industry standard for professional and amateur digital-audio systems. This is likely a holdover from the earliest days of the compact disc, when digital technology simply could not sample any faster (successive formats like the DVD and SACD use much higher sample rates). Recordists and manufacturers did not randomly arrive at a rate of 44.1 kHz, however. That number was the

---

1 Samples of this kind are, of course, entirely different from the excerpts of previously recorded materials, also called "samples", which DJs and producers use to create sample-based musics like hip hop, techno and other forms of electronic dance music.

product of a complicated mathematical reasoning the late engineer Harry Nyquist first proposed. David Franz (2004: 26) provides a remarkably cogent explanation, worth reproducing here in full:

> Digital recording is like taking pictures of music at a speed determined by the sample rate. In order to reconstruct an accurate continuous analog sound from digital samples, we need to take over 40,000 samples per second. That is referred to as the "sample rate". If the sample rate is set to 44.1 kHz, your digital recording device takes 44,100 "pictures" of your input audio signal every second. Each picture — each sample — captures the amplitude (level) of the audio signal at that moment. So, when even one second of analog signal is recorded digitally, there are thousands of samples to represent it as digital information . . . The American engineer Harry Nyquist figured out that the sample rate must at least double the frequency (pitch) that we want to represent in order for it to sound accurate to our ears. That is, our sound "camera" has to snap at least twice as fast as the wave is cycling in order for us to get a good picture of its waveform. Because we can only hear sounds up to 20 kHz, we only need to sample at twice that frequency, 40 kHz. This formula is known as the "Nyquist theorem".

Whatever its sample rate, each time a digital-audio device samples a sound source it defines what it hears as a particular binary value. In other words, samples are quantized, or digitally mapped, to discrete digital values. During quantization, samples are converted into digital words which are discreet sequences of binary digits (bits), each as long as the bit-depth of the digital-audio device itself. When a device has a bit-depth of only 1-bit, for instance, samples are quantized to a value of either 1 or 0; such a limited bit-depth measures only the presence and absence of sound. A bit-depth of 2-bits, on the other hand, doubles the number of quantization levels available for quantization up to four, in which case the device can begin to measure pitch and volume; a bit-depth of 3-bits generates eight quantization levels; and so on (see **Figure 1.20**).

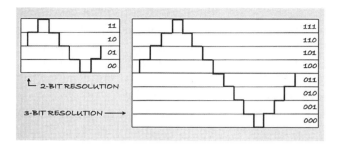

Figure 1.20 A 2-bit resolution with four quantization levels and a 3-bit resolution with eight quantization levels. The most commonly used resolutions are 16-bit, and 24-bit, which offer 65,536 and 16,777,216 quantization levels, respectively (adapted from Franz 2004: 38–9).

Increasing bit-depth increases resolution, which is the number of quantization levels a digital-audio device can use to map, or quantize, sounds to discrete binary values. Compact discs require a 16-bit resolution even though most digital-audio devices now allow recordists to track at resolutions of more than 24-bits. Though this may seem like yet another purely academic consideration, discrepancies in resolution can lead to a number of practical problems during tracking and once tracking is complete. Compact discs and CD-players comprise a 16-bit system, for instance. When recordists track for compact disc using modern 24-bit equipment, they have to dither what they record to a resolution of 16-bits. Far from a merely procedural consideration, the dithering process can induce a number of distortions. As Thomas Rudolph and Vincent Leonard (2001: 4) explain:

> It would appear that the standard ... compact disc format (16-bit sampling and 44.1 kHz sample rate) is ideal. However, the hardware that controls these signals is not perfect and can affect the overall sound quality. For example, when an analog signal is converted to a digital signal, and in the conversion process is slightly altered, a distortion called "quantization noise" occurs. "Aliasing", another form of signal corruption, happens when the analog-to-digital

converter misreads the signal and produces a lower frequency. To reduce signal distortion, some systems record at sampling rates of 44.1 kHz but with 20- or 24-bit resolution. This allows for greater dynamic range and reduced distortion or noise during production. However, before the CD is recorded, the signals must be "dithered" down to 16-bit. "Dithering" is the name given to the process of reducing the number of bits in each digital word or sample. This process involves adding some white noise to the signal. Using a process called "noise-shaping", this noise is usually switched to areas of the audio spectrum to which our ears are less sensitive, above 10 kHz.

Example 1.6   Bitcrushing

Example 1.6 uses a "bitcrusher" to emulate the audible byproduct of "down-sampling" digital-audio without dithering and noise-shaping. The bit-depth of the original track is successively reduced with each subsequent reiteration of the vibraphone sample. Example 1.6 begins with a full iteration of the primary sample, at a 24-bit resolution; then, for the second iteration, at 0:09, the resolution is down-sampled to 16-bits. After this point, the resolution is reset four more times: at 0:19 it is set to 10-bits; at 0:28 it is set for 8-bits; at 0:38 it is set for 4-bits; and, then, at 0:46, it is returned to its original setting, specifically, 24-bits. After only 9 seconds, noise accrues. Initially, it sounds like white noise, but it very quickly grows in intensity and the track is increasingly garbled.

3.1 Workstation Capacities

The workstation paradigm has been embraced by so many record-ists that the capacities of digital-audio workstations themselves now underwrite modern Recording Practice in its entirety. This is not to say that recordists only use workstations to track their records now. In fact, some recordists conspicuously, and vocally, avoid the workstation paradigm altogether. Tool, for instance, when recording the album *10,000 Days*, used reel-to-reel tape technology and analog processors exclusively. Similarly, when Pearl Jam released *Riot Act*, they marketed the record as an "anti-ProTools statement". As drummer Matt Cameron (cited in Hodgson, Starr and Waterman 2009: 438) put it:

> This [*Riot Act*] is definitely our [read: Pearl Jam's] anti-ProTools record. To us, a song like "Can't Keep" is proof that it's more interesting hearing musicians in a room playing hard, with the tempo fluctuating as the band heats up. Perfection is boring.

Producer Steve Albini, who has been anything but shy about his own anti-digital point-of-view, recently echoed Cameron's concerns. As Albini sees it, the emergence of the workstation paradigm is a lamentably amateurish development in Recording Practice:

> driven by non-technical people, wanting to get involved in recording, without investing time, and money, in equipment, and learning about it. Most small semi-professional studios are run this way . . . There is a lot of use of ProTools in professional studios, but this is mostly for the special effects it allows, not for sound quality. These special effects soon fall out of fashion, and I don't think this trend will define studios permanently. Do you remember when real drummers were told to sell their drum kits, because drum machines were going to take over? That same false prophesy is happening with regard to analog tape machines, and ProTools now. It is a trend, and it will have some permanent impact, but it doesn't replace analog systems, which are more durable, sound better and are more flexible (cited in Benni 2002).

Musical luddism aside, most recordists see at least some value in the workstation paradigm — even as they acknowledge that a vast and quantifiable discrepancy exists between the sounds that analog and digital technologies can produce. During the mid-2000s, the number of workstation users increased exponentially. Not surprisingly then, during that same period the functional capacities of workstations themselves came to exert an increasingly profound influence on the way that pop records were made. Records are now often made through a combination of transduction, direct-injection and sequencing techniques; and though I risk invoking the ire of a great many practicing recordists in saying so, I do not think it matters all that much which particular workstation recordists ultimately choose to adopt. Almost every workstation shares most of its functionality with every other workstation (I say 'almost' because, unlike most other workstations, Adobe Audition is not a MIDI host, which precludes its use in most electronic musics). Only the workflow, that is, the sequence of mouse-clicks that are required to make use of those capacities — and particular synthesis, sampling and signal processing capabilities — changes from DAW to DAW.

Most workstations are organized around the metaphor of a multi-track mixing console. The arrange window in a workstation, which is where the lion's share of work is done, features a series of channel-strips, or, tracks, organized sequentially as on a multi-track mixing console. Each track can be assigned to: (i) a General MIDI (GM) instrument; (ii) a virtual synthesizer; (iii) a sampler; (iv) a drum machine; or (v) real-audio, which means it will be used to store transduced or direct-injected digital-audio. Each channel-strip in turn features a set of open plug-in slots, reserved for algorithmic signal processors (e.g., reverb, delay or distortion), and a set of open send slots reserved for bussing (i.e., auxiliary sends). A recordist need only assign a plug-in to a particular track or bus a track to a send channel with processors active to significantly alter the dynamic and frequency content of that track.

Once they have assigned an instrument to a channel-strip — and, if they so desire, signal processing plug-ins — recordists can then input musical information. They do so by: (i) step inputting; (ii) real-inputting; and (iii) digital-audio tracking. I will now explain each of these techniques in the order that I list them.

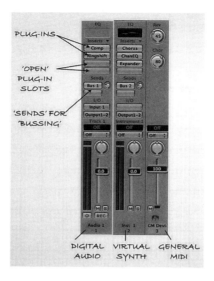

Figure 1.21   Digital-audio, virtual synthesis and General MIDI tracks in the LogicPro 7.2 workstation, with bus and plug-in slots noted.

STEP-INPUTTING

Step-inputting encapsulates all that modern sequencing, especially computer-based sequencing, requires of recordists. To step input musical information so it becomes part of the sequence of musical events that a workstation triggers on playback, recordists enter ticks into either a matrix editor (a.k.a. MIDI grid) or a step sequencer. The matrix editor is located in the arrange window of a workstation, while the step sequencer is located on the instrument interface itself.

Matrix editors divide the audible spectrum into pitches — stacked vertically, usually according to the metaphor of a piano keyboard — and rhythmic subdivisions (see **Figure 1.22**). Recordists step input ticks, that is, vertical and horizontal values, into the matrix editor to indicate where in the audible spectrum, at what volumes and for how long, the assigned instrument should generate sound. If the matrix editor doesn't suit their workflow preferences, however, recordists might instead opt to use a step sequencer (see **Figure 1.23**). Most virtual drum machines,

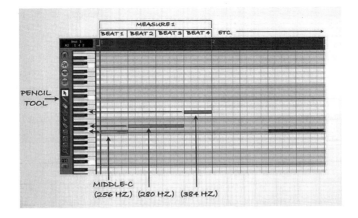

Figure 1.22 The matrix editor (a.k.a. MIDI grid) in the LogicPro 7.2 workstation, with four ticks (entries) of varying length and velocity (volume) inputted. The ticks were entered using the pencil tool noted on the far-left of the matrix editor below.

for instance, are equipped with a step sequencer: a row of rectangular slots, flipped onto their side, representing eighth-, sixteenth- and thirty-second-note subdivisions of the global tempo.

Table 1.7 Tracks on Kanye West's *808s & Heartbreak* featuring obviously step input drum machine and synth-bass parts. Though almost any hip hop record could demonstrate the sound of step input sequencing, West's *808s & Heartbreak* is comprised almost exclusively of virtual synthesis, Roland 808 drum machine, and obviously auto-tuned vocal tracks .

Record	Track
Kanye West, *808s & Heartbreak*	1. Say You Will
	3. Heartless
	5. Love Lockdown
	7. RoboCop
	8. Street Lights
	9. Bad News

Drum machines (and samplers) are usually armed with libraries of:
   (i) hits (or, impulse samples) comprised of single component musical
      units like a single kick drum hit or a rim shot, which recordists

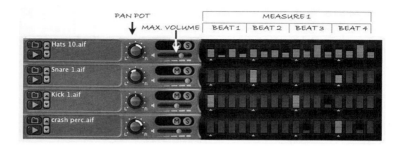

Figure 1.23 The step sequencer on an iDrum virtual drum machine. Horizontal position designates when, in a 4/4 bar, a sample should sound, and vertical height designates the volume.

sequence together to create broader musical patterns like beats, grooves, riffs and fills;

(ii) loops, which are longer samples usually comprised of already-sequenced beats and riffs that can be used to create larger arrangements; and, finally,

(iii) open slots, which recordists can fill with self-produced samples.

Recordists choose a sample and a time in the sequence for that sample to trigger, by inputting ticks on the step sequencer. If they want a kick drum sample to sound on beats 1 and 3 of a common time (4/4) measure, for instance, and a snare drum sample to sound on beats 2 and 4, recordists need only select the desired samples from the sample library and tick

Figure 1.24 A sample library menu for snare hits on the iDrum virtual drum machine pictured in Figure 1.23 above. The horizontal and vertical values in the step-sequencer do not change when recordists choose a different sample, only the sample that those values trigger.

the corresponding slots on the step sequencer (see **Figure 1.24**).

Example 1.7   Step-Sequencing And Samples
Example 1.7a demonstrates the sound of step-input sequencing using a virtual iDrum drum-machine. The same four-bar sequence is repeated six times throughout the example. Every subsequent iteration of the sequence triggers a different set of drum hits, that is, a different set of sample hits was used for each iteration, even as the step-input sequence itself remains the same. Example 1.7b follows the same protocol as Example 1.7a, but using various software synthesizers.

REAL INPUTTING

Real inputting provides workstations with the same information that step-inputting provides. When recordists real input a sequence, however, they *perform* that sequence in real time on a connected instrument, usually a MIDI controller, while the workstation is set in record mode. Recordists typically opt to real input their sequences when step-inputting creates an overly precise sequence of sound events; or, alternatively, when the sequence they want to input is very complex, and step-inputting thus presents an overly time-consuming option. In fact, recordists have recently begun to openly rebel against the mechanical precision of step inputting, opting to intentionally mis-align the tempo of component samples with the global tempo of tracks. They may also use differing swing-quantization settings for various sequences in a multi-track production, which algorithmically misaligns the rhythmic symmetry of MIDI ticks. Flying Lotus' *1983, Los Angeles, Cosmogramma, Reset* and *L.A. EP 1 × 3*, and Prefuse 73's *Preparations* and *Everything She Touched Turned To Ampexian*, clearly illustrate this principle at work in the modern pop soundscape (see **Table 1.8**).

Table 1.8 Tracks by Prefuse 73 and Flying Lotus with obvious tempo misalignments.

Record	Track
Prefuse 73, *Preparations*	3. Aborted Hugs 4. The Class of 73 Bells 5. Girlfriend Boyfriend 7. Prog Version Slowly Crushed 11. I Knew You Were Gonna Go 12. Pomade Suite Version One 13. Preparation Outro Version
Prefuse 73, *Everything She Touched Turned To Ampexian*	1. Periodic Measurements of Infrequent Smiles 2. Hairy Faces (Stress) 3. Parachute Panador 5. Punish 8. Dec. Machine Funk All ERA's 9. Get Em High 11. When Is A Good Time? 12. Fountains Of Spring 13. Whipcream Eyepatch 14. Regalo 16. Oh Is It 17. Four Reels Collide 18. Fingertip Trajectories 21. Yuletide 23. No Lights Still Rock 25. Digan Lo 27. Pitch Pipe 29. Formal Dedications
Flying Lotus, *Reset*	2. Vegas Collie 3. Massage Situation 6. Dance Floor Stalker
Flying Lotus, *1983*	1. 1983 5. Shifty 7. Pet Monster Shotglass 8. Hello 9. Untitled #7

(*continued*)

Record	Track
Flying Lotus, *Los Angeles*	2. Breathe . Something/Stellar Star
	3. Beginner's Falafel
	4. Camel
	6. Comet Course
	8. Golden Diva
	9. Riot
	10. GNG BNG
	12. Sleepy Dinosaur
	14. SexSlaveShip
	16. Testament (feat. Gonja Sufi)

After they real-input control information into a workstation, recordists can always use the matrix editor to revise the recorded performances. Among other things, recordists can adjust: (i) pitch information; (ii) timing information; (iii) events in the sequence itself (i.e., they can delete ticks and move them to different horizontal locations); (iv) velocity (i.e., volume) information; and (v) which virtual instrument, or samples, the sequence triggers. In doing this, recordists use the matrix editor to adjust only those participatory discrepancies which they

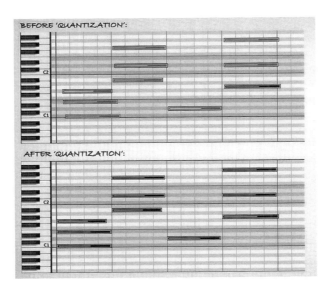

Figure 1.25   Matrix editor before and after tempo quantization, which automatically aligns tracks to absolute horizontal (rhythmic) values.

deem overly distracting, leaving intact the general impression of a live performance which real-inputting conveys.

REAL-AUDIO

Alongside their sequencing, synthesis and processing capacities, digital-audio workstations also provide: (i) a storage site for digital-audio tracks produced by transduction and direct-injection; and (ii) a suite of post-production processors called plug-ins (I explain signal processing in Chapter 2). Arming a real-audio track in the arrange window of the workstation, that is, enabling the record button on the track, routes all incoming audio onto that track. As it records audio data, the workstation renders it in waveform format, within that armed (recording) track. What results is an 'audio object', as seen in **Figure 1.26**. Once the workstation renders an audio object, recordists can re-tailor it to suit the needs of any given project. They can re-size the audio object, for instance, should they want a longer or shorter duration (see **Figure 1.27**). Recordists can also move the resulting re-sized audio object, back-and-forth within the track-slot, should they desire a different start and stop time (see **Figure 1.28**). Finally, record-ists can copy, cut and paste an audio object, or a segment of an audio object, as they might a word or phrase in a word processor; and they can loop the resulting (pasted or copied) audio objects such that they repeat however often they see fit (see **Figure 1.29**). Some workstations also allow recordists to force warp an audio object so that a defined region of the object triggers at a faster or slower rate than the rest of the object.

Figure 1.26   An 'audio object' in Apple GarageBand. Note that the 'audio object' begins shortly after the downbeat of measure 1 and ends on beat 3 of measure 2.

Figure 1.27   The same audio object as in Figure 1.26, re-sized to end precisely on the downbeat of measure 2.

Figure 1.28   The re-sized audio object from Figure 1.26, moved to beat 1 of measure 1.

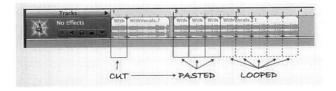

Figure 1.29   The audio object from Figure 1.26, but with beat 1 cut and pasted to the downbeat of measure 2, copied to beats 2 and 3 of measure 2, and then looped five times.

Example 1.8   Tracking: Putting It All Together

Example 1.8, an original demo track entitled "Devil Take A Bow," follows the modern workstation paradigm of Recording Practice, which is to say, transduction, direct-injection and sequencing all figure. The entrance of each track, and a basic description of the way it was recorded, is listed in Table 1.9 below. Readers will find it easiest to hear the tracking techniques if they use headphones, and monitor at a relatively moderate level.

Table 1.9   First entrance of tracks, and the method used to track them, in Example 1.8.

Time	Track	Tracking Method	Comments
0:00	field recording (thunder storm)	transduction, distant placement	large diaphragm condenser, set for omni response, aimed out a window
0:17	lead-vocals	transduction, close placement	large diaphragm condenser, set for cardioid, placed 1.5 feet from mouth
	acoustic guitar	transduction, close placement	small diaphragm condenser, cardioid, 6″ from 12th fret of guitar, aimed at the hole
0:41	acoustic violin	transduction, close placement	large-diaphragm condenser, set for omni, placed 1.5 feet from violin
0:46	synth pad	step-input sequencing, direct-injection	sequenced using the matrix editor on an early workstation keyboard, direct-injected onto an open track
0:52	electric bass	DI-transduction tandem	electric bass is direct injected, and transduced at amp, using a dynamic microphone placed within 3″ on-axis
1:20	timpani	transduction, distant placement	large diaphragm condenser, set for omni response, placed 6 feet away

(continued)

Time	Track	Tracking Method	Comments
1:24	violin section	transduction, distant placement	overdubbed single violinist four times, using a large diaphragm condenser, set for omni, placed 3+ feet from the violin for each pass
1:26	orchestral bell	transduction, distant placement	large diaphragm condenser, set for omni response, placed 6 feet away
1:26	drum machine	step-input sequencing, direct-injection	sequenced using the step sequencer on a virtual drum machine, direct-injected onto an open track
1:58	electric piano	real-input sequencing, direct-injection	sequenced using an early workstation keyboard, direct-injected onto an open track
2:18	electric bass solo	transduction, room placement	a large-diaphragm condenser room mic, set for omni, added to the original DI-transduction tandem; the signal is further treated with auto-wah and slight vocoding
2:56	slapback vocal	transduction, room placement	room mic is added to the lead-vocal track, creating a slight slapback
3:29	electric bass solo	transduction, room placement	a large-diaphragm condenser room-mic, set for omni, added to the original DI-transduction tandem, for overdubbed arpeggios; no auto-wah or vocoding
3:39	vocal screams	transduction, distant placement	large diaphragm condenser, set for omni response, placed 8+ feet from mouth; signal time-stretched and severely distorted

Chapter 2

Signal Processing

EQ, Dynamics, Distortion,
Feedback, Delay, Modulation

After tracking, recordists are ready to process the audio signals they gathered. Signal processing is modifying an audio signal by inserting a "signal processor" — that is, a device designed to modify audio signals in particular ways — into the audio chain, and manipulating its adjustable parameters. This practice plays a crucial role in modern Recording Practice. All manner of harmony, rhythm and melody are conveyed to listeners in a processed state on record now, and recordists are expected to be as proficient at signal processing as they are at tracking, mixing and mastering. As Kevin Ryan and Brian Kehew (2008: 266) explain, the modern recordist now:

> has at his fingertips a nearly infinite array of effects. From traditional standbys such as reverbs and delays, to more modern techniques such as convolution and emulation, the selection is endless and — for better or worse — instantaneous. Effects are now a ubiquitous commodity.

It should come as no surprise, then, that recordists have become extroverted in their use of signal processing. Whereas signal processing was

once used to preserve the realism of a recorded performance, a majority of pop records now feature what John Andrew Fisher (1998) calls
"nonveridic" applications, which is to say, they do not sound as though
they were, or even like they could be, performed live. Of course, what
sounds veridic and nonveridic varies from time to time and place to
place. A veridic punk rock production, for instance, will sound totally
different than, say, a veridic hardhouse track. Moreover, what sounded
nonveridic decades ago can epitomize veridic production values today.
What ultimately matters, in an analytic sense, is that recordists continue
to make a fundamental distinction between what they do in the studio
and on stage, and that they deploy a variety of signal processing techniques to do so. In Alexander Case's (2007: xix–xx) words:

> The most important music of our time is recorded music. The
> recording studio is its principle musical instrument. The recording
> engineers and music producers who create the music we love know
> how to use signal processing equipment to capture the work of art-
> ists, preserving realism or altering things wildly, as appropriate . . .
> Equalization is likely the most frequently used effect of all, reverb the
> most apparent, delay the most diverse, distortion the most seductive,
> volume the most under-appreciated, expansion the most under-
> utilized, pitch shifting the most abused, and compression the most
> misunderstood. All effects, in the hands of a talented, informed and
> experienced engineer, are rich with production possibilities.

In the following chapter of this field guide, I examine common signal
processing techniques which recordists routinely use to craft their
recorded musical communications. I have organized this chapter into
a series of discreet entries, each devoted to one of six different signal
processing techniques, specifically: (i) equalization, (ii) dynamics,
(iii) distortion, (iv) feedback, (v) delay and (vi) modulation (I examine
reverb processing in Chapter 3). What follows is only an introduction to
signal processing in modern Recording Practice. Signal processing is an

immense, and immensely complicated, musical craft which I can only very briefly survey within the confines of this field guide. Readers who familiarize themselves with the signal processing techniques surveyed in the chapter below can nevertheless expect to hear signal processing at work everywhere in modern pop.

1. EQUALIZATION

Equalizers (EQs) adjust the amplitude of audio signals at particular frequencies. They are, in other words, frequency-specific volume knobs. Recordists originally used equalizers to compensate for the distorted frequency response of early microphones. If a microphone exaggerated, say, the upper-midrange (1 to 7 kHz) of a sound source, recordists inserted an equalizer into the audio chain, attenuated all signal in that range and, in so doing, adjusted the equalizer until the recorded sound matched, or, was equalized with, the sound source. However, as Roey Izhaki (2008: 205) explains:

> equalizers used today are not employed to make one sound equal to another, but to manipulate the frequency content of various mix elements. The frequency virtue of each individual instrument, and how it [fits within] the overall frequency spectrum of the mix, is a paramount aspect of mixing. Operating an equalizer is an easy affair, but understanding frequencies and how to manipulate them is perhaps the greatest challenge mixing has to offer.

Recordists use equalizers to manipulate component frequencies within the input spectrum. That is, recordists use equalizers to adjust the volume of those particular frequencies which, combined, comprise the total spectral content (frequency content) of a recorded sound. "All musical instruments create sounds with multiple frequencies, called complex waveforms, even if only playing one note," writes David Franz

(2004: 190). "Depending on the particular note played, an instrument will produce the specific pitch for that note (known as the fundamental pitch) plus additional pitches with lower amplitudes (known as harmonics and overtones) that color the overall sound." Ultimately then, through equalizing recordists adjust the volume of the component frequencies in a sound source and, thus, its timbre.

Example 2.1   Input Spectrum

Example 2.1 sweeps a Bandpass filter, set to filter out all but a sliver-thin frequency band, through a sample comprised of a harmonically rich synthesizer pad and a step-input drum sequence. The sample initially sounds with its full frequency content. The sample then repeats with the Bandpass filter activated. The filter sweeps down through the audible spectrum, from 20 kHz to 20 Hz, and back up to 20 kHz again. Finally, the sample sounds once more in its original unfiltered state.

There are numerous EQs on the market. However, recordists chiefly use five basic kinds: (i) parametric; (ii) semi-parametric; (iii) graphic; (iv) peak; and (v) program. Though each of these equalizers has its fairer features, parametric and graphic EQs remain most common (Toulson and Ruskin: 2008). Parametric equalizers allow recordists to determine every parameter of equalization, including:

   (i) 'band', that is, where in the frequency spectrum to equalize;
  (ii) 'Q-value', that is, how much of the frequency spectrum to equalize; and
 (iii) 'amount', that is, the amount of equalization, or, the size of the boost or cut (attenuation) to apply.

A 'graphic' equalizer, on the other hand, features only a sequence of fixed bands, and the Q-value of each remains predetermined. Users of graphic EQs thus choose only the amount of boost or cut to apply to each fixed band, and only as the predetermined Q-value proscribes. The width of each band on a 10-band graphic EQ is one octave, meaning that the input spectrum can be adjusted in only octave swaths; the width of each band on a 31-band graphic EQ, on the other hand, is one third of an octave.

DEPTH EQUALIZATION

Aside from 'hyping' tracks — that is, equalizing tracks to produce unorthodox musical timbres — recordists use a number of equalization techniques. Recordists commonly use equalization to increase the 'depth' of a mix, for instance. Human ears tend to interpret duller sounds, specifically, sound sources which lack upper-midrange and high-frequency content, as less proximate than sounds with a plethora of such components (sounds with more high-frequency content also tend to sound louder, which only further increases their perceived proximity). In Roey Izhaki's (2008: 207) words:

> Low frequencies bend around obstacles and are not readily absorbed. High frequencies are exactly the opposite. These are some of the reasons for which we hear more low-frequency leakage coming

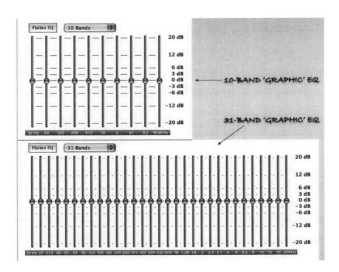

Figure 2.1   A 10-band (above) and 31-band (below) graphic equalizer.

from within venues. Our brain decodes dull sounds as if coming from further away, a reason for which our perception of depth is stretched when under water. We use this 'darker-equals-further' phenomenon to enhance, if not perfect, the front-back impression of various instruments [in a mix].

Recordists regularly use this quirk of human hearing to their advantage. Introducing equalization boosts and cuts at select frequencies across a mix, to emphasize the high-frequency content of some tracks and the bass and midrange of other tracks, recordists increase the general impression of depth which that mix creates. The long crescendoing sample that sounds from 0:08 to 0:37 in Eric Prydz's "Call On Me" provides an instructive example. Comprised entirely of a well-known vocal phrase sampled from Steve Winwood's "Valerie" — specifically, the singer's repeated request for his love interest, Valerie, to "call on me" — the sample initially sounds with all of its midrange and high-frequency content muted. Over the course of a 29-second fade-in, however, Prydz broadens the spectral profile of the sample until its full frequency content finally sounds at 0:35, after which point Prydz triggers another sample from the Winwood original — "I'm the same boy I used to be" — and "Call On Me" begins in earnest. Prydz repeats this technique without any accompaniment just over one minute later, at 1:49 into "Call on me"; and again with full accompaniment at 2:31. In all three cases, as Prydz broadens the input spectrum of the Winwood sample, he also increases its proximity, and thus the general impression of depth which the mix creates.

MIRRORED EQUALIZATION

Another common equalization technique is mirrored equalization. This practice entails using EQs to give tracks with similar frequency components complimentary spectral contours (frequency profiles). Recordists wedge equalization boosts and cuts into a mix at select frequency ranges where instruments would otherwise overlap and compete for audibility. For instance, bass guitar and kick drum usually fight for the same frequency space on rock records; both instruments present overlapping frequency ranges and they thus compete for audible prominence in those ranges. Only making matters more difficult, the kick drum and bass guitar are usually paired in a pop production, meaning that they are typically arranged to sound at roughly the same times. Recordists thus routinely apply equalization boosts on the kick drum in roughly the same regions they cut on the bass guitar, and vice versa, that is, they mirror their equalizations for both instruments.

When applied to tracks 'panned' to either side of the stereo plane in a mix, mirrored equalization can enhance the perceived width of a mix. Recordists often equalize electric guitar parts differently, and when appropriate, pan the tracks to opposite sides of the stereo spectrum (if they work with an experienced band, both guitarists should already mirror their equalizations). The distinct spectral contours that both electric guitars subsequently take prompts listeners to localize a different sound source for each, located in the extreme left and right periphery of the mix, respectively. Applying a very brief delay of, say, 8 to 45 milliseconds to only one of the panned tracks can further enhance the impression of width this technique creates (Izhaki 2008: 168–76).

Mirrored equalization is characteristic of a number of rock productions. However, perhaps the most obvious examples are heard throughout the Strokes' *Is This It?*. Every track on the album features mirrored equalization at least once. The most obvious example is "Last Night," track seven on *Is This It?*, which features an abrupt transition from mono to stereo imaging on the electric guitars after exactly 10 seconds. Throughout the record, in fact, Albert Hammond Jr.'s and Nick Valensi's guitar parts are mirrored and panned either moments before or precisely when Julian Casablancas' vocals enter, a mixing move which wedges more space into the center of the mix for Casablancas' vocals to fill. This technique is clearly audible at 11 seconds into track six,

"Alone Together"; 11 seconds into "Is This It?"; 14 seconds into "The Modern Age"; 7 seconds into "Soma"; 10 seconds into "Last Night"; and 16 seconds into "New York City Cops."

Table 2.1   Examples of mirrored equalization on Wolfmother's *Cosmic Egg*. Like most records by the Strokes, *Cosmic Egg* features mirrored equalization at least once on every track.

Record	*Track (Entrance of Mirrored EQ)*
Wolfmother, *Cosmic Egg*	1. California Queen (0:11)
	2. New Moon Rising (0:00)
	3. White Feather (0:09)
	4. Sundial (0:11)
	5. In The Morning (0:00)
	6. 10,000 Feet (0:11)
	7. Cosmic Egg (0:14)
	8. Far Away (1:07)
	9. Cosmonaut (0:00)
	10. Pilgrim (0:10)
	11. Eyes Open (0:00)
	12. Back Round (0:28)
	13. In The Castle (1:30)
	14. Caroline (0:22)
	15. Phoenix (0:06)
	16. Violence Of The Sun (1:01)

2. DYNAMICS

While equalization reshapes the amplitude of an audio signal at select frequencies, 'dynamics processors' react to, and reshape, the amplitude of an audio signal across the frequency spectrum. They are, in other words, "automatic volume knobs," as Bill Gibson (2005: 5) explains. Most often, users select a threshold, expressed in decibels, which serves as an automatic trigger for the device. When the amplitude of the input signal registers either above or below that threshold, the dynamics processor either amplifies or attenuates the input signal by a select amount, called the 'ratio' or 'range', depending on the device used and how it is set. Recordists can furthermore specify how quickly, and for how long, they want the processor to work after it has been triggered, by setting unique 'attack' and 'release' times, respectively. The most common dynamics processing techniques used today are: (i) compression/limiting; and (ii) gating. I will now examine these techniques, in order.

COMPRESSORS/LIMITERS

"A compressor and limiter both operate on the same principle," according to Bill Gibson (2005: 9):

> The only difference between these dynamic processors is the degree to which they affect the signal that exceeds the threshold. Whereas a compressor functions as a gentle volume control — which, normally, should be transparent and seamless to the audio process — a limiter is more extreme, radically decreasing the level of the signal that passes above the threshold. Each of these tools has a distinct and important purpose for the creation of professional sounding audio ... When used [correctly] a high-quality compressor/limiter is transparent throughout the majority of the audio material, while performing important level control during peak amplitude sections.

Only making matters more difficult for the inexperienced processor, "there is nothing built in to human hearing that makes it particularly sensitive to the sonic signatures of compression," as Alexander Case (2007: 161–162) notes:

> There is no important event in nature that requires any assessment of whether or not the amplitude of the signal heard has been slightly manipulated by a device. Identifying the audible traits of compression is a fully learned, intellectual process that audio engineers must master. It is more difficult than learning to ride a bicycle. It is possible that most other people, including even musicians and

avid music fans, will never notice, nor need to notice, the sonic fingerprint of compression. [Recordists] have this challenge all to themselves.

Compression is comprised of five basic adjustments: (i) threshold; (ii) ratio; (iii) attack; (iv) release; and (v) knee. As noted, compressors feature a threshold which users set to a particular decibel value; the compressor triggers (turns on) whenever the amplitude of the input signal exceeds that value. Once triggered, the compressor attenuates the input signal according to a selected attenuation ratio. If the input signal registers, say, 6 decibels over the selected threshold and the attenuation ratio is set for 3:1, the resulting compressed signal will rise only 2 decibels above the threshold; set for a ratio of 3:1, the compressor allows an output of only one-decibel-above-the-threshold per every three-decibels-above-the-threshold the processor registers. A ratio setting of 10:1 or higher results in 'limiting', that is, compressors that limit the dynamic range of an audio signal such that it never exceeds a selected decibel value, though most recordists use a dedicated limiter to achieve this effect nowadays. Compressors thus compress the distance between a waveform's peaks and valleys, which is to say, they compress

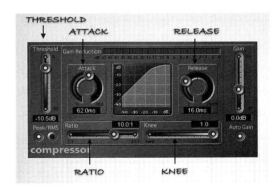

Figure 2.2   A typical compressor interface, with adjustable parameters noted.

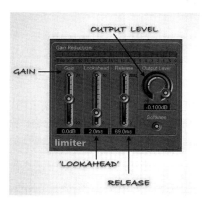

Figure 2.3 A basic limiter interface, with adjustable parameters noted.

the dynamic range of audio signal, while limiters limit the peak amplitude of audio signal to an absolute decibel value.[2]

PUMPING

Compression is easiest to hear when it is creatively misused. The most
common, and obvious, misuse for compression produces what recordists call 'pumping', that is, "audible unnatural level changes associated
primarily with the release of a compressor" (Izhaki 2008: 160). While
there is no single correct way to produce pumping — Case (2007: 160),
for instance, notes that the effect results from selecting "too slow or too
fast . . . or too, um, medium" attack and release settings — pumping
usually accrues when recordists fail to assign a long enough release
time to adequately handle a decaying signal:

> One of the few times compression can be clearly heard, even by
> untrained listeners, is when it starts pumping . . . The audio signal
> contains material that changes level in unexpected ways. It might be

---

2 I should also note that both compressors and limiters have gain functions which
influence how much attenuation of an audio signal ultimately obtains.

steady-state noise, the sustained wash of a cymbal, or the long decay of any instrument holding a note for several beats or bars. Listeners expect a certain amplitude envelope: the noise should remain steady in level, the cymbals should slowly decay, etc. Instead, the compressor causes the signal to get noticeably louder. This unnatural increase in amplitude occurs as a compressor turns up gain during release. (Case 2007: 160)

Example 2.2   Pumping

Example 2.2 demonstrates the sound of pumping. A percussion sample sounds for the first 10 seconds with a notable amount of compression applied. The release setting is then reduced to produce the characteristic sound of pumping; and, after 10 seconds, the setting is returned to its initial setting, at which point the pumping stops. This process repeats, every 10 seconds, for the remainder of Example 2.2. The easiest way to hear the pumping in this example is to use headphones, and focus on the decay and release profile of each cymbal hit.

Pumping is now a common technique in rock and electronic dance music. House, techno and IDM (Intelligent Dance Music) records all very often feature the technique, as do tracks by modern rock bands like Radiohead and, periodically, the Strokes. Flying Lotus' *1983*, *Los Angeles* and *Cosmogramma* are replete with examples, as are most instrumental records by the late hip hop producer J Dilla, though readers may find it easier to hear the technique at work in a Top 40 rock production rather than in experimental IDM or hip hop. Phil Selway's drum track for Radiohead's "Exit Music (For A Film)" provides a celebrated example. From the time they enter at 2:51, Selway's drums are increasingly compressed to the point of pumping; and pumping is particularly audible on the cymbal-heavy portion of Selway's performance from 3:20 to 3:36. In fact, the cymbal crash which sounds from 3:26 to 3:28 of "Exit Music (For A Film)" pumps so dramatically, and so obviously, that producer Nigel Godrich may as well have foregone the compressor and simply automated a volume swell on the cymbals using a parametric or graphic EQ. Pumping is also clearly audible on the electro percussion loop which underpins Radiohead's "Idiotheque," track eight from the band's groundbreaking album *Kid A*, especially in the wild dynamic fluctuations that characterize the snare sample's sustain and release profile after the entrance of the sampled pads at 0:11. Benny Benassi's "Finger Food," which opens *Rock and Rave*, offers another clear example; and pumping is likewise clear on the ride cymbals throughout Portishead's "Pedestal," track nine on *Dummy*.

Table 2.2   Flying Lotus tracks with obvious compression-induced pumping.

Record	*Track*
Flying Lotus, *1983*	1. 1983
	2. Sao Paulo
	5. Shifty
Flying Lotus, *Los Angeles*	10. GNG BNG
Flying Lotus, *LA EP 1x3*	2. Rickshaw
	4. RobertaFlack (feat. Dolly)
Flying Lotus, *Cosmogramma*	2. Pickled!
	3. Nose Art

SIDE-CHAIN PUMPING

A more advanced, if heavy-handed, application of dynamics processing entails use of a compressor's 'side-chain' feature. A compressor's 'side-chain' uses the amplitude envelope (dynamics profile) of one track as a trigger for a compressor used in another track. Applied to, say, a synth pad, a compressor which is side-chained to a kick drum playing regular four-on-the-floor quarter notes will compress (attenuate) the synth pad when the amplitude of the kick drum surpasses the threshold setting of the compressor. This produces a sequence of quarter-note volume-swells in the synth pad, offset from each iteration of the kick drum by a selected release time. The result is similar to pumping but side-chain pumping fluctuates according to the amplitude of another track, and regardless of the properties of the compressed track.

Example 2.3   Side-chain Pumping

Example 2.3 demonstrates one of the most common applications for the side-chain technique in modern electronic dance music, namely, to produce pumping on a synth pad. Throughout this brief example, the side-chain function on a compressor, applied to the synth pad, is applied to the percussion sample, and successively engaged and disengaged five times.

Side-chain pumping has found a special place in the hearts of house, techno, IDM, hip hop, dubstep and drum 'n' bass recordists lately. However, Eric Prydz's "Call On Me" is largely credited with having popularized the technique, even if Daft Punk's "One More Time" could easily make a claim for that honor. "Call On Me" features obvious side-chain compression on the synth pads whenever the kick drum sounds (i.e., 0:00–0:25, 0:37–0:50, 0:52–1:03, 1:08–1:19, 1:30–1:45 and 2:16–2:42) and a conspicuous absence of side-chain compression whenever the kick drum is tacit (i.e., 0:26–0:37, 0:51–0:52, 1:03–1:08, 1:19–1:30, 1:46–2:16 and 2:43–3:00). The side-chain pumping effect is

Figure 2.4   The same compressor plug-in from Figure 2.2, side-chained to the kick drum (track 2) in a multi-track production.

clearly audible during the first 15 seconds of the track, when only the kick drum and a synth pad sound in tandem, but it is also abundantly clear in subsequent sections, especially from 0:39 to 1:50.

Another clear example of side-chain pumping can be heard on Madonna's "Get Together," track two on *Confessions On A Dance Floor*. During the song's 38 second introduction, the amplitude envelope of the synth pads remains constant, making the side-chain pumping that sputters in on those pads with the entrance of the kick drum at 0:38 all the more conspicuous. Finally, the synth arpeggios which sound between 1:28 and 1:55 of Benny Benassi's "My Body (feat. Mia J.)" are also instructive. From 1:28 to 1:42, the kick drum sounds the obligatory 'four-on-the-floor' pulses and the side-chained compressor on the synth follows dutifully along; between 1:42 and 1:55, however, the kick is tacit and the synth track repeats completely unattenuated (some commentators have actually taken to calling side-chain compression 'Benassi pumping', since the Italian DJ makes such extensive use of the technique).

Table 2.3   Obvious examples of side-chain pumping on records by Flying Lotus, Justice, Lone, and Armin Van Buren's *A State Of Trance 2009* compilation.

Record	Track
Flying Lotus, *Reset*	1. Tea Leaf Dancers
	3. Massage Situation
Flying Lotus, *1983*	1. 1983
	4. Orbit Brazil
	7. Pet Monster Shotglass
	8. Hello
Flying Lotus, *Los Angeles*	2. Breathe . Something / Stellar Star
	8. Golden Diva
	10. GNG BNG
	17. Aunties Lock/Infinitum (feat. Laura Darlington)

(*continued*)

Record	Track
Armin Van Buren, *A State Of Trance 2009*	1. Never Fade Away 2. Change Your Mind 4. Riddles In The Sand 5. Fractal Universe 6. Iselilja 7. Miami Vibe 8. Deep Down 9. Helpless 10. You Walk Away 11. Faces 12. Nothing At All 16. Find Yourself (Cosmic Gate Remix) 17. Inside Of You 22. Rosaires 27. Look Ahead 28. Come To Me
Lone, *Ecstasy & Friends*	1. To Be With A Person You Really Dig 2. Sungrazer Cascade 3. Paradise Backyard Jam 4. Arcade 5. Waves Imagination 6. Endlessly 8. Love Heads 9. Karen Loves Kate 10. Go Greenhills Racer 11. Apple Hi
Justice, *Cross*	1. Genesis 4. Newjack 5. Phantom 6. Phantom II 8. Tthhee Ppaarrttyy 9. DVNO 12. One Minute To Midnight

NOISE GATES

As compressors attenuate signal above the threshold, noise gates attenuate signal which registers below the threshold. Unlike compressors, however, these gates attenuate signal by a fixed amount, called the

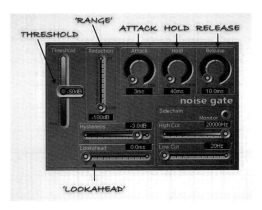

Figure 2.5 A typical noise gate with adjustable parameters noted.

range. Recordists chiefly use gates to reduce the input signal to silence at quiet intervals, which can require a range of more than 80 decibels of immediate reduction, though the device has plenty of other established uses. Aside from 'attack' and 'release' settings, gates also typically feature a 'hold' setting, which determines the length of time — usually anywhere from zero to three seconds — the gate remains active once the signal which triggered it has subsided under the threshold. Most gates also feature a 'look-ahead' function, which delays the input signal by millionths of a second, so the gate can examine its amplitude and determine a 'soft', that is, a gradual, response to any portions of the input signal which require attenuation.

GATED REVERB

Though gates are often used to remove background noise from the quieter portions of noisy tracks, they also have their creative misuses. One of the best known misuses for gating is the 'gated-reverb' effect, which producer Steve Lillywhite and engineer Hugh Padgham famously used to craft Phil Collins' notoriously massive drum timbre on Peter Gabriel's "Intruder." Recorded in a cavernous barn with room-mics distributed at strategic intervals to capture the kit's ambient reflections in the room, the resulting drum track was compressed first and then gated. Lillywhite and Padgham used compression to ensure that Collins' drum hits and their ambient reflections sounded dynamically equivalent, the usual amplitude envelope of a Top 40 drum-kit in this case replaced by a cavernous, elongated 'decay' and 'sustain' profile; while the gate truncated the release profile of each hit, ensuring an almost instantaneous transition from sound to silence. Lillywhite and Padgham then applied different release settings on the gates for each component drum track, allowing about a quarter-note of sustain on the kick drum and only an eighth-note of sustain on the snare, for instance. As Albin J. Zak (2001: 80–81) explains:

> The effect in this case is one of textural clarity . . . The gated ambience on the drums resolves a physical contradiction: it evokes the size associated with large, open ambient spaces while at the same time confining the sound to a clearly delineated place in the track. Limiting each eruption of sonic intensity to a short burst solves the problem of preserving textural clarity without diminishing the ambient drums' visceral power . . . With the ambient decay continuously truncated, there is a sense of things being always interrupted, of their natural course being curtailed and controlled by a dominating force.
>
> And the strange behavior of the sound in this atmosphere dictates the terms of our acoustic perception. Because it makes no sense in terms of our experience of the natural sound world, rather than perceiving the ambience as space, we are reoriented to hearing it simply as an extension of the drums' timbre.

MULTI-LATCH GATING

Another celebrated misuse for gating, which I call 'multi-latch gating', can be heard on David Bowies "Heroes," track three on the middle record from his and Brian Eno's so-called "Berlin Trilogy" (i.e., *Low*,

Heroes and *Lodger*). "Heroes" (1977) tells the story of a doomed couple, living on either side of the Berlin Wall, whose clandestine meetings Bowie claimed to have observed from the windows of Hansa "By The Wall" Tonstudio while he, Brian Eno and producer Toni Visconti recorded there. The track features a number of quirky production techniques which have long since become the stuff of legend for subsequent generations of recordists.

Likely the most celebrated production quirk on "Heroes" is the treatment Visconti devised for Bowie's lead vocal. Vicsonti tracked Bowie using three different microphones, distributed variously throughout Hansa's cavernous live room, specifically, at a distance of 9 inches, 20 feet and 50 feet, respectively. Applying a different gate to each microphone, Visconti ensured that signal made it through to tape only when the amplitude of Bowie's vocals became sufficiently loud to surpass each gate's threshold. Moreover, Visconti muted each microphone as the next one in the sequence triggered. Bowie's performance thus grows in intensity precisely as ever more ambience infuses his delivery until, by the final verse, he has to shout just to be heard.

This multi-latch system was, apparently, a common recording technique in the classical genre. Visconti is nonetheless typically credited with having invented multi-latch gating in rock, perhaps indicating how little sharing of notes went on between rock and classical recordists in the middle- and late-1970s. In any event, the distanced effect which multi-latching generated on "Heroes" is obviously reinforced by Visconti's treatment of Bowie's backing vocals during the final verse and chorus. Beginning at 4:28, it is the backing line which appears driest and loudest in the mix; the conventional dynamic relationship between lead and backing vocals is, in this case, reversed so Bowie's lead vocals are buried far back in the mix while his backing vocals swell to the fore. The more Bowie shouts just to be heard, in fact, the further back in the mix Visconti's multi-latch system pushes his vocal tracks, creating a stark metaphor for the situation of Bowie's doomed lovers: shouting their love for one another over the Berlin Wall, the more passionate their (undoubtedly fictional) love grew the further apart they must have felt.

ENVELOPE FOLLOWING

Just as compressors can side-chain to a different track than the one they attenuate, so too can gates key to another track than the one they attenuate. Keyed to a vocal track, for instance, a gate on an electric guitar part will only open to allow sound through when the amplitude of the vocal track exceeds its threshold. One of the more obvious and creative uses for keyed gating produces 'envelope following': the deliberate refashioning of one amplitude profile either to match or, at the very least, to closely imitate another. This technique has become particularly popular in modern electronica productions, especially on trance records. Alex Case (2007: 184–185) explains:

> Insert a gate across a guitar track, but key the gate open with a snare track. The result is a guitar tone burst that looks a lot like a snare, yet sounds a lot like a guitar. This kind of synthesized sound is common in many styles of music, particularly those where the sound of the studio — the sound of the gear — is a positive, such as trance, electronica, and many other forms of dance music (always an earnest adopter of new technology). A low-frequency oscillator, carefully tuned, can be keyed open on each kick drum for extra low end thump. Sine waves tuned to 60 Hz or lower will do the job. Distort slightly the sine wave for added harmonic character or reach for a more complex wave (i.e., sawtooth). The resulting kick packs the sort of wallup that, if misused, can damage loudspeakers. Done well, it draws a crowd onto the dance floor.

In fact, so prevalent is envelope following in modern trance that some commentators now refer to the process as "trance gating". Trance DJs routinely key sustained synth pads to more rhythmically active tracks

in order to produce the characteristic syncopated sound of trance gating; the technique can clearly be heard, for instance, beginning at 1:11
on DJ Nexus "Journey Into Trance." Trance gates can be produced any
number of ways, including via a dedicated trance gate plug-in which
combines sequencing capacities with a keyed gate. The synth sequence
is keyed, internally, to a rhythmic sequence which recordists can either
step-input or real-input. However, as Doug Eisengrein (2007) argues:

> A still common yet more creative use for [keyed gating] involves
> a noise gate in conjunction with any form of rhythmic music.
> Dance-floor tracks such as techno or synth-pop can be enhanced
> by placing a gate on a synth line or pad and using a sharp repetitive
> sound such as a hi-hat, clap or conga loop for the key input. Now,
> each time the relevant percussive element triggers the gate, the synth
> line will be chopped up, resulting in a rhythmically locked arpeggio
> of sorts. I can imagine you trance addicts licking your chops now
> in anticipation of your next studio session. By adding this simple
> ingredient into the stew, your tracks can churn and bubble along
> just a little bit funkier.

Table 2.4   Examples of trance gating on DJ Nexus' *Groove Theory*.

Record	*Track (Entrance of Trance Gate)*
DJ Nexus, *Groove Theory*	2. Feel The Groove (1:02–1:58; 2:14–3:19)
	6. Spaced Out (0:28–4:04)
	7. A Journey Into Trance (1:11–4:07)
	8. Mind Body and Soul (0:00–0:59; 1:23–2:10, etc.)
	9. Tribal Dance (1:51–2:20)
	10. Dust It Off (0:00–1:43)
	11. Movin N Groovin (0:00–1:03; 2:38–3:23)
	12. Body Movin (0:00–0:29; 0:47–2:57)
	13. Hold On (Nexus Dub House Mix) (0:00–0:12)
	15. Raise Your Hands To Heaven (0:45–1:14)
	16. Im A Beat Junkie (2:09–2:23)
	19. Only In My Dreams (1:03–2:02; 2:04–3:59)

Envelope following is sometimes used to tighten a sloppy performance. In funk and disco, for instance, rhythmic precision was a key ingredient but the unique way that each musician interpreted the global pulse of a song played an equally crucial role. Nile Rodgers famously used keyed gating on a number of Le Chic productions to superimpose his rhythmic feel onto tracks performed by other musicians. As Rodgers (cited in Buskin: April 2005) recalls:

> There was the gimmick of my rhythm playing — which was pretty accurate, pulsing on the money — being used as a trigger for other instruments that weren't playing nearly as funky. On the very first record that we recored, "Everybody Dance," we did it with one of my jazz-musician friends playing clavinet. He was not funky at all. So, when you hear that really cool solo that he plays on the song, it's actually him just playing whole notes while the rhythm is keyed by my guitar. That was our very first recording, and [producer] Bob Clearmountain taught us how to do that. He said, 'Oh man, the keyboard player sucks! Why don't you play the rhythm Nile, and just let this guy play whole notes . . . We used that trick quite successfully later on, the most successful being on the Diana Ross song "Upside Down," where I keyed the funky rhythm of the strings.

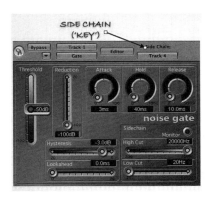

Figure 2.6   The same noise gate seen in Figure 2.5, but keyed to a vocal track (track 4).

Example 2.4   Envelope Following

Example 2.4a demonstrates the sound of envelope following, using a drum sample and a synth pad. The synth pad initially sounds without gating; and, then, at precisely 0:16 into the track, a gate — keyed to the kick, and snare, on the drum sample — is applied. At 0:24, the drum track is faded to silence, leaving only the synth pad, which continues along until 0:32, at which point the gate is bypassed, and the synth pad fades to silence. Examples 2.4b through 2.4d follow the same protocol as Example 2.4a, but using a different synth pad sounds.

Imogen Heap demonstrates another creative use for envelope following in her breakout hit from 2005, "Hide and Seek." Heap's production for the song is remarkably sparse, given how lushly orchestrated it sounds on first blush. Sung into a Digitech Vocalist Workstation harmonizer, Heap's lead-vocals (which are manually doubled) and a few overdubbed vocalizations provide the song's only melodic content, while the harmonizer, set in 'vocoder mode', automatically fills in the song's background harmonies, using the pitches that Heap performs on a connected keyboard while she sings. Keyed to Heap's vocal line, the gate on the harmonizer only opens when Heap sings, and it abruptly attenuates the signal to silence during each pause in her delivery. The effect is strangely unsettling, as though a chorus of synthesizers were singing along with Heap, leaving only bits of reverb and delay to trail off into the periodic silences.

DUCKING

Another common use for keyed gating is to 'duck' the amplitude of one signal under another, that is, to make one track quieter whenever another gets louder. To achieve this effect, recordists insert a modified gate — a gate with its 'ducking' function engaged — or a dedicated 'ducker' into the audio chain of whichever track they want to attenuate. They then key the ducking mechanism to the track they want to make more prominent in the mix. Whenever the amplitude of the ducking signal registers above its threshold, the gate attenuates the volume of the ducked signal by a fixed range. As Roey Izhaki (2008: 377) explains:

> Say we want the full slap of the kick but the distorted guitars mask much of it. We can reduce this masking interaction by ducking the distorted guitars whenever the kick hits. It can be surprising how much attenuation can be applied before it gets noticed, especially when it comes to normal listeners. Whether done for a very brief moment, or for longer periods, ducking is an extremely effective way to clear some space for the really important instruments. Indeed, it is mostly the important instruments serving as ducking triggers and the least important instruments being the ducking prey.

Some analysts have noted that ducking closely resembles side-chain pumping. However, most agree that it is attenuation by a specified range which characterizes ducking, rather than the variable attenuation which a side-chained compressor creates. In Case's (2007: 183–184) words:

> The alert reader may note that a compressor with a side-chain input should achieve nearly the same thing [as a ducker]. The ducking process . . . is attenuating a signal when the threshold is exceeded — the very goal of compression. Background music is attenuated when the voice goes above the threshold. The trouble with using compression for this effect, and the reason some . . . gates provide this feature, is the presence of that critical parameter: range. Not available on most compressors, range sets a maximum amount of attenuation, useful in many . . . gating effects. In the case of ducking, it is likely that the music should be turned down by a specified, fixed amount in the presence of the speaking voice. No matter the level of the voice, the music should simply be attenuated by a certain finite amount based on what sounds appropriate to the engineer, perhaps 10–15 dB. Compression would adjust the level of the music constantly based on the level of the voice. The amplitude of the music would modulate constantly in complex reaction to the level of the

voice. Compression does not hit a hard stop because compressors do not typically process the range parameter. Therefore, look to noise gates for the ducking feature.

The most often cited example of ducking is its broadcast application: "when the DJ speaks, the music is turned down," summarizes Izhaki (2008: 374). However, one of the most common ducking techniques used on rock and electronica records today is to duck reverb and delay processing under dry vocal tracks (recordists typically use the metaphors of 'wet' and 'dry' to designate, respectively, a signal with and without obvious reverberation or delay processing). As I noted occurs on David Bowie's "Heroes," for instance, the more that ambience pervades a track, the more muffled and distant it sounds. Recordists can combat this muffling effect by inserting a ducker into the reverb and delay line (e.g., a send/return track), keyed to the dry track. The dry track thus ducks its own reverb and delay, so the reverb and delay is notably attenuated each time the amplitude of the dry track exceeds the ducker's threshold.

A clear example of this technique can be heard on Céline Dion's "The Power Of Love." Produced by Canadian David Foster, "The Power Of Love" has all the hallmarks of a Dion track from the early 1990s. Every detail of Foster's production seems geared to showcasing Dion's trademark massive vocals, which range from a whisper to straightforward 'belting' numerous times throughout the song. The ducking effect is most obvious during the first verse and chorus, however, as the lush reverb and delay on Dion's vocals swell to the fore each time she pauses. The end of the first vocal line in the first chorus — "because I'm your lady" — provides the song's clearest example, as the echoing delay and thick reverb on Dion's vocals swell to audibility the very second she stops singing. Interestingly, as the song progresses and Foster's layered arrangement becomes increasingly dense, the ducking effect becomes less pronounced. By the second verse, at 1:23, Foster has dispensed with the delay on Dion's vocals completely, though the reverb remains constant and ducked throughout the song. The effect is also exceedingly clear on Adele's "Cold Shoulder."

Table 2.5   Clear examples of lead-vocal tracks ducking their delay lines on Perry Farrell's vocals for Jane's Addiction and Porno For Pyros. Readers should note that the effect is applied variably across each track; it is clearest on the louder portions of Farrell's delivery in tracks listed below.

Record	Track
Jane's Addiction, *Nothing's Shocking*	2. Ocean Size 4. Ted, Just Admit It 5. Mountain Song
Jane's Addiction, *Ritual De Lo Habitual*	1. Stop 2. No One's Leaving 4. Obvious 6. Three Days
Porno For Pyros, *Porno For Pyros*	4. Cursed Female 5. Cursed Male 7. Bad Shit 8. Packin' 9. Black Girlfriend

DUCKING SYSTEMS

As with all aesthetic limits, the only limitation on what can be ducked, and how ducking should be done, exists in the imaginations of recordists. Any track can duck any other track so long as both tracks contain sufficient amplitude. To combat masking, for instance, some recordists forego mirrored equalization techniques altogether and instead duck the bass guitar under the kick drum. This produces a subtle side-chain pumping effect which effectively wedges space into the mix for the kick drum to fill, but only when it and the bass guitar sound in tandem. Similarly, recordists working in the 'heavier' genres will often duck rhythm-guitar under lead-guitar tracks. And, in most genres of electronic dance music, recordists sometimes duck everything under the kick drum and snare, though this is most often done using side-chained compressors, as I note above.

Some recordists go even further, however, creating 'ducking systems': one track ducks another track, which in turn ducks another track, which is set to duck another track, and so on. This systems approach to ducking, which resembles the multi-latch gating system described above, produces a sequence of pronounced dynamic fluctuations that seem to flex randomly, even as they follow the internal logic of the ducking system. Portishead's "Biscuit" provides an illustrative example. The main 8-second sample which underpins the track, audible in its entirety from 0:12 to 0:20, features at least the following ducking sequence during its first iteration: (i) the opening kick, on the downbeat of bar one, ducks everything but the Fender Rhodes; (ii) the second kick, which sounds like it is accompanied by some kind of sub-bass, on beat two, ducks everything which precedes it, including the vinyl hiss, the Fender Rhodes and the resonance of the first kick and snare hit; and (iii) the second snare hit ducks everything which precedes it. This opening sequence is simply the most obvious. Numerous other, less overt ducking sequences occur throughout "Biscuit."

3. DISTORTION

Once it is input into a device, even the most minute change in the waveform of an audio signal qualifies as "distortion". Though there are many different kinds of distortion, recordists and musicians are mostly concerned about amplitude distortion, that is, changes in the amplitude of a signal. When the volume of an input signal is too great for a device to handle, or when it is magnified beyond what the device is equipped to convey, the transient peaks of its waveform are often radically limited, a process recordists call "clipping" (Stark 2005: 79). Solid-state and digital technology tends to clip immediately, "hard-clipping" the input waveform into what Alexander Case (2007: 97) calls a "squareish" shape. "Tube" and "analog" gear, on the other hand, will respond to over-abundances of amplitude gradually, generating a beveled s-curve,

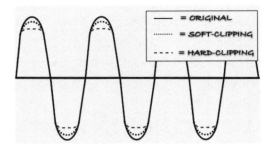

Figure 2.7 An undistorted, soft-clipped and hard-clipped waveform.

or, soft-clipped shape (see Figure 2.7). In either case, amplitude distortion almost completely transforms the input waveform, and in so doing, significantly alters its spectral content.

Perhaps no genre so enthusiastically embraced distortion as rock 'n' roll (and, more recently, the gabbercore techno genre). As Robert Walser (1993) notes, the recordists and musicians who invented rock 'n' roll championed distortion as a staple timbre, incorporating it into productions with wild abandon during the middle- and late-1950s. It was arguably this predilection, in fact, which most obviously set rock 'n' roll apart from tamer competitors during its formative years, though the genre's suggestive rhythms did little to endear it to conservative listeners. As Ikutaro Kakehashi (cited in Fukuda 2001: 69), a key player in the development of fuzz distortion, remembers:

> Nowadays there are various kinds of distortion. But back then, in the 1950s, well, clipping was all we could use. That's why we [read: BOSS] had to go ahead with development without an idea of what was right, without knowing what standard we should be aiming for ... The top players of the time sounded pristine. None of the top players used fuzz ... That was the cycle that we were caught up in. I wonder if it was Hendrix who pulled us out? When he became popular, fuzz suddenly took off.

THE SLASH AND BURN METHOD

Rock recordists have developed an extremely broad palette for distortion. Timbres such as "overdrive", "fuzz", "distortion" and "feedback", among others, are now integral to numerous subgenres of popular music. At first, though, rock musicians and recordists had very few tools for creating distortion. Early champions of the timbre like urban blues guitarist Muddy Waters and Brit-Rock pioneer Dave Davies had little choice but to slash the speaker-cones of their amplifiers to create distortion. Or, they intentionally patched into old amplifiers with malfunctioning circuitry and burnt-out tubes to generate the timbre of distortion, as did bebop trailblazer Charlie Christian and journeyman R&B star Ike Turner.

The Kinks' breakthrough hit from 1964, "You Really Got Me," provides a clear illustration of this slash and burn technique for creating distortion. A crucial volley in the 'first wave' of the British Invasion, "You Really Got Me" generates much of its much ballyhooed brutal and anarchic excitement through the distortion which permeates Dave Davies power-chord guitar riff. This riff is heard most iconically during the first three seconds of the track. Davies created this distortion by taking a razor blade to the speaker-cone of a small 8- or 10-watt Elpico amplifier, and he combined the output from that amplifier with signal split to his standby Vox AC30 amplifier; and, meanwhile, older brother and singer Ray Davies quietly reinforced the riff on a Fender telecaster while his brother played (Hunter 1999). As Dave Davies (cited in Hunter 1999) remembers:

> I was getting really bored with this guitar sound — or lack of an interesting sound — and there was this radio spares shop up the road, and they had a little green amplifier in there next to the radios. It was an Elpico — I've got a picture of it on my web site — and I twiddled around with it and didn't know what to do. I tried taking the wires going to the speaker and putting a jack plug on there and plugging it straight into my AC3O. It kind of made a weird noise, but

it wasn't what I was looking for. I started to get really frustrated, and I said, "I know! I'll fix you!" I got a single-sided Gillette razorblade and cut round the cone . . . from the centre to the edge, so it was all shredded but still on there, still intact. I played and I thought it was amazing, really freaky. I felt like an inventor! We just close-miked that in the studio, and also fed the same speaker output into the AC3O, which was kind of noisy but sounded good.

THE OVERDRIVE METHOD

Rather than slash and burn their amplifiers, early pioneers of distortion could also simply "overdrive" the gain (volume); this technique was arguably the first distortion to regularly permeate pop records. Electric guitarists produced overdrive by driving (boosting) the gain on their guitars and amplifiers into non-linear regions, which is to say, well past the point-of-distortion. Charlie Christian, for instance, whose work with distortion during the late-1930s and early-1940s was at least as visionary as his guitar playing, had only a 15-watt Gibson EH-150 amplifier, equipped with a 10-inch speaker cone and a single 6L6 RCA vacuum-tube, to project his ES-150 hollow-body electric guitar past the Big Bands and Swing Orchestras he played with (Hunter 2008). Competing with, say, the Benny Goodman Orchestra, whose main goal was to rile listeners to dance, the natural tendency would have been to crank the gain as far up, that is, as loud, as possible.

Unlike other kinds of distortion, overdrive developed within an almost entirely tube-based environment: solid-state technology would not come to market until almost two-decades after the likes of Charlie Christian and Les Paul first cranked the volume on their amplifiers (Kyttala 2009). Overdrive, then, is usually associated with the sound of tube-based gear cranked, or, overdriven, into its non-linear region. Tube amplifiers gradually squash and compress an input signal as it distorts, creating a soft-clipped waveform. The distortion this gradual compression generates does not usually reach the same amplitude, nor

does it sound as dissonant, as the distortion that hard-clipping generates. In Daniel Thompson's (2005: 245–246) words:

> Clipping occurs when the amplitude of the input signal is too
> great for the device to handle. The upper portions . . . of the wave
> are either rounded off or drastically cut by the device, yielding a
> changed waveform. The exact result of this [is] called harmonic
> distortion . . . When solid-state devices distort, this generates a
> waveform that resembles a square wave. In doing so, it also generates
> the harmonic components of a square wave, notably odd harmon-
> ics. By contrast, tube-based gear, which uses vacuum tubes instead
> of transistors for internal amplification, as well as analog tape, will
> start to gently distort before even reaching the so-called 'point of
> distortion', and subsequently eases into distortion gradually . . . Soft
> clipping is heard to be more musical and more pleasant than hard
> clipping, and is often referred to as sounding 'warm', where hard
> clipping is said to sound 'harsh' or 'cold'.

A celebrated landmark in the early development of distortion can
be heard on Les Paul's overdriven guitar part for "Bugle Call Rag,"
which he recorded live with the Nat King Cole Trio at the Los Angeles
Philharmonic Auditorium on 2 July 1944. The recording was first in a
series of critically celebrated live albums that Norman Granz produced
from the Philharmonic stage throughout the 1940s and early 1950s.
Recently released as track three on the compilation album *Jazz At The
Philharmonic*, "Bugle Call Rag" documents a fairly conventional bebop
performance from the mid-1940s, replete with the obligatory 'head-
and-solos' arrangement, orderly turn-taking for the improvisations
(even if the sequence of solos seems to have been determined on the
spot) and the requisite frantic pace.

Entertaining as his performance on the electric guitar is, it is Les
Paul's subtly overdriven tone which proves most compelling. Equipped
with one of the guitarist's hand-wound 'super-hot' pickups, the guitar
Paul used at this time was already prone to producing amplitude

distortion regardless of which particular amplifier it patched into. Every note that Paul picks throughout "Bugle Call Rag" is thus overlain with a soft veneer of overdrive though the distortion becomes notably opaque on the syncopated accents Paul adds beginning at 1:33.

"Bugle Call Rag" is, admittedly, not the most obvious example of overdrive on record. However, it is one of the earliest examples and, as such, provides an invaluable document of one musician's efforts to consciously incorporate overdrive into his performance practice. Over time, musicians would become much more extroverted in their use of the effect. One need only sample rock records produced in the mid- and late 1960s by, say, Jimi Hendrix ("Purple Haze"), Cream ("Sunshine Of Your Love"), the Beatles ("Helter Skelter" and "Everybody's Got Something To Hide Except For Me And My Monkey"), Buffalo Springfield ("Mr. Soul"), the Rolling Stones ("Gimme Shelter"), the Who ("My Generation"), the Kinks ("All Day And All Of The Night"), Led Zeppelin ("Good Times Bad Times"), CSNY ("Ohio") and Pink Floyd ("Set The Controls For The Heart Of The Sun") to grasp how quickly the rock world became infatuated with the timbre.

One of the first lead vocal tracks to feature overdrive can be heard on the Beatles' "I Am The Walrus," arguably the band's most notorious psychedelic offering from the acid rock era after only "Revolution 9." Pathologically insecure about his singing, John Lennon routinely insisted that producer George Martin 'pour ketchup' on any vocal tracks he recorded, that is, Lennon insisted that Martin should process his vocal tracks extensively. Though Martin apparently had deep reservations about doing this, the producer nevertheless seems to have complied with Lennon's every request (Martin and Hornsby 1994). Thus on the night of 5 September 1967, in Abbey Road Studio One, Martin and engineer Geoff Emerick felt free to overdrive Lennon's vocal line for "I Am The Walrus" before it reached tape. The duo overdrived the volume on the (REDD.47) preamplifier in the (REDD.51) mixing console they used that night, and to increase the likelihood of distortion they even had Lennon sing through a rewired 'talkback' microphone on the mixing console (Emerick and Hornsby 2006). The duo then doubled (copied) the overdriven track using an Automatic Double Tracking (ADT) machine (see "Doubling", pg. 130) (Ryan and Kehew 2008: 466). Though Lennon's vocals are consequently overdriven throughout "I Am The Walrus," the distortion is particularly opaque on the words "me" (0:25), "together" (0:25–0:29), "how" (0:30) and "come" (0:44), and throughout the final strophe (2:53–3:16) and extended outtro, especially on the singer's emphatically absurd "jooba-joobas" between 3:23 and 3:34.

THE STOMP-BOX METHOD

Aside from arranging tacit sections, the slash and burn method of generating distortion obviously mandated use of distortion throughout the entirety of a production. Slashing the speaker cone on an amplifier, or boosting the volume of an amplifier with a loose connection, ensured that every tone it output bore the sonic imprint of distortion. However, distortion was not always appropriate throughout a song. Recordists were thus forced to make difficult decisions about whether a production could include distortion at all.

Beginning in the early 1960s, however, corporations such as Gibson Electronics brought stand-alone signal processing units to market that afforded instrumentalists unprecedented control over when, and for how long, distortion should permeate their performances. Affectionately dubbed 'stomp-boxes' by users, these processors were (and still are) designed for insertion into the audio chain as an intervening stage before final amplification. Each stomp-box lays flat on the floor at the foot of musicians who, at any point during a performance, can stomp the large button on top to activate its effect (some devices, such as wah-wah and expression pedals, use a 'treadle', that is, a large foot-activated potentiometer). Moreover, each stomp-box usually features a series of dials and switches so recordists can individually adjust each processing parameter to taste. When a stomp-box is disengaged, the input signal is routed directly to output through a so-called 'bypass' circuit.

Simply activating a stomp-box completely transforms the timbre of electric instruments. The timbral complexity of rock music thus blossomed once stomp-boxes hit the market and, within less than a decade, stomp-boxes had re-shaped signal processing into a core rock 'n' roll performance technique. By 1967, in fact, now legendary rock guitarists like Jimi Hendrix and Pete Townshend could arrange entire improvisations around a core repertoire of stylistically unique signal processing techniques, with only the odd bits of straightforward performance practice thrown in for good measure. Hendrix's iconoclastic rendering of the American national anthem, "The Star Spangled Banner," at the Woodstock Music and Art Fair in 1969, and his performance of "Wild Thing" at the Monterey Pop Festival two years before, remain lasting and widely celebrated early monuments to this development in rock performance practice.

THE MAESTRO FUZZ-TONE FZ-1

The first stomp-box to reach market was Gibson Electronics Maestro Fuzz-Tone FZ-1, which made its American debut in spring of 1962. This device provided distinctive 'fuzz' distortion to any guitarist who could afford the device. Though nothing definitive has been written about the origin of the FZ-1 'fuzzbox', an apocryphal creation myth for the device nonetheless circulates in modern rock criticism and in collecting publications.

According to this legend, a Nashville studio musician named Grady Martin accidentally stumbled onto the fuzz sound while he worked a session for Marty Robbins, specifically, to record "Don't Worry." While Martin setup to record a 6-string bass part, either a connection in the mixing board came loose or a tube somewhere along the audio-chain burnt-out . . . nobody seems to know for sure. Either way, the signal for Martin's bass quickly degraded and, eventually, distorted completely.

Though conventional wisdom said that the resulting fuzz should be erased, engineer Glen Snoddy showcased the timbre by way of a 6-string bass solo during the song's bridge (1:25 to 1:43). Unorthodox and risky as it was, Snoddy's gamble paid off: not only did "Don't Worry" become the first hit record to feature what would soon be a staple timbre in modern country and rock music, but it topped the country charts and made Number Three on the Billboard pop charts.

The next year, in 1961, guitarist Billy Strange further popularized the fuzz tone by applying it to his lead-guitar work on Ann-Margaret's first Top 20 hit in the U.S., namely, "I Just Don't Understand"; and he used the timbre again on Bob B. Soxx and the Blue Jeans' "Zip-a-Dee-Doo-Dah," which made the American Top 10 in 1962 no doubt thanks in large part to the production work of Phil Spector. Guitarist Big Jim Sullivan used the fuzz timbre for his guitar solos on P. J. Proby's "Hold Me" and "Together," using fuzzboxes custom-made by famed electronics whiz Roger Mayer. Then came the Ventures, a prolific American surf rock band who counted themselves among the many listeners happily shocked by these records. So inspired was the band by the fuzz timbre, in fact, that they tasked their friend, session stalwart Red Rhodes, with devising a reliable means of reproducing fuzz for their records. A few months later, Rhodes presented the band with a custom-made fuzzbox which they used, in turn, on their Top 5 novelty number, "2000 Pound Bee."

Meanwhile, Glen Snoddy continued to engineer country sessions. Many of the musicians Snoddy engineered requested fuzz for their productions, and on other sessions Snoddy himself suggested the timbre. Demand for fuzz amongst country recordists soon reached the tipping point as records by the likes of Merle Haggard, Buck Owens, Waylon Jennings, Wanda Jackson and Kay Adams, among many others, showcased the timbre (see **Table 2.6**). Snoddy thus set to work devising a reliable means of producing fuzz for sessions and, late in 1961, he hit upon the solution of a stomp-box. Convinced that he had a potential money-maker on his hands, Snoddy pitched the device to

Gibson Electronics who gladly shared Snoddy's vision. The result was the production of the first Maestro Fuzz-Tone FZ-1 in the spring of 1962 (Meiners 2001).

Table 2.6 Country tracks from the 1960s featuring fuzz distortion (adapted from http://blog.wfmu.org/freeform/2007/11/country-fuzz-sp.html).

Artist	Track
Marty Robbins	Don't Worry
Carl Butler	Wonder Drug
Claude Gray	Stone Heart
Darrell McCall	Got My Baby On My Mind
Glen Garrison	City Of Sin
Ferlin Husky	I'll Sail My Ship Alone
Wilis Brothers	Ruby Ann Soft Shoulders, Dangerous Curves
Wanda Jackson	This Gun Don't Care Who It Shoots
Jimmie Rodgers	Rhumba Boogie
Skeeter Davis	If I Had Wheels
Kay Adams	Little Pink Mack Big Mac
Phil Baugh	One Man Band
Jean Shepard	My Mama Didn't Raise No Fools
Johnny Darrell	Mental Revenge
Chesley Carroll	Hippie From Mississippi
Waylon Jennings	Six Strings Away
Buck Ownes	Who's Gonna Mow Your Grass?
Grady Martin	The Fuzz

By the time Gibson manufactured the first FZ-1, a market for the fuzz timbre was clearly emerging in select rock and country music communities across North America and England. That said, it would still take a few more years for that market to reach anything like widespread proportions. Despite the initial optimism of Gibson's marketing and sales personnel, who managed to convince retailers to purchase no less than 5,458 units of the FZ-1 in 1962 alone, sales of the FZ-1 fizzled. After its initial marketing push, Gibson managed to ship only three of the fuzzboxes throughout 1963 and 1964 (Meiners 2001).

Everything changed in 1965, however. That year Keith Richards used the Maestro Fuzz-Tone FZ-1 for the iconic chorus riff on the Rolling Stones "(I Cant Get No) Satisfaction." When the track topped the charts on both sides of the Atlantic Ocean in August of 1965, sales of the FZ-1 climbed into the thousands. Between August and December of 1965, a span of only four months, every last commercially available FZ-1 sold; and Gibson manufactured, and sold, an additional 3,454 units in January of 1966 alone (Meiners 2001). By December of 1966, just 16 months after "(I Cant Get No) Satisfaction" reached pole-position on the charts, Gibson had shipped and sold a staggering 15,540 Maestro Fuzz-Tone FZ-1 fuzzboxes (Meiners 2001).

An early artifact of stomp-box processing can be heard at 0:35 of the Rolling Stones "(I Cant Get No) Satisfaction." Having completed the first verse, for which Richards uses an unprocessed tone, the guitarist somewhat sloppily stomps on the FZ-1 for the return of the chorus riff and a button-click clearly penetrates the mix (the sound is similar to the clicking noise made by a retractable ballpoint pen). Another click can be heard at 1:35. This time, however, Richards stomps on the device roughly 1 second too late and the first two pitches of the chorus riff sound without fuzz. Finally, at 2:33, Richards prematurely stomps the FZ-1, adding fuzz to the last pitch of the song's ramp section. Recognizing his mistake, the guitarist immediately stomps the fuzzbox off and a button-click once more penetrates the mix.

Despite its comic quirks, Richards' performance on "(I Can't Get No) Satisfaction" clearly established fuzz as a staple timbre in rock. Other guitarists almost immediately followed his lead in adopting fuzzbox processing as a core technique. Jeff Beck, for instance, used a Sola Sound MK I fuzzbox on the opening riff for the Yardbirds' "Heart Full Of Soul," as did Paul McCartney on his doubled electric bass track for the Beatles' "Think For Yourself"; and Dave Davies reportedly did the same on the Kinks' "All Day And All Of The Night," mercifully sparing his amplifiers any further injury. Meanwhile, Jimi Hendrix developed a tone almost wholly defined by fuzz, opting for chiefly American fuzzboxes like the Mosrite Fuzzrite and the Dallas Arbiter Fuzz Face, and countless other units custom-made by the likes of Roger Mayer. And, of course, Jimmy Page made fuzz a staple timbre of heavy metal and hard rock, incorporating distortion into the heavier portions of *Led Zeppelin I* and *Led Zeppelin II* by way of, most famously, Sola Sound's MK II fuzzbox, a Gibson overdrive pedal custom-made once again by Roger Mayer, a Marshall 1959 SLP amplifier and a small 15-watt Supro practice amplifier, both cranked to their limits.

By the early 1970s, the fuzzbox market had become crowded. Sola Sound introduced the British public to domestically manufactured fuzzboxes in 1965, marketing its MK I, MK II and VOX Tone Bender fuzzboxes to great success. The next year, in 1966, Mosrite sold its first Fuzzrite fuzzbox in America and the Dallas Arbiter Group brought to market the notorious Fuzz Face, both of which would quickly become 'go to' devices for the likes of Jimi Hendrix, Eric Clapton, David Gilmour, Carlos Santana, Pete Townshend and Jimmy Page. Finally, in 1971, Electro-Harmonix released its Big Muff, which defined the sound of distortion in British and North American progressive rock for the next two decades. In fact, the Electro-Harmonix Big Muff continues to figure in guitar rigs for some of the world's most influential rock bands, including the Smashing Pumpkins, Mudhoney, Mogwai, Sonic Youth and the White Stripes.

Table 2.7 Some celebrated stomp-box distortion units, and their users.

Manufacturer	Pedal	Users
Gibson Electronics	Maestro Fuzz Tone FZ-1	Keith Richards
Sola Sound	MK I	Pete Townshend, Jeff Beck, Jimmy Page
Sola Sound	MK II	Jeff Beck, Jimmy Page, Eric Clapton

(continued)

Manufacturer	Pedal	Users
Dallas Arbiter Gr	Fuzz Face	Jimi Hendrix, Eric Clapton, Jimmy Page, Eric Johnson
Shin-ei	Companion FY-2	Jim Reid, William Reid, Johnny Greenwood
Univox	Super Fuzz	Pete Townshend, Eric Clapton, J. Masics
Fender	Fender Blender	Billy Corgan, Kevin Shields, Bilinda Butcher
Electro-Harmonix	Big Muff	Carlos Santana, David Gilmour, Billy Corgan, James Iha, J. Masics, Jack White, Stuart Braithwaite, James "Munky" Shaffer, Thurston Moore, Lee Ranaldo, Kim Gordon, Steve Turner, Mark Arm, Kurt Cobain

RE-AMPING

Since the time of FZ-1s, recordists have developed a highly nuanced understanding of the various distortions their amplifiers and processors can be made to generate. This tacit knowledge now forms the basis of an increasingly common processing technique called 're-amping'. When musicians track parts with their processing effects activated — when they track with, say, distortion and chorus effects actively processing the signal — there is little they can do later if the effects conflict with or mask other tracks in the production. Recordists have thus taken to tracking parts without processing, only to process the signal later through a practice called re-amping.[3] This entails sending the dry signal through various amplifiers, stomp-boxes and outboard gear, and re-tracking the newly processed signal through a combination of close-mic, distance-mic, room-mic and direct-injection techniques.

---

3 Mastering engineers also re-amp a fair bit now. Tasked with re-mastering dated records, they routinely re-amp the original dry tracks through modern processors and amplifiers to help update the sound.

Now that re-amping is common, recordists are expected to be tremendously knowledgeable about the various timbral modifications available to them through the gear they use. Each particular amplifier, microphone, preamplifier, outboard processor, stomp-box effects pedal, audio interface and cable is but another signal processing device, so far as modern recordists are concerned. Riku Katainen (2008), guitarist for the Finnish metal band Dauntless, clearly demonstrates this expertise in his blog entry for the weekend of 28 November to 1 December 2008, which describes the re-amping procedure he undertook to craft both the rhythm and lead-guitar tones on Dauntless' *Execute The Fact*:

> I started out tone hunting with [a] very basic combination: Tubescreamer + Mesa/Boogie Dual Rectifier + Mesa/Boogie Rectifier 4x12" . . . I removed the Tubescreamer and took ProCo Rat distortion and boosted the amp with it. OMG! It had some "Swedish death metal" flavour, but not as extreme as Boss HM2 would have been . . . Then the problems started . . . [A]fter two broken fuses and one faulty power tube, we could not use the Mesa. We had to start from the beginning and find the same sound from a Peavey 5150 II. To our surprise we managed to match it 98 % . . . We were very happy and re-amped all the rhythm guitars through this combination: Little Labs Redeye, ProCo Rat Distortion, Peavey 5150II, Mesa[-] Boogie Rectifier 4x12," Shure SM57, MS Audiotron MultiMix, RME Fireface 800. I wanted to keep it simple, so I recorded the cab with only one microphone . . . I used the basic on-axis "dustcap edge" placement . . . After the rhythm guitars were done, I changed the boost pedal to Tubescreamer to make it slightly smoother for lead guitars . . . and I was done.

Re-amping does not always require such a compartmentalized process, however. Live re-amping, that is, re-amping done during live tracking sessions, played a crucial role in shaping the notoriously lo-fi timbre of Julian Casablancas' lead vocals on the Strokes' *Is This It?* and *Room On Fire*, for instance. Each track on these records features the same 'hyped' vocal timbre, which was the product of a re-amping system that Casablancas himself devised, in conjunction with the band's producer, Gordon Raphael. When Casablancas recorded demonstration tracks for what would become *Is This It?*, the vocalist used only an Audio-Technica 4033A condenser microphone, patched through a small 8-inch Peavey practice amplifier, with its bass knob turned all the way down. When it came time to re-record tracks for *Is This It?* Casablances could think of no reason to change this signal chain — it had worked for demonstration recordings, the singer reasoned, so why should he change it just because a major label was now involved? Though he acknowledged the merit in Casablancas' reasoning, Raphael nonetheless pushed the singer to consider more professional options, most of which included singing vocal overdubs into a Neumann TLM103 large-diaphragm condenser microphone. After what was apparently a difficult and protracted back-and-forth between the singer and his producer, Casablancas and Raphael eventually reached a happy compromise. As Raphael (Buskin 2002) himself remembers:

> I would usually work with Julian for an hour just to get the voice tone. Until the final result was achieved he would be extremely suspicious and unhappy, and invariably the final result would have some kind of messiness or not-quite-rightness about it, at which point he would smile and say, "This is great." So, that was one technique, and then the second technique was something that Julian had discovered on his own at home while making the demos. He liked to sing through his Peavey practice amp, which is about eight inches tall, and I'd mike that with a Neumann TLM103, so he'd still be singing into the Audio-Technica [4033a] — Julian found the Neumann distasteful! — but I'd still be "Neumanning" it in order to get the exact details of what this horrible little amp sounded like. He wanted it shitty, but not too shitty. He would always say things like, "This sound needs to have its tie loosened."

SPECIFIC USES FOR DISTORTION: SECTIONAL DISTORTION

Three more common uses for distortion require attention, namely, 'sectional' distortion, 'lift' distortion and 'reinforcement' distortion. Of these, sectional distortion is easiest to hear: recordists simply use distortion for only one or two sections of a song to achieve its obvious effect. A definitive feature of grunge records made in the early 1990s, sectional distortion characterizes records by the likes of Nirvana, the Smashing Pumpkins, Alice In Chains, Stone Temple Pilots, Pearl Jam and countless other bands. Each of these groups crafted a slew of hit productions almost universally divisible into (i) quiet and timbrally-subdued verses and (ii) massively distorted, exploding choruses. Some of the best-known productions to feature this device include: Nirvana's "Smells Like Teen Spirit," "In Bloom," "Lithium," and "Lounge Act," from the band's breakthrough album *Nevermind*, and "Heart Shaped Box" from the band's last album *In Utero*; Alice In Chains' "Rooster" and "Would?" from *Dirt*; the Smashing Pumpkins' "Today," from *Siamese Dream*, and "Bullet With Butterfly Wings" from *Mellon Collie And The Infinite Sadness*; and Soundgarden's "Black Hole Sun" from *Superunknown*.[4]

---

4 Of course, fans will know that Soundgarden's "Black Hole Sun" is an exception to the band's usual output. In Anderson's (2007: 123) words: "'Black Hole Sun', which would win a Grammy for Best Hard Rock Performance, was a massive watershed moment for grunge, sadly occurring at the end of its reign of supremacy in the post-Cobain era. The song was a massive molten slab of melodic rock, a mid[-]period [Led] Zeppelin riff wrapped in a wave of druggy psychedelia. The lyrics seem to be about Armageddon (or some sort of cataclysmic event that seems pretty biblical), and the words match up perfectly with the music underneath, as the tension and discomfort in the verses give way to the bombast and destruction in the chorus. Curiously 'Black Hole Sun' is one of the few Soundgarden songs that follow the traditional quiet verse/loud chorus dynamic that grunge made famous — the band always seemed to go from being loud to being extremely loud."

SPECIFIC USES FOR DISTORTION: LIFT DISTORTION

'Lift' distortion differs from sectional distortion in a number of ways. Most obviously, lift distortion is typically applied to individual tracks in a multi-track production. Recordists often use lift distortion to emphasize the attack profile of electric or synthesized bass tracks. This affords recordists a rare opportunity to 'lift' tracks which might otherwise be buried (overwhelmed) in a mix, without having to apply a straightforward volume boost to those tracks. As Alex Case (2007: 98) puts it, "any single track of a multitrack project fighting to be heard in a crowded mix can achieve distinct audibility through the harmonic lift that comes from at least a little well chosen distortion." Far from a quick fix, however, lift distortion shifts the spectral location of the masking problem, forcing recordists to clear room elsewhere in the mix for the lift itself:

> The harmonic energy associated with distortion can cause masking of other signals. That is, a vocal that had been perfectly intelligible and a snare drum that formerly cut through the mix can both become more difficult to hear when distortion is added to the electric guitar. Spectral masking is very much in play. Distortion, like equalization, must be strategically used . . . [It] affects not only the [distorted instrument] but also instruments that occupy similar spectral regions (Case 2007: 100).

Though lift distortion has shaped the Top 40 since at least 1965, when Paul McCartney patched into a Sola Sound MK I fuzzbox to overdub a distorted bass part for The Beatles' "Think For Yourself," the device has most recently captured the attention of electronica recordists. The Chemical Brothers' "Loops Of Fury" provides an early example, though the duo applies distortion to the synth-bass track only variably on the record, allowing the track to sound dry at 3:29, for instance, and lifted at 3:46. Benny Benassi's "Satisfaction" from his electro-house debut, *Hypnotica*, and Cassius' "The Sound Of Violence" from *Au Rêve*, use lift distortion throughout; both productions provide ideal demonstrations of the device in that they feature distortion as an integral component of the synth-bass timbres (rather than an aggressively dissonant addition). Since he produced *Hypnotica*, Benny Benassi seems to have adopted lift distortion as a common technique. On his most recent record, *Rock and Rave*, Benassi uses lift distortion on every cut, though it is clearest on: "Finger Food," "My Body (feat. Mia J)," "Who's Your Daddy (Pump-kin Remix)," "Rock 'n' Rave," "I Am Not Drunk," "Free Your Mind — On The Floor (feat. Farenheit)," "Come Fly Away (feat. Channning)" and "Eclectic Strings."

Example 2.5   Lift Distortion
Throughout Example 2.5, a muddy and buried synth bass track is lifted and, in the process, brought to the fore of an electronica mix. The synth bass track is lifted at 0:27. The lift is then bypassed at 0:44, before it is reinstated for the remainder of the track at 1:01.

SPECIFIC USES FOR DISTORTION: REINFORCEMENT DISTORTION

According to Roey Izhaki (2008: 453):

> just like the parallel compression technique, where a compressed version is layered underneath the original, signals are sometimes distorted and then layered below the original [see "Mastering" for more on parallel compression techniques]. This gives [recordists] added control over the amount of distortion being added. Consequently, this lets [recordists] drive the distortion harder to produce a stronger effect, but then layer it underneath at lower levels so it is not too obvious.

Though any track could theoretically benefit from the select application of this kind of "reinforcement" distortion, the technique is most often applied to rock vocals. As Izhaki notes (2008: 453), the distinctive technique involves starting with an original track (call it "O") and then layering a heavily distorted "double" of "O" (call it "C") "under" (i.e., at a quieter volume than) the original track "O" (which remains dry and undistorted). Given that the reinforcing (distorted) track "C" is intentionally buried by recordists, reinforcement distortion can very easily go undetected by listeners, comprising a felt rather than heard element of productions.

Reinforcement distortion does not necessarily require signal processing. Jimmy Miller, for instance, often reinforced Mick Jagger's vocals on the more energetic numbers he produced for the Rolling Stones by having Jagger or Keith Richards shout a second take, which he then buried deep in the mix. "Sympathy For The Devil," for instance, features a shouted double in the right channel throughout, though the track is faded so that it only sporadically breaches the threshold of audibility; "Street Fighting Man" offers another obvious example. "Let It Bleed" provide another example of shouted (manual) reinforcement distortion, though Miller buried the shouted reinforcement track so far back in the mix that it takes headphones and an entirely unhealthy playback volume to clearly hear. By the time Miller produced the shambolic *Exile On Main Street*, however, he had dispensed with such preciousness altogether: the producer regularly pumps Jagger's and Richards' shouted reinforcement tracks to an equal level with the lead-vocals on the album. The first cuts on the album, "Rocks Off" and "Rip This Joint," and the ninth and tenth tracks, "Loving Cup" and "Happy," provide superb demonstrations of the technique. Other examples on the album include: "Casino Boogie," "Torn And Frayed," "Sweet Black Angel," "Turd On The Run," "Ventilator Blues" and "All Down The Line."

Example 2.6 Reinforcement Distortion

Example 2.6 features manual reinforcement distortion throughout, in the context of an original rock mix entitled "Pushing Up Daisies." The distortion is particularly clear on the word "daisies" in the choruses; the reinforcement tracks are, moreover, panned to either side of the stereo spectrum, each time they sound. During the song's bridge — which begins: "bow down abject, humbled, and pray . . ." — the shouted reinforcement track sounds on the left side of the stereo spectrum, at a very low level. For clarity, headphones are recommended, as is a moderate playback volume.

More recently, in the early and middle 1990s, processed reinforcement distortion found a welcome home in Top 40 alternative rock productions. The Breeders' "Cannonball" clearly showcases the technique, particularly during the introduction (0:00–0:15) and pre-chorus (i.e., 1:24–1:31), and throughout the second strophe (1:08–1:14). The Wallflowers' "One Headlight" also makes effective, albeit subtler, use of the reinforcement technique, specifically, on Jakob Dylan's overdubbed backing vocals; each successive chorus on the track features a slightly more distorted version of Dylan's backing line until, by the third chorus (at 3:57), his voice sounds more like a dot-matrix printer than anything else. "Gratitude," "So What'cha Want?," "Time For Livin'," "The Blue Nun" and certain portions of "The Maestro," from The Beastie Boys' *Check Your Head*, likewise feature reinforcement distortion on Mike D's, Ad Rock's and MCA's vocal tracks. And, perhaps most famously, Nirvana made copious use of the device on "Smells Like Teen Spirit," "Lithium" and "In Bloom" from *Nevermind*; "Sliver" from the B-sides and rarities compilation *Incesticide*; "Heart Shaped Box" and "Pennyroyal Tea" from *In Utero*; and on the posthumous "You Know You're Right."

4. FEEDBACK

Feedback is a special case distortion (Stark 2005: 5).[5] The often shrill timbre accrues when the input and output of an audio system — say, a microphone and speakers — combine to create a mutually reinforcing "feedback loop". A feedback loop is created when a signal enters an input, usually a microphone or a guitar pickup, and exits through loudspeakers. The amplified signal is subsequently received again through the input and is sent back through the amplifier, and back through the input, and back through the amplifier, and so on, "until a steady howl or whistle is heard" (Stark 2005: 195). As David Franz (2004: 115) explains:

> Except when they want Jimi Hendrix-like guitar feedback, most people try to avoid feedback in studio environments. Acoustic feedback is created when two magnetic pickups (i.e., microphone and speaker) feed each other the same audio signal. An audio signal going into the mic comes out of the speaker back into the mic and so forth, creating a loop. This feedback loop is the result of the signal building upon itself and creates a sometimes painful and injurious noise. Feedback at high decibel levels can cause hearing loss — not to mention damage to equipment.

Feedback loops remain intact, and usually ever intensifying, until a fresh audio signal is input (by the same device) and the "loop materials", that is, the physical materials which resonate at the feedback frequencies, are made to vibrate at different rates, thus breaking the loop.

---

5 For those who are aware of such distinctions, I follow the industry convention and use the term "feedback" as a shorthand for "acoustic feedback." Other forms of feedback, such as "electrical feedback" and "negative feedback" exist; interested readers are encouraged to consult Glenn D. White and Gary J. Louie (2005: 146) for more.

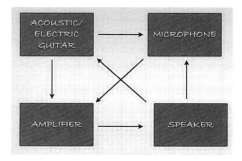

Figure 2.8   Block diagram of the signal-flow for a common feedback loop.

PITCHED FEEDBACK AND WHAMMY SLAMMING

Rock musicians and recordists are often far more interested in provoking and manipulating feedback than they are in preventing it from ever arising. Since guitarists like Jimi Hendrix and Pete Townshend first destroyed their amplifiers to produce the timbre during the late 1960s, a bona-fide technique for provoking and manipulating feedback has emerged. Guitarists boost the volume on their amplifiers and turn to face the speaker cone(s) with their guitars, either sustaining a pitch or leaving the strings to resonate unhindered; the requisite feedback loop will then generally accrue. As Robert Clarke (2005) explains:

> the amplifier closes the loop between the input and output [and] the [amplified] sound can [only] further enhance the vibrations of the guitar. If the gain is excessive, this enhancement results in instability dubbed 'feedback' by the musician. In such cases, the guitar starts vibrating excessively at a particular frequency and this vibration produces an audible tone. For [acoustic] guitars this typically occurs at lower frequencies ranging between 100 and 200 Hz. A similar mechanism occurs when amplifying the output of an electric guitar. Structural vibrations induced by acoustic feedback can magnify the signal generated by the sensors embedded in the guitar to pick up its sound, which leads to instability.

Once they have established the requisite loop, guitarists then change the resonating feedback frequencies by changing the angle between guitar and amp. This physical movement re-dimensions the feedback loop and, in turn, alters its resonance, allowing guitarists to create pitched-feedback melodies comprised entirely of feedback. A clear example of this technique can be heard during the guitar solo for Tool's "Jambi" on the album *10,000 Days*. Robert Fripp's lead guitar work for David Bowie's "Heroes" provides another clear example: the guitarist's pitched-feedback lines sound prominently in the right channel from 0:06–0:16 and 0:19–0:26, and in the left channel from 0:35–0:41, of the extended cut of the song which appears on the album (i.e., as opposed to the curtailed single release). As producer Toni Visconti (cited in Buskin: October 2004) recalls:

> Fripp [stood] in the right place with his volume up at the right level and getting feedback . . . Fripp had a technique in those days where he measured the distance between the guitar and the speaker where each note would feedback. For instance, an 'A' would feedback maybe at about four feet from the speaker, whereas a 'G' would feedback maybe three and a half feet from it. He had a strip that they would place on the floor, and when he was playing the note 'F' sharp he would stand on the strip's 'F' sharp point and 'F' sharp would feedback better. He really worked this out to a fine science, and we were playing this at a terrific level in the studio, too. It was very, very loud, and all the while he was [creating] these notes — that beautiful overhead line — Eno was turning the dials [on the filter bank of his EMS VCS3 synthesizer, which Fripp patched into] and creating a new envelope. We did three takes of that, and although one take would sound very patchy, three takes had all of these filter changes and feedback blending into that very smooth, haunting, overlaying melody you hear.

A celebrated live demonstration of pitched-feedback took place during the first minute of the Jimi Hendrix Experience's performance of "Wild

Thing" at the Monterey Pop Festival on 18 June 1967. Captured for posterity by famed 'rockumentarian' D. A. Pennebaker, as scene 17 of his documentary film *Monterey Pop*, Hendrix begins the performance by provoking feedback from his Marshall 'stack' amplifier and speaker cabinet. Warning the front row to guard their hearing — actually, he recommends they plug their ears — Hendrix impulsively grabs the whammy bar on his Fender Stratocaster and upends the instrument, stabbing the neck downwards between his legs. A convulsive dance ensues: swooning, shaking, swaying from side-to-side, Hendrix struggles to embody each unorthodox sound that he coaxes from his guitar and amplifier. More pitched-feedback and whammy-slamming, that is, manipulation of the whammy bar, ensues until, after about a minute, Hendrix subtly checks his tuning and cues the band to enter.

Actually, by the time Hendrix played Monterey he had already demonstrated some of the more radical possibilities of pitched-feedback and whammy-slamming. Track nine on the guitarist's debut record, *Are You Experienced?*, specifically, "Third Stone From The Sun," provides something like a master class demonstration of both techniques. Between 2:34 and 5:12 of the track, Hendrix never once picks a string on his guitar, relying almost totally on pitched-feedback and whammy-slamming instead. When the guitarist slams (presses) down on the whammy bar, as he does at 2:27 for instance, the string tension on his guitar slackens, producing what sounds like a slow-motion downward glissando; and when he pulls up on the bar, as at 3:43, the opposite effect is heard.

FEEDBACK LEAD-INS

Though Jimi Hendrix remains feedback's Dionysian image, and Robert Fripp its Apollonian avatar, neither guitarist was first to feature the distortion on record. In fact, feedback has been an integral component of the Top 40 soundscape since at least December of 1964, when the Beatles' "I Feel Fine" reached pole-position on both the British and North American pop charts, becoming the first chart-topper to showcase feedback distortion in so doing. "I Feel Fine" begins with the sound of a single note plucked percussively by Paul McCartney on his electric bass. Producer George Martin then orchestrates a cross-fade to pure feedback, generated by John Lennon using a Gibson J-160E semi-acoustic guitar leaned against an unspecified amplifier. Thus does "I Feel Fine" present listeners with a six second musique concrète sound-sculpture before anything like a pop song can be said to emerge. As Paul McCartney (cited in Emerick and Hornsby 2006: 94–95) remembers:

> John had a semi-acoustic Gibson guitar. It had a pick-up on it so it could be amplified . . . We were just about to walk away to listen to a take [of 'I Feel Fine' (1964)] when John leaned his guitar against the amp . . . and it went, "Nnnnnnwahhhhh!" And we went, "What's that? Voodoo!" "No, it's feedback." "Wow, it's a great sound!" George Martin was there so we said, "Can we have that on the record?" "Well, I suppose we could, we could edit it on the front." It was a found object — an accident.

Feedback lead-ins would soon become industry standard in pop productions. Producer Chas Chandler, for instance, used the device on Jimi Hendrix's "Foxey Lady," the producer grafting feedback onto a hammered and pulled guitar trill during the song's 10-second introduction. George Harrison would overdub a feedback lead-in comprised solely of pitched-feedback and whammy-slamming onto the first few seconds of the Beatles' "It's All Too Much." And, a short while later, Hendrix himself would adopt the technique to introduce "Crosstown Traffic," track three on the guitarist's self-produced *Electric Ladyland*. Other more recent feedback lead-ins can be heard on: the first 18 seconds of the Strokes "New York City Cops," track seven on the European release of *Is This It?*; the first minute of Ben Folds Five's "Fair"; the opening 45 seconds of Midnight Juggernauts' "Road To Recovery"; Nirvana's "Radio Friendly Unit Shifter"; the first few seconds of the Jesus And

Mary Chain's "Tumbledown" and "Catchfire"; and, briefly, in the intro-
ductions for the Stone Roses' "Waterfall," Porno For Pyros' "Tahitian
Moon," Tool's "Stinkfist" and the Cure's "Prayer For Rain."

TRANSITIONAL FEEDBACK SWELLS

Combined with a quick volume swell, feedback can also function as a
transitional device. In this case, electric guitarists provoke feedback a
few bars before the beginning of a heavier, or, at the very least, a more
energetic, section of a song, only to break the loop by picking something on the downbeat of that section, the distortion mixed to an ever
louder volume all the while before. Though examples abound on rock
records made since the time of The Beatles — guitaristic bands like
Meshuggah and Tool tend to be exceedingly fond of this device — arguably the gold-standard for transitional feedback is Weezer's "My Name
Is Jonas," track one on the band's eponymous debut CD. Recorded some
time between August and October of 1993, at Electric Lady Studios in
New York City, and produced by ex-Cars frontman Ric Ocasek, "My
Name Is Jonas" begins with only a finger-picked acoustic guitar and a
tambourine rattling in the background. A massive wall-of-feedback
quickly swells to the fore, however, and the song transitions into the
first of its many heavy sections (i.e., 0:06–0:12, 0:15–0:55, 1:03–1:06
and 1:10–3:08).

The Strokes have made transitional feedback yet another signature
mixing move, featuring the device at least once on each of their first
three records. "Reptilia" provides likely the clearest example: feedback
grows in intensity from 0:06 to 0:12, at which point Albert Hammond Jr.
picks the downbeat of the first verse and the feedback loop immediately
breaks. The same thing happens on "New York City Cops"; feedback
swells from 0:15 to 0:17, even as feedback from another amplifier trills
unabated, at which point Hammond Jr. plucks the downbeat of the
main riff and the song begins in earnest. And, finally, the device clearly

figures from 0:07 to 0:12 of "Juicebox," track three on the band's *First Impressions of Earth*.

FEEDBACK FADE-OUTS

Recordists will sometimes opt to feature a cacophony of feedback to end tracks. Most often this is done to generate, rather than relieve, emotional tension. In most cases, a track builds to some kind of release, thematically and musically, before it cross-fades immediately to feedback; and in turn, the feedback is almost always faded-out to silence. This suggests that whatever emotional issues a song explores — and, more often than not, feedback fade-outs figure in the ending for songs which explore decidedly dark themes — they remain unresolved at song's end. Consider, for instance, the conclusion to tracks like Nine Inch Nails' "Mr. Self Destruct" and "Corona Radiata"; and Modwheelmood's remix of Nine Inch Nails' "The Great Destroyer."

The Jesus And Mary Chain proved themselves extremely fond of the feedback fade-out in the mid-1980s and early-1990s. In fact, some might argue that, barring the band's sophomore offering (*Wastelands*), the Jesus And Mary Chain fashioned an entire career out of catchy pop hooks, cavernous reverberation times, and megalithic doses of feedback. The duo's debut record, *Psychocandy*, prominently features ear-splitting feedback on almost every track, for instance. But even on later tracks, like "Reverence," feedback ebbs and swells unabated throughout the production; the Reid brothers even go so far as to feature feedback in the lead role during the bridge of "Reverence," from 1:50 to 2:08. Other tracks on the Jesus And Mary Chain's *Reverence* feature feedback in a subtler role, the distortion faded-in and faded-out as a tactile texture at various points (i.e., "Teenage Lust," "Sugar Ray," "Good For My Soul" and "Catchfire"). And still other tracks on the same album feature straightforward feedback fade-outs, including "Teenage Lust," "Tumbledown," "Catchfire," "Sundown" and "Frequency."

5. DELAY

The "simple delay line" is the building-block of all delay processing techniques. Recordists feed an audio signal into a delay line. That delay line then shunts the input signal directly to output, and in turn splits a copy of the signal, stores it somewhere for a certain period of time and then sends it to output as well (see **Figure 2.9**). Recordists then fine-tune the delay line by adjusting its: (i) "delay time" setting, that is, the amount of time which elapses between the arrival of the shunted input signal and its delayed copy at output; (ii) "mix" setting, that is, the amount of input signal and delayed signal which the delay line outputs; and, finally, (iii) "feedback", that is, the amount of the output signal which gets routed back to input for another round, and hence the length of time that the delayed signal will remain active.

Recordists have crafted a staggeringly diverse array of musical techniques just by adjusting the three parameters I list above. For instance, to create reverberations, an effect I examine in greater detail in the next chapter, recordists need only adjust the delay time setting on a delay line for any value less than 40 milliseconds. To emphasize the comb-filtering which delay times of under 40 ms inevitably induce, the recordist may furthermore increase the mix setting on a delay line so the amount

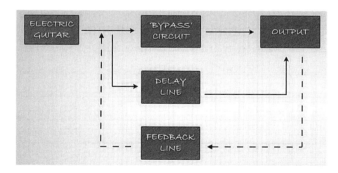

Figure 2.9   Block diagram of the signal-flow for a typical simple delay-line, in this case tied to an electric guitar. Note that the feedback line is represented by a dotted line to indicate that feedback is a variable component in the simple delay-line.

of direct and delayed signal sent to output is roughly equivalent. Of course, multi-track productions are continuously evolving; should an echo sound wind up being more appropriate than reverberations, recordists can simply readjust the delay time setting on the delay line to a value of more than 50 ms. And, finally, should they want those echoes to continue repeating well after the delayed signal has faded to silence, recordists can increase the feedback setting on the delay line until the desired number of echoes accrue.

TAPE DELAY

Recordists initially had no choice but to use analog tape machines to add delay to an audio signal. Alex Case (2007: 224) explains:

> Before the days of digital audio, a common approach to creating delays was to use a spare analog tape machine as a generator . . . During mixdown, the machine is constantly rolling, in record mode. The signal is sent from the console to the input of the tape machine in exactly the same way one would send a signal to any other effects unit — using a spare track bus. That signal is recorded at the tape machine and, milliseconds later, is played back. That is, though the tape machine is recording, it remains in repro mode so the output of the tape machine is what it sees at the playback head . . . The signal goes in, gets printed onto tape, the tape makes its way from the record head to the playback heard (taking time to do so), and finally the signal is played back off tape and returned to the console. The result is tape delay.

Decades have passed since the heyday of tape, however. Recordists now, as a rule, chiefly use digital (algorithmic) processors to create their (digital) delay lines. That said, demand for the distinctive sound of tape delay remains sufficiently high amongst recordists to warrant inclusion of at least one digital tape delay emulator in the suite of processing plug-ins which come bundled with most digital-audio workstations. These tape delays, as they are known, emulate the distinctive 'warble' and 'flutter' of old tape machines, that is, they simulate the subtle (and not so subtle) variances in pitch which accrue given imprecise and irregular tape speeds, just as they emulate the low-frequency bias of tape in general — "tape can be looked at as having a LPF [low pass filter] with its cut-off frequency dependent on the tape speed and quality," notes Roey Izhaki (2008: 384). Digital tape delays thus filter progressively more high-frequency content from each subsequent echo in a simple delay line, as did the analog machines on which they are modeled.

SLAPBACK ECHO

'Slapback echo' remains one of the most iconic tape delay sounds in modern pop and rock. Initially comprised of only a single distinct echo, delayed by anywhere from 75 ms to 200 ms, the sound of slapback echo achieved early prominence on records produced by Sam Phillips for his Sun Records imprint in the mid-1950s. Celebrated examples of slapback can be heard on the vast majority — though, contrary to popular belief, not on all — of Elvis Presley's so-called 'Sun Sides'. Slapback figures, for instance, on Presley's lead-vocal, and Scotty Moore's lead guitar, tracks for: "Mystery Train," "Baby, Let's Play House," "Blue Moon Of Kentucky," "Tomorrow Night," "Trying To Get To You" and "I'll Never Let You Go (Little Darlin')." However, though Presley's vocals provide the most iconic demonstrations of slapback, the effect is, to my ears, much clearer on Jerry Lee Lewis' lead vocals for many of his own Sun sides, especially "Whole Lotta' Shakin' Goin' On" and "Great Balls Of Fire."

The role that tape machines themselves played in shaping the sonic character of slapback was crucial. When Phillips sold his contract with Elvis Presley to RCA in 1957, for instance, Presley's new producer, Chet Atkins, famously struggled — and ultimately failed — to reproduce the distinctive slapback echo Phillips devised for Presely at Sun Records.

This was in large part because the tape machines at RCA ran at a different speed than the ones at Sun. As Atkins (cited in Wadhams 2001: 48–49) himself recalls:

> In order to recreate the slapback echo sound that had characterized all of Elvis' Sun records, a speaker was placed under a stairwell out in the hall. We were recording on those RCA machines and they ran at a different [tape] speed than the Ampex machine we used at Sun. So we were careful about trying to capture the Sun sound. And, of course, we didn't, but it was enough to fool people. But not enough to fool all of the RCA executives in New York. Displeased with the new records, they initially wanted to have Sholes go back to Nashville and have Elvis re-record the materials. The idea soon got vetoed, and following the release of 'Heartbreak Hotel,' the fears were quickly forgotten.

The difference between the vocal treatment on, say, Presley's "Mystery Train" and "Heartbreak Hotel" clearly demonstrates the crucial role that the mechanical idiosyncrasies of tape machines themselves once played in determining the sound of slapback. Once upon a time, in fact, expert listeners could hear the brand of tape used to make a record. According to Daniel J. Levitin (2006: 3):

> When [my] band broke up . . . I found work as a producer of other bands. I learned to hear things I had never heard before: the difference between one microphone and another, even between one brand of recording tape and another (Ampex 456 tape had a characteristic "bump" in the low-frequency range, Scotch 250 had a characteristic crispness in the high frequencies, and Agfa 467 a luster in the mid-range). Once I knew what to listen for, I could tell Ampex from Scotch or Agfa tape as easily as I could tell an apple from a pear or an orange.

The sort of particularity which Levitin describes has long since vanished, however. Most recordists now use digital (algorithmic) plug-ins to create slapback echoes, which means that idiosyncratic differences in the mechanical operations of a processor seldom shape the sound of delay nowadays. Recordists simply shut the feedback setting on their delay processor completely off, so the delay line produces only a single echo, or for a very low value, so relatively few echoes accrue. Though the specific delay time settings that recordists use to create slapback may vary in accordance with the demands of each particular production, delay times generally range between about 70 ms to 200 ms. Moreover, though recordists usually opt to include more than one slapback echo, they still tend to restrict the feedback setting so it generates no more than three or four echoes.

Slapback echo remains the most referentially fixed of all delay processing techniques. When combined with particular instruments, performance styles and compositional techniques, slapback can clearly reference the sound of rockabilly and rock 'n' roll records produced during the mid- and late 1950s. It is no surprise, for instance, that Robert Plant's lead vocals on Led Zeppelin's "Rock n Roll," the band's homage to early rock 'n' roll, features a slapback echo throughout. As Alex Case (2007: 223) writes:

> A staple of 1950s rock . . . music fans pretty much never heard Elvis without [slapback]. Solo work by John Lennon, therefore, often had it. Guitarists playing the blues tend to like it. Add a single audible echo somewhere between about 80 ms and as much as 200 ms, and each and every note shimmers and pulses a bit, courtesy of the single, quick echo. On a vocal, slap echo adds a distinct, retro feeling to the sound. Elvis and his contemporaries reached for this effect so often that it has become a cliché evocative of the period. Pop-music listeners today have learned to associate this effect with those happy days of the 1950s.

As Case notes, the distinctive retro sound of slapback is everywhere apparent on John Lennon's *Rock 'n' Roll*. An homage to 1950s rock 'n' roll in general, *Rock 'n' Roll* features 18 cover-versions of the rock 'n' roll genre's most canonic tracks, including "Be-Bop-A-Lula," "Ain't That A Shame," "Sweet Little Sixteen," "Peggy Sue," "Bony Maronie," "Since My Baby Left Me" and "Stand By Me." Co-produced by Phil Spector and John Lennon himself, every track on *Rock 'n' Roll* features some kind of slapback echo on the lead vocal track(s), even if the comparatively quick delay time settings on the vocals for "Stand By Me," "Peggy Sue" and "Just Because," for instance, produces something much more like doubling than anything else. That said, on tracks like "Be-Bop-A-Lula," "You Can't Catch Me," "Do You Want To Dance," "Sweet Little Sixteen," "Slippin' And Slidin'," "Bony Moronie" and "Angel Baby," the slapback echo is equally as prominent as Lennon's lead-vocal itself.

More recently, slapback echo came to occupy a prominent position in the rockabilly, jump blues and psychobilly revival that ascended to prominence during the early and mid-1990s. This revival was spearheaded by the likes of Brian Setzer, Colin James and the Reverend Horton Heat. Lead vocals, electric guitars and acoustic bass all regularly feature slapback on their albums, including: the Brian Setzer Orchestra's *Guitar Slinger*, *The Dirty Boogie*, and *Vavoom!*; the first three volumes of Colin James' *Colin James and the Little Big Band*; and the Reverend Horton Heats' *Smoke 'Em If You Got 'Em*, *It's Martini Time*, *Space Heater*, and *Spend A Night In The Box*. So focused was the Reverend Horton Heat on reproducing the sound of classic 1950s rock 'n' roll records, in fact, that the psychobilly rocker re-recorded *Smoke 'Em If You Got 'Em* in its entirety on two-track tape when the initial multi-track masters failed to yield the requisite retro sound and feel. Precursors of the revival, such as the Stray Cats, likewise prominently feature slapback on their records. Setzer's lead vocals for, among other tracks, the Stray Cats "Rock This Town," "Rumble In Brighton," "Runaway Boys" and "Blast Off" all provide clear examples.

Example 2.7   Slapback Echo

Example 2.7 demonstrates the sound of slapback echo, applied to the lead-vocal track of an original composition by Mark Collins, called "Grind Me Down." The first verse and refrain feature no delay processing; the slapback echo is only applied at the outset of the second verse. During the song's heavier conclusion, another delay plug-in is added to the lead-vocal track. Every setting on that delay plug-in is exactly the same as the settings used to create the slapback echo, but the delay-time setting, and feedback amount, are both increased, so more, and longer, echoes accrue (i.e., the slapback echoes generate echoes of their own). Readers should also note the entrance of mirrored electric guitars at 1:58.

DOUBLING

Singers and musicians have doubled their parts for centuries. Some singers even adopt the technique as a definitive characteristic of their vocal sound. One would be hard pressed to find Elliott Smith, for instance, singing anything on a record which is not doubled; and the likes of John Lennon and Kurt Cobain relied heavily on the technique as well. Until the mid-1960s, recordists had no choice but to overdub doubled tracks. This was a grueling, labor-intensive process which most musicians came to detest intensely. It was this distaste for manual double-tracking, in fact, which prompted Ken Townsend, an engineer who worked at Abbey Road Studios in the mid- and late 1960s, to invent the first signal processor designed to automatically, that is, electronically, double tracks. Townsend dubbed the machine, appropriately enough, the Automatic Double Tracking (ADT) machine. In Wayne Wadhams' (2001: 123) words:

> John [Lennon] liked to double and triple his vocals for a thicker, fuller sound, but he was also impatient, and dreaded the tedious process required to get both the pitch and timing of each syllable exactly right on a second or third pass. This led to the discovery of ADT (Automatic Double Tracking). Thenceforth, when a good lead

vocal track was complete, it was played back into a second recorder equipped with a variable speed control. By manually varying the record and playback speed of the second machine, a "copy" vocal came back perhaps twenty milliseconds (twenty thousandths of a second) after the original vocal. This signal was then mixed with the actual lead vocal and recorded onto an open track of the original tape. The result sounded like a perfectly doubled lead vocal. ADT was subsequently used on almost every lead and background vocal track of Revolver.

The Beatles eagerly adopted ADT as both an efficiency-aid and a powerful aesthetic tool. Vocal tracks on Beatles records released after *Revolver* regularly feature ADT; in fact, the band took to using ADT on a number of instrumental tracks as well. To produce an effected sound using ADT, Martin would pan both the input signal and its ADT-delayed copy to the same horizontal position in a mix. To emulate manual doubling, however, Martin panned the tracks to opposite sides of the stereo spectrum. Ryan and Kehew (2008: 297) explain:

When the original signal and delayed signal were panned to the same spot in the stereo picture, a distinctive sound emerged. The presence of two separate sounds could be discerned but the signal sounded affected: it did not sound entirely like natural double-tracking. This, of course, was one of the qualities that greatly attracted The Beatles to the effect, aside from its time saving benefits. However, when the two signals were panned to different parts of the stereo image, the double-tracking effect could be quite convincing indeed. A listen to the brass in "Savoy Truffle" illustrates this nicely; with the original signal panned to one side and the delayed signal panned to the other, the illusion of two separately overdubbed parts was remarkable. The vocals on "Ob-La-Di, Ob-La-Da" and "Birthday" were handled similarly. Quite often on later Beatles records, this effect was used to create a lush stereo image, an especially useful effect when only four tracks were available.

Table 2.8   Examples of ADT vocal tracks on Beatles records (all stereo releases).

Record	Track
The Beatles, "Paperback Writer/Rain"	Rain
The Beatles, *Revolver*	Eleanor Rigby I'm Only Sleeping And Your Bird Can Sing Doctor Robert
The Beatles, *Sgt.Pepper's Lonely Hearts Club Band*	With A Little Help From My Friends Lucy In The Sky With Diamonds Being For The Benefit Of Mr. Kite Lovely Rita Good Morning, Good Morning
The Beatles, *Magical Mystery Tour*	Blue Jay Way I Am The Walrus
The Beatles, *Yellow Submarine*	All Together Now Hey Bulldog It's All Too Much
The Beatles, *The Beatles*	Ob-La-Di, Ob-La-Da I'm So Tired Birthday Helter Skelter
The Beatles, *Abbey Road*	Mean Mr. Mustard Polythene Pam She Came In Through The Bathroom Window

Since the heyday of ADT, recordists have had the benefit of digital processors for doubling. Recordists simply insert digital processors into the audio chain for a track, and they set the delay time for a period of anywhere from 20 ms to 50 ms. As I explain later, this delay time setting can be modulated (modified) using a low frequency oscillator (LFO), to emulate so-called "participatory discrepancies", that is, subtle differences in delivery which accrue given more than one performance of a musical line, but this usually requires panning the input and doubled tracks to different positions along the stereo spectrum. When recordists do not require participatory discrepancies, however, they simply set the delay time for 20 ms to 50 ms, and they shut the feedback setting completely off (or, sometimes, to an extremely low setting). Clear examples of this technique at work in the modern pop soundscape can be heard in the lead-vocal tracks for: Boston's "More Than A Feeling"; Led Zeppelin's "Immigrant Song," "The Song Remains The Same," "Trampled Under Foot," "Kashmir" and "Nobody's Fault But Mine"; and, more recently, during the refrain of the Jesus And Mary Chain's "Reverence" and throughout Porno For Pyros' "Orgasm."

This all said, recordists still often opt to manually double vocal tracks, especially when the goal is to thicken (add prominence to) those tracks. Further emphasis can be applied by panning both tracks to either side of the stereo spectrum. Elliott Smith, for one, uses this technique extensively on his self-produced *Either/Or*. "Speed Trials," "Between the Bars," "Rose Parade" and "Angeles," for instance, all feature manually doubled vocal tracks panned to either side of the stereo spectrum. Tracks like "Alameda" and "Pictures of Me," on the other hand, feature doubled tracks panned to the same horizontal locations, at the front-and-center of Smith's mixes for those cuts. Smith also combines centered and panned double tracks at various points on certain tracks. "Cupid's Trick," for instance, features centered vocals until the song's explosive chorus, when a call-and-response between centered ("shooting me up") and panned ("it's my life") double tracks emerges. "2:45 AM" features centered vocals until 1:58, when Smith introduces double-tracked vocals on either side of the stereo spectrum; and the album's concluding cut, "Say Yes," features centered vocals for only its first 17 seconds, after which point Smith doubles the vocals and pans both tracks to either stereo extreme.

In the hip hop genre, manual doubling is often introduced to emphasize only certain words in a lyric, usually — though by no means always — terms used to end phrases. This can work to reinforce the thematic content of a lyric, even if its primary function is simply to buttress the flow (delivery) of rapping MCs. Readers can select basically any hip hop album at random and be assured that at least one or two tracks on the album will prominently feature this device. Clear demonstrations can be heard on: Jay-Z's "99 Problems"; the Wu Tang Clan's "Wu-Tang Clan Ain't Nothin' Ta F' Wit"; House Of Pain's "Jump Around" and "Shamrocks and Shenanigans"; the Beastie Boys' "Intergalactic" and "So What'cha Want"; and the Pharcyde's "Oh Shit" and "Drop." **Table 2.9** elucidates the position of manual doubling on select records by the Beastie Boys from the 1980s and 1990s.

Table 2.9   Examples of selective manual doubling on records by the Beastie Boys.

Record	Track
The Beastie Boys, *Licensed To Ill*	1. Rhymin' and Stealin' 3. She's Crafty 7. Fight For Your Right 8. No Sleep Till Brooklyn 11. Brass Monkey
The Beastie Boys, *Paul's Boutique*	2. Shake Your Rump 3. Johnny Ryall 5. High Plains Drifter 6. The Sounds Of Science 8. Hey Ladies 13. Shadrach
The Beastie Boys, *Check Your Head*	1. Jimmy James
The Beastie Boys, *Ill Communication*	1. Sure Shot 5. Root Down
The Beastie Boys, *Hello Nasty*	1. Super Disco Breakin' 6. Body Movin' 7. Intergalactic 16. The Negotiation Limerick File

ECHOES (UNSYNCED)

Delay time settings of more than 50ms produce echoes. Common sense would seem to suggest that, when recordists opt to introduce echoes, those echoes should always be in sync with the tempo of tracks, so each echo metrically subdivides the global pulse. If echoes propagate at a rate which somehow clashes with the underlying meter of a song, they can easily induce timing errors, and confusion, especially when delay times are set for anything longer than an eighth-note value. This said, recordists continue to feature unsynced echoes on their productions. In fact, there are numerous reasons why recordists might opt for unsynced rather than synced echoes. According to Roey Izhaki (2008: 391):

> First, very short delay times, say those shorter than 100 ms, seldom play a rhythmic role or are perceived to have a strictly rhythmical sense. Second, for some instruments tempo-synced echoes might be masked by other rhythmical instruments. For example, if we delay hi-hats playing eighth-notes and sync the delay time, some of the echoes will overlap with the original hits. Triplets, three-sixteenth-notes and other oblique durations can often prevent these issues while still maintaining some rhythmical sense. Perhaps the advantage of out-of-sync delays is that they can draw some more attention, being contrary to the rhythm of the song. This might work better with occasional delay appearances, where these off-beat echoes create some tension that is later resolved.

Most often, it is the latter function which Izhaki describes, namely, added emphasis, which compels recordists to unsync echoes. The fact that unsynced echoes naturally avoid masking each other, while synced echoes are prone to masking, only makes the unsynced option all the more attractive. While the Edge's guitar playing in general demonstrates basically every delay processing technique in the modern rock record-ist's toolbox, his guitar work for "Stuck In A Moment You Can't Get Out Of," track two on U2's *All That You Can't Leave Behind*, provides a particularly clear demonstration of the unsycned principle at work in modern rock. Just before the song's pre-chorus at 0:29, the Edge's dry guitar is suddenly delayed. The dry track remains on the left side of the stereo plane while the delay line is bussed (sent) to an open channel on the opposite side. Because the Edge subdivides the basic tempo of the track with a sequence of straight quarter- and eighth-note arpeggios at this point, producer Daniel Lanois had little choice but to unsync the delay line. Synchronized echoes would have overlapped the dry line, potentially inducing masking and, perhaps most egregiously in the soft rock world that U2 dominates, inducing inappropriate dissonances each time the harmony changes. Lanois further buttresses the dry track against masking through spatial separation, panning both tracks to opposite sides of the stereo spectrum.

Beyond solving masking issues, panning also works to produce an effect like mirrored equalization in the pre-chorus for "Stuck in A Moment You Can't Get Out Of." Sent to either extreme of the stereo spectrum, the dry guitar track and its echoes prompts listeners to widen the perceptual width of the mix. Practical experience teaches the human ear to associate echoes with large spaces. Somebody shouts into a cavernous space and, after a certain period of time, the length of which is wholly dependent on the size of the space itself (longer delay times denote larger spaces), their voice reflects back as an echo. Knowing this, when listeners hear the Edge's dry guitar track emanate on the extreme left and, shortly after, bounce back as an echo on the extreme right, practical experience suggests a large horizontal space between the sound source (the electric guitar) and its reflections (echoes), which perceptually wedges even more room into the center of the mix for Bono's vocals.

Table 2.10   Unsynced delay on Edge's guitar tracks for U2's *All That You Can't Leave Behind* and *Vertigo*.

Record	Track (Entrance; Channel)
U2, *All That You Can't Leave Behind*	1. Beautiful Day (0:29; right channel)
	2. Stuck In A Moment You Can't Get Out Of (0:38; left channel)
	5. Kite (0:06; left channel)
	7. Wild Honey (0:38; dry: left, delay: right)
	9. When I Look At The World (0:10; left channel)

(*continued*)

Record	Track (Entrance; Channel)
U2, *Vertigo*	3. Sometimes You Can't Make It On Your Own (1:01; left channel) 5. City of Blinding Lights (0:12, left channel; 0:16, right channel) 9. One Step Closer (0:30; left channel) 10. Original Of The Species (0:00 and 1:17; dry: left, delay: right)

MULTITAP ECHOES (SYNCED)

Despite its widespread use in pop, the feedback mechanism in a traditional delay line can be seriously limiting for recordists. "Echoes are spaced at regular intervals, their level drops in a predictable way and their frequency content is correlated," notes Izhaki (2008: 388). And this regularity is not always appropriate. Rather than a run of uniformly diminishing quarter-note echoes, each panned to the left side of the stereo plane, for instance, a mix may require: a run of six quarter-note echoes on the right side of the stereo plane, three sixteenth-note echoes on the left side, and then a sequence of crescendoing triplet eighth-note echoes panned back-and-forth across the stereo plane. While such a sequence would undoubtedly produce a totally bizarre effect, the control and flexibility required to create it is nonetheless necessary at times, given the unique demands of certain productions.

To create a run of independent echoes, each with its own timing, volume and stereo location, recordists turn to so-called multitap delay processors. These processors allow recordists to set distinct delay times, volumes, pan positions and feedback settings for each echo the processor produces. Obviously, this sort of control relies on digital means. However, it is possible to use non-digital means. Converting a tape delay into a multitap processor would require fitting its component tape machines with, say, eight moveable playback heads, each with its own amplifier — a feat that only Pierre Schaffer, Pierre Henry, Terry Riley and other avante-gardists seem likely to bother attempting.

Indeed, multitap echoes only obviously began to permeate the Top 40 soundscape during the mid-1970s, when digital multitap processors first made market *en masse*.

Since multitap plug-ins have become standard in the suite of digital processors which are now bundled with most digital audio workstations, the multitap delay line has achieved a newfound prominence in modern electronica. In fact, electronica productions feature multitap processing in a primarily rhythmic role now, with recordists multitapping irregular sequences of echoes to generate rhythmic propulsion and momentum for tracks. Though examples of multitapping abound on modern electronica records, Tosca's "Suzuki" provides an exceptionally clear demonstration. The track begins with a single harmonic, percussively plucked on an electric bass, followed by a sequence of regularly diminishing echoes. When the harmonic repeats, however, it is followed by a multitapped sequence of echoes that randomly ping-pong back-and-forth across the stereo spectrum: right-right-left-right-left-right-left-left-right-left-left-left-left, et cetera. Compared with the regularized echo-delay heard on, say, the electric bass line which introduces Porno For Pyros' "Pets," the multitapped echoes on "Suzuki" clearly belong to an entirely different genus.

6. MODULATION

Modulation processors are a more complicated class of delay processor which use a low frequency oscillator (LFO) to modulate a delay line. This seemingly simple modification enables a surprisingly vast array of effects. As Alex Case (2007: 214) summarizes:

> The modulation section of a delay unit relies on a simple LFO. Instead of modulating the amplitude of a signal, as might be done in an AM (amplitude modulation) synthesizer, this LFO modulates the delay time parameter within the signal processor. Rate is the

frequency of the LFO. Depth is the amplitude of the LFO. Shape, of course, is the type of LFO signal . . . These three parameters give the recording engineer much needed control over the delay, enabling them to play it like a musical instrument. They set how fast the delay moves (rate). They set the limits on the range of delay times allowed (depth), and they determine how the delay moves from its shortest to its longest time (shape).

LFOs oscillate (produce) 'infrasonic' frequencies, which is to say, frequencies that fall below the threshold of audibility (i.e., under 20 Hz). The human ear thus typically interprets the infrasonic frequencies which an LFO produces as pulsating rhythms rather than discrete pitches. If recordists modulate the amplitude envelope (dynamics profile) of a synth pad using an LFO set to oscillate at 6 Hz — if the amplitude of a synth pad were made to rise to peak amplitude, and fall to base amplitude, in the shape of an undulating 6 Hz sine wave — the volume of the synth pad would rise and fall six times per second, that is, at a rate of 6 Hz. If, on the other hand, the LFO were set to oscillate twice as fast, the volume of the synth pad would rise and fall at a rate of 12 Hz. In either case, the modulation produces the dynamic quivering which musicians call tremolo.

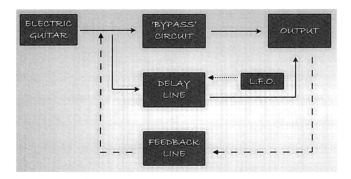

Figure 2.10   Simplified block diagram of the signal-flow for a simple delay-line with modulating LFO. The feedback line is again represented by a dotted line to indicate that it is a variable component.

'Modulation rate' determines how quickly a particular modulation should occur per second. Not surprisingly then, the modulation rate of a modulation processor is usually expressed in Hertz. Most often, recordists apply the LFO on a modulation processor to its delay time setting. If an LFO is applied to a delay time setting of 10 ms, then, a common modulation: (i) raises the delay time to 15 ms; (ii) lowers it to 5 ms; and, then, (iii) raises it back up to 10 ms again. If recordists set the LFO to oscillate at 6 Hz, the modulation described above occurs six times per second, that is, the delay time modulates from 15 ms to 5 ms six times per second. If, on the other hand, the LFO were set to modulate at a rate of, say, 2 Hz, the modulation would accrue only twice per second.

"Modulation depth", on the other hand, describes the amplitude of the modulating waveform and, thus, the strength (amount) of the modulation it produces. In most cases, modulation depth is expressed as a percentage value of whichever setting the processor modulates. If a delay line is set for a delay time of 20 ms, for instance, and record-ists set the modulation depth for +/—50%, the modulated signal rises and falls in exactly 10 ms increments, however often per second the modulation rate setting dictates. If the depth is set for only +/—25%, on the other hand, the processed signal only rises and falls in 5 ms increments. And, of course, if it is set for +/—75%, it rises and falls in 15 ms increments.

'Modulation shape' describes the (sometimes variable) shape of the modulating waveform. If recordists choose a sinusoidal shape, for instance, the modulation sweeps smoothly from base to peak setting at a rate and strength determined by the modulation rate and the modu-lation depth settings, respectively. Should recordists choose a square waveform, however, the modulation snaps immediately between those settings, as the modulating waveform snaps immediately from crest to trough. Though different waveforms produce wildly divergent modu-lations, variable modulation shape settings are exceedingly rare on modern modulation processors. Some flangers, for instance, still allow recordists to shape the modulating frequency into either a sinusoidal or triangular form — not a terribly dramatic variance, in any event — but most modulation techniques require only a sinusoidal shape.

FLANGING

Flanging is one of the oldest modulation processing techniques in the recordist's toolbox. Innovated by pioneer recordists like Les Paul, while they worked with rudimentary tape delay systems, flanging was initially an entirely tactile, or, manual, technique. To produce the effect, recordists smudged their fingers against the metal flanges that held the tape-reels on a tape machine in place. In doing this, recordists impeded the capstan from cycling as usual thereby varying the delay time setting according to the amount of pressure they applied. Delay times were usually short — recordists could expect to vary the delay time setting up to 85 milliseconds without breaking the capstan — so flanging regularly provoked comb-filtering. Moreover, because delay times varied constantly according to the manual pressure which recordists applied with their fingers and thumbs, the resulting comb-filter swept back-and-forth across the frequency spectrum, creating the whooshing sound which recordists still, to this day, associate with flanging. Longer delay times shifted the notches in the comb-filter ever lower in the frequency spectrum, while shorter delay times raised them to ever higher regions.

Nowadays, of course, everyone but purists use digital plug-ins for flanging. These plug-ins do exactly what tactile flangers did, only they use algorithms rather than manual force to vary the delay time setting. As such, digital plug-in processors tend to produce a more obviously regularized cyclic tonal variance (i.e., the whoosing sound they create moves up-and-down the audible spectrum in a more mechanically precise way). Moreover, modern flangers often route a portion of their output back to input for another round of flanging, which only makes the comb-filtering all the more severe. Whatever technology they use, though, recordists have made flanging an extremely common term in the pop lexicon. Flanging is most obvious when it is applied globally, that is, to whole productions. One of the earliest known examples of this can be heard during the psychedelic interludes between chorus and verse on the Small Faces' "Itchycoo Park" (i.e., 0:50–1:07, 1:40–2:05, and 2:20–2:46); but any track from **Table 2.11** below will suffice to demonstrate its sound.

Table 2.11   Tracks with clear sectional flanging.

Recordist	Track (Entrance of Flanged Sections)
Jimi Hendrix	Axis Bold As Love (2:47)
The Eagles	Life In The Fast Lane (3:38)
Jane's Addiction	Standing In the Shower (1:44)
The Stone Roses	Made Of Stone (3:30)
Red Hot Chili Peppers	Dani California (3:47)

Example 2.8   Sectional Flanging

Example 2.8 demonstrates another conventional use for sectional flanging, namely, to conclude a song. In this case, the final minute of "Grind Me Down," from Example 2.7, fades-in. The final three iterations of the chorus are flanged; and the flanger, itself, is adjusted for sufficiently intense settings to provoke its characteristic whooshing sound, which many analysts liken to the sound of an airplane flying overhead.

CHORUSING

A distant cousin of flangers, chorus processors send audio signal through one or more simple delay-lines— some processors use more than 50 delay lines — using an LFO to modulate the delay time setting of each. Though this obviously resembles the signal-flow for flanging, chorusing does not usually require a feedback line to route its output back to input. As the input signal shunts directly to output, the first modulated delay-line outputs a copy which is delayed by however long the LFO's modulation rate, depth and shape settings dictate; a second modulated delay-line then delays and modulates the first modulated delay-line; a third modulated delay-line delays and modulates the second line; a fourth line delays and modulates the third; and so on. When all of these modulated delay lines combine at output, a sequence of so-called "pitch modulations" accrue, that is, cyclic variances in pitch (Lehman: 2009).

Example 2.9 Chorusing
Example 2.9 demonstrates a characteristic product of chorusing: pitch modulation. The electric guitar part on an original downtempo track, called "Sea Horse," is gradually subjected to ever increasing amounts of chorus beginning at 0:07. Listeners will likely interpret the product of chorusing as a cyclic de-tuning of the guitar's pitch. At 0:38, the chorus is bypassed, and the original un-chorused guitar track reappears and fades-out to silence.

Chorusing is easiest to hear when recordists set the LFO for a particularly fast and deep rate and depth. These fast and deep settings produce a characteristic warbling sound, which is the product of pitch modulation. Such deep chorus effects are typically applied to electric guitar and piano tracks in a pop production. **Table 2.12** below lists a number of obvious examples of chorused electric guitar tracks, on hit records released since the late 1970s, and early 1980s, which many historians, and critics, consider to have been a golden age for the chorus effect.

Table 2.12 Obviously chorused electric guitar tracks, which produce the distinctive warbling of deep settings, on records released since the early-1980s.

Recordist	Track (Entrance of chorused guitar track)
Fripp & Eno	Evensong (clearest beginning at 0:37)
Nirvana	Come As You Are (from 0:00 but clearest at chorus 0:48)
Mike Stern	Swunk (0:00)
Satellite Party	Mr. Sunshine (0:19, in right channel)

PHASING

Phasers are a "special case" modulation processor. Rather than a simple delay line, phasers use all-pass filters to reshape the frequency content of an input signal. Among the many things they do, all-pass filters shift the phase of the input signal — for our purposes: they delay the input signal — at a rate determined by wavelength. Low frequencies, which have longer wavelengths, thus shift (delay) at a slower rate than do higher frequencies. Neil Morley (2009) explains:

> the phase of a low frequency [and] . . . a higher frequency will be phase shifted by different amount[s]. In other words, various frequencies in the input signal are delayed by different amounts, causing peaks and troughs in the output signal which are not necessarily harmonically related.

Notches, that is, muted frequency ranges, subsequently accrue at frequencies where the phase-shift induced by the all-pass filters is precisely 180-degrees. This emulates the effect of comb-filtering and, when a modulating LFO is applied to the phase rate of those filters, the notches subsequently sweep back-and-forth across the frequency spectrum.

   Table 2.13 cites a number of progressive rock records released during the mid-1970s which feature clearly phased electric guitar and electric bass tracks. While it may be patently obvious to readers that the tracks noted in **Table 2.13** feature some kind of comb-filtering, many will nevertheless find it difficult to determine whether that filter is the product of flanging, chorusing or phasing. And yet, this is a crucial distinction for many recordists.

FLANGE, CHORUS AND PHASE: TELLING THEM APART

To say with confidence whether a track was flanged, chorused or phased can be extremely difficult. All three techniques are, after all, variations on the same basic process (i.e., modulating the delay time setting on one or more delay lines). Nonetheless, flanging, chorusing and phasing each have unique audible traits. Chorusing is likely easiest to distinguish because it is the only modulation processing technique that produces pitch modulations. Flanging and phasing are more difficult to distinguish. Both techniques create a comb filter in the input signal, and both sweep that comb filter up-and-down the audible spectrum. However, flanging does so in the service of producing a more severe comb filter than phasing creates — the tonal distortion which flanging produces more obviously transforms the input signal, especially when recordists opt to engage the feedback option — and flanging also tends to create harmonic notches much higher in the audible spectrum, which produces a whoosing sound like a low-flying airplane passing by overhead. The audible effects of phasing are usually restricted to a kind of midrange variance, without harmonic relation to the input signal.

The Fender Rhodes track which introduces Led Zeppelin's "No Quarter" provides an ideal case study. The track is obviously the product of modulation processing of some sort; and, moreover, the modulating LFO obviously oscillates at a fast and deep setting. This produces a sound that, on first blush, clearly resembles the warbling that chorusing creates. However, closer inspection reveals a conspicuous absence of pitch modulations, which rules out chorusing as a possibility. The warbling might be the product of flanging, then, but the ascending and descending high-frequency whoosing that flanging creates is also absent. This leaves phasing as the only option and, indeed, close inspection of the track reveals a cyclically varied comb-filter, focused primarily in the midrange of the input spectrum, which characterizes that process.

Example 2.10   Chorusing -vs.- Flanging -vs.- Phasing

Example 2.10 juxtaposes the characteristic sounds of chorusing, flanging and phasing. The same acoustic guitar track sounds throughout this example. At 0:06, the guitar fades-out, only to fade-in again at 0:09 with chorusing active. The process repeats three more times, with: (i) flanging, rather than chorusing, active (0:26); (ii) phasing, rather than flanging, active (0:46); and, finally, (iii) without any processing whatsoever (1:04). Example 2.10 then fades-out to silence.

Table 2.13   Clearly phased electric guitar tracks and one electric bass track on progressive rock records released during the mid-1970s, focusing particularly on Pink Floyd's recorded repertoire.

Recordist	Track (Entrance of Phased Track)
Robin Trower	Bridge of Sighs (0:00)
Led Zeppelin	The Rover (0:05)
Pink Floyd	Speak To Me/Breathe (1:13)
Pink Floyd	Brain Damage (0:00)
Pink Floyd	Shine On You Crazy Diamond, pt. II (4:06)
Pink Floyd	Shine On You Crazy Diamond, pt. VI (0:15)
Pink Floyd	Sheep (0:22; 5:33)

Example 2.11   Signal Processing: Putting It All Together

Example 2.11 demonstrates all six signal processing techniques elucidated in the preceding chapter of this field guide, in the context of an original rock mix called "Stains." An analysis of the mix is provided in Table 2.14 below. Again, it is recommended that readers use headphones, and a moderate volume, to audition the track.

Table 2.14 First entrance of clearly processed tracks in Example 2.11

Time	Track	Process
0:00	Electric guitar	Distortion
0:04	Electric guitar	Feedback lead-in (overdubbed)
0:14	Electric bass	Slight lift distortion, mirrored EQ with kick drum
	Drum kit	Cymbals side-chained to duck under kick and snare
	Electric guitars	Distortion, mirrored and delayed to increase width
0:38	Lead-vocal	Compression, unsynced delay multi-tapped to left/right
	1/4-note comp guitar	Chorus
1:58	Electric guitar	Overdrive (mono imaging)
2:20	Electric guitar	Distortion, mirrored and delayed to increase width
2:37	Electric guitar	Feedback fade-out
2:41	Entire mix	Chorus
	Entire mix	Fade-out

Chapter 3

Mixing

The Space of Communications

Though we have seen that both tracking and signal processing ramify at mix level, recordists have developed mixing into a craft all its own. When they mix a record, recordists organize its component tracks into a particular spatial arrangement. Recordists typically liken this space to a three-dimensional canvas which requires careful balancing front-to-back, side-to-side and top-to-bottom. As Bobby Owsinski (2006: 8) explains:

> Most great mixers think in three dimensions. They think 'tall, deep and wide', which means making sure all the frequencies are represented, making sure there's depth to the mix, and then giving it some stereo dimension. [With] the tall dimension . . . essentially you're trying to make sure that all the frequencies are properly represented. Usually that means that all the sparkly, tinkly highs and fat, powerful lows are there. Sometimes it means cutting some mids. Clarity is what you aim for . . . You achieve [depth] . . . by introducing new ambience elements into the mix. You usually do this with reverbs and delays (and offshoots like flanging and chorusing) but room-mics, overheads, and even leakage play an equally big part.

The panning or wide dimension is placing a sound element in a soundfield in a way that makes a more interesting soundscape, such that you can hear each element more clearly.

Every record is mixed. Even when recordists do not consciously mix a record — even when recordists move directly from tracking to mastering — records always present some spatial arrangement of sound more than just sounds *per se* and, as such, they are always mixed. In fact, recordists mixed long before multi-track mixing consoles came to market. Phonograph and gramophone records, for instance, were clearly mixed. Recordists who worked with such acoustic technology simply had to arrange themselves into often awkward formations around the recording bells of phonographs and gramophones while they tracked to mix their records. In Virgil Moorefield's (2005: 1) words:

> In the early days of recording, the record producer in the modern sense did not exist. Perhaps the closest thing to production in the 1890s is the image of Fred Gaisberg, who ran the first recording studio, holding an opera singer by the arm and moving her closer or further away from the gramophone's horn, according to the dynamics of the passage being sung.

Once upon a time, then, mixing was holistically ingrained within the tracking process. Producers like Fred Gaisberg guided singers towards, and away from, the gramophone's horn and, in so doing, he mixed their performances. And for the next six decades very little changed, though recordists eventually learned to use microphone placement to refine the proximal location of tracks in a mix. The emergence of mixing as a 'separate phase' procedure in record-making coincided with the concomitant emergence of the multi-track paradigm of record production. Mixing became a way to manage some of the more overwhelming complexities which multi-tracking suddenly interjected into the production process. Bobby Owsinski (2006: 2) explains:

In the early days of recording, there really wasn't mixing *per se*, because the record medium was mono and a big date used only four microphones. Over the years, recording developed from capturing an unaltered musical event to one that was artificially created through overdubs, thanks to the innovation of Selsync (the ability to play back off of the record head so that everything stayed in sync), introduced in 1955. The availability of more and more tracks from a tape machine begot larger and larger consoles, which begot computer automation and recall just to manage larger consoles fed by more tracks. With all that came not only an inevitable change in the philosophy of mixing, but also a change in the way that a mixer listened and thought.

1. BOUNCING

Though recordists were slow to take advantage of the possibilities that multi-track technology had to offer, by the mid-1960s most successful recordists insisted that at least two four-track tape machines were needed to make a commercially viable record. A seemingly insatiable hunger for more and more tracks seized the industry, which led to the development of a mixing technique known variously as: 'mixing-as-you-go', 'reducing', 'bouncing', 'bouncing-down' and '4-to-4'. Whatever it was called — recordists eventually settled on 'bouncing' — this practice represents the first multi-track mixing technique in the modern 'separate phase' sense.

To clear track-space for the ever growing number of overdubs which recordists suddenly required, mix engineers bounced tracks from one 4-track tape machine onto one or more open tracks on another connected machine. Because bouncing inevitably led to a notable degradation in sound quality (given the low-frequency bias of tape in general, high-frequency content was successively obscured with each successive bounce) bouncing became a mixing skill like any other. By 1966 a capable mixing engineer could bounce tracks such that the inherent sacrifice in sound quality the process entailed was rendered moot, particularly when considering the more detailed arrangements bouncing enabled. In fact, many recordists continue to describe this era as a kind of golden age for mixing. In Andy Johns' (in Owsinski 2006: 3) words:

> You know why *Sgt. Pepper's* sounds so good? You know why *Are You Experienced?* sounds so good — almost better than what we can do now? It's because, when you were doing '4-to-4' (bouncing from one 4-track machine to another), you mixed as you went along. There was a mix on two tracks of the second 4-track machine, and you filled up the open tracks and did the same thing again. Listen to "We Love You" by the [Rolling] Stones. Listen to *Sgt. Pepper's* [by The Beatles]. Listen to "Hole In My Shoe" by Traffic. You mixed as you went along. Therefore, after you got the sounds that would fit with each other, all you had to do was adjust the melodies. Nowadays, because you have this luxury of the computer and virtually as many tracks as you want, you don't think that way anymore.

By 1966, bouncing was arguably industry standard in the rock world. To create Jimi Hendrix's "Are You Experienced?," for instance, engineers Eddie Kramer and George Chkiantz bounced the track no less than three times (McDermott with Kramer and Cox 2009: 44). The first take featured four tracks recorded live-off-the-floor, specifically, (i) Hendrix's electric guitar; (ii) Noel Redding's electric bass; and (iii—iv) a stereo reduction of Mitch Mitchell's drum kit. To clear room for "backward elements" (i.e., reverse-tape special effects), and a piano, Kramer and Chkiantz then bounced Hendrix's guitar track to an open slot on a connected tape machine, and they reduced Redding's bass and Mitchell's drums to the second open track, which left tracks three and four open for overdubs. To make space for Hendrix's lead-vocals, a final reduction mix was prepared. Track one was still reserved for Hendrix's electric guitar, and track two had the reduction mix of Redding's

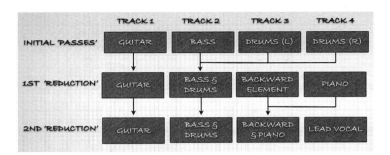

Figure 3.1 Reduction mixes for the Jimi Hendrix Experience's "Are You Experienced."

electric bass and Mitchell's drums. Track three, meanwhile, reduced the 'backward element' and piano tracks which were overdubbed onto tracks three and four before, which left track four available for Hendrix's vocal overdubs.

Another group who made copious use of bouncing was The Beatles. By 1967, in fact, the band had made bouncing a common component of their tracking and mixing processes; and when simple bouncing would no longer suffice, the band had their producer George Martin sync two four-track tape machines together so all eight tracks from both machines could be reduced onto open tracks on another four-track machine, leaving even more tracks available for overdubbing. Psychedelic tracks like "I Am The Walrus" arguably pushed this mixing practice to an absurd and complicated limit:

> [George] Martin decided that Take 20 had been the best take . . . so a reduction mix was made, bouncing the strings and horns together in order to free up some space . . . The [laughing] voices [heard in the song's conclusion] were recorded onto track 3 of Take 25. The orchestra and chorale recordings on Take 25 had to be merged with The Beatles' instruments and vocal on Take 17. Track 2 of Take 17 had been left free for this purpose. What Martin would ultimately do is manually sync Take 17 with Take 25, and bounce

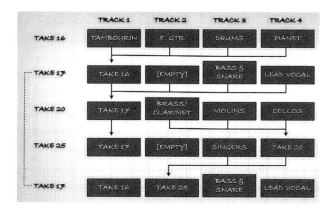

Figure 3.2 Reduction mixes used to mix The Beatles "I Am The Walrus"

the orchestra and choir on Take 25 down to track 2 of Take 17. All subsequent mixing could then be done without having to sync the two machines. And, if necessary, the bounce could be done in pieces (this appears to have been done: close listening shows that the orchestra is slightly out of sync with the rhythm track on some sections and not in others, likely the result of having been bounced in pieces). (Ryan and Kehew 2008: 466)

2. PAST-TENSE AURAL NARRATIVES

As complicated a procedure as bouncing could be, mixing has arguably grown exponentially more complicated since the time of four-track tape. The modern pop recordist now deploys a number of specialized tools and techniques to fuse the component tracks in their multi-track productions into coherent three-dimensional shapes. And yet a formalized "best-practice" protocol for mixing remains notably absent; the mixing process remains a stubbornly entrepreneurial and firmly individualized process. Albin Zak (2001: 143) explains:

The many and varied approaches that recordists take to mixing
reflect the same issues as other aspects of the record making process
— style of music, personal preferences, contingencies of the project,
and so forth. Some build a mix beginning with the drums, some
begin with the vocal. Some push up all the faders from the beginning, and work from there. Others proceed one part at a time. Some
fashion the mix after an image of a live performance, while others
are intent on creating a sonic world without real-world counterpart.
Some kinds of music call for a hazy texture, others for sharp clarity.
Some emphasize the groove, others the lyrics. Some recordists use
minimal sound processing, others use it extensively.

In fact, recordists generally claim technology as the very least of all the
tools they use to mix a record. The ingenuity and skill of mixing engineers carries the day, recordists usually claim. "While the equipment
someone chooses to use is, of course, an important creative decision,"
writes Maureen Droney (2003: 5), "what's more important is the ability
to know what you want that equipment to do for you." As Phil Ramone
(2002: 4) puts it:

Engineers use many of the same tools, and yet they create mixes
that are quite different from each other . . . Technology is constantly
changing; equipment is constantly evolving; and every new generation must either follow or break the rules of the past. Engineers like
Al Schmitt, Leslie Ann Jones, and Chuck Ainlay all learned in different kinds of formal settings, and yet they carry forward a certain
tradition. In listening to their work, one understands that the great
engineers know how to make technology work for them. No matter
how many tracks are recorded, at some point an engineer must use
his or her skill to marry a combination of elements, from great live
recordings to sampled drum sounds, while still ensuring that the
record grooves. And of course, lest we forget who is the star of the
music, they must also ensure that the vocal sound is superb!

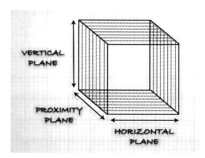

Figure 3.3   The three dimensional planes of a mix, as envisioned by recordists, specifically, (i) the vertical plane, (ii) the proximity plane, and (iii) the horizontal plane. Note that these dimensions most obviously correspond with stereophonic reproduction; mono mixes still hear directionally, however.

Whichever technology they use, and however they use it, recordists shape an aural perspective to sound when they mix. This aural perspective is comprised of three fundamental components: (i) the horizontal (width) plane; (ii) the proximity (depth) plane; and (iii) the vertical (height) plane. Situating tracks along these planes, recordists construct a past-tense aural narrative which tells how a particular sequence of sound events was once (ideally) heard, even if what the mix (ideally) hears could never be reproduced in a live performance context. A mix doesn't just fuse the component tracks of a multi-track production into "a composite image of an apparently unitary musical performance," as Zak (2001: 141) contends. In doing this, each mix also fuses the component tracks in a multi-track production into a past-tense aural narrative which explains how an "apparently unitary musical performance" was once (ideally) heard.

The following chapter details the aural perspective which each mix represents; and it surveys a number of common techniques that recordists use to shape and refine that perspective. I have already explained a number of mixing techniques which obtain during tracking and signal processing. This chapter is primarily concerned with alerting readers to the various spatializations these techniques, and mixing techniques in general, interject over the course of a recorded musical communication. Ultimately then, this section details the most common story-telling techniques that modern mixers use to shape those past-tense aural narratives.

3. HORIZONTAL PLANE

The horizontal plane runs side-to-side across a stereo mix. **Table 3.1** lists a number of tracks, culled from recent records from a variety of genres, which feature clearly delineated horizontal planes. As is evident from this table, a number of patterns recur on modern pop records which suggest the existence of some guiding principles, though no hard-and-fast rules govern where recordists should situate tracks along the horizontal plane of a mix. For instance, accompaniment tracks are almost always situated along the periphery and back-center of pop mixes while lead tracks — like vocals and soloing electric guitars — are almost always mixed to the front-and-center. Meanwhile, backing vocals, like those heard throughout Pink Floyd's *Dark Side Of The Moon*, only very rarely wind up at the same horizontal position as lead vocals in a pop mix; even as kick drum, electric bass and snare drum tracks are almost universally mixed to the same, or a similar, horizontal place. As David Franz (2004: 187–188) summarizes:

> The kick drum, snare drum, bass, and lead vocal/instrument tracks are usually centered in the stereo image. Toms and cymbals are usually panned, but not totally hard-left and [hard-]right, because that doesn't sound very realistic . . . Keyboards are often panned left and right for stereo spread and guitar tracks are often doubled, with each track panned to create a wide stereo image. Stereo pairs [stereo mic configurations] are also common on horns, strings, and even percussion, to provide expanded sonic width and balance. It's also

cool to have particular instruments only on one side of the stereo spectrum.

Table 3.1 Clearly delineated horizontal planes on records released since 2000. The tracks noted in the right column are clearest; other tracks appear throughout the production.

Track	Excerpt	Comments
Adele, "Chasing Pavements"	0:09–0:23	Fender Rhodes (left), vocals and bass (center), electric guitar with tremolo (right)
Boards Of Canada, "Color Of The Fire"	0:00–1:45	Time-stretched field recording of child and synth (center), ping-pong echoes of child panned (left and right)
Bon Iver, "Flume"	0:00–3:39	E-bow acoustic guitar #1 (left), vocals, acoustic guitar, electric bass (center), e-bow acoustic guitar #2 (right)
Cut & Copy, "Midnight Runner"	0:24–1:04	Electric guitar (left), bass, vocals, snare and kick (center), backing vocals (right)
Empire Of The Sun, "We Are The People	0:00–4:27	Acoustic guitar #1 (left), vocals, kick, bass (center), acoustic guitar #2 (right)
Fergie, "Big Girls Don't Cry"	0:00–0:43	Acoustic guitar (left and right), vocals, hi-hats, ride (center)
Weathervanes, "Big Ups"	0:00–0:56	Banjo (left), vocals, rim shots, bass, synth (center), tinkly glockenspiel (right)
Wilco, "Wilco (The Song)"	0:00–2:59	Electric guitar #1 (left), bass, vocals, snare and kick (center), electric guitar #2 (right)
Kanye West, "Say You Will"	0:00–4:32	808 pong effect #1 (left), bass, vocals (center), 808 pong effect #2 (right), choir pad (left and right)
Yeah Yeah Yeahs, "Gold Lion"	0:00–3:07	Acoustic guitar (left), kick, snare, vocals (center), electric guitar (right)
Zero 7, "Swing"	0:00–1:34	Organ, ride cymbal, glockenspiel (left), acoustic guitar, hand-claps, vocals, kick (center), Fender Rhodes (right)

3.1 Mono's Demise: Stereo-Switching

The horizontal plane, and the mixing techniques which construct it, are a relatively recent addition to Recording Practice. Well into the 1960s, in fact, long after stereophonic technology came to market, stereo mixing remained a largely neglected craft, especially in British recording studios. Records were made primarily for mono (monaural) reproduction, that is, for transduction via sound systems with only one channel regardless of the number of loudspeakers used. Stereo — and, thus, the horizontal plane — was simply "not a factor in early rock recording," Albin Zak (2001: 148) explains:

> Although techniques for recording and reproducing binaural sound had been in existence since the late 1920s, it was only with the advent of magnetic tape that stereo began to make inroads into the home listening environment. In the late 1940s, tape recorders became popular consumer items, and stereo tapes offered a sound experience closer than ever to the acoustic conditions of live performances. But it was not until 1957 that record companies finally agreed among themselves on a standard system for producing stereo records. Even then, however, the format was intended not for the mass market but for audiophiles, who were, for the most part, collectors of classical recordings. The prime artifact of rock 'n' roll was the mono 45-rpm single, the staple of both teenagers' record collections and AM radio, which did not broadcast in stereo.

Perhaps more importantly, Zak (2001: 148) continues:

> mono recordings represented an aesthetic frame for musicians and producers, who had grown up with them. Phil Spector, for instance, never really took to stereo. When it became the standard format in the record industry, he began sporting a button demanding 'Back to MONO' . . . Brian Wilson, too, believed that mono was the preferable format because it gave the recordist more precise control over the sound image.

Despite the bitter protests of many mono enthusiasts, by the end of the 1960s stereophonic reproduction had usurped monaural reproduction as the new paradigm in pop. Pop Recording Practice became, suddenly, binaural. The abruptness of this transition cannot be over-emphasized; stereo technology presented a massive rupture in the way that recorded musical communications were made and heard, and recordists had little choice but to accommodate its peculiar dual-hemisphere demands. In 1967, for instance, when George Martin and The Beatles completed work on *Sgt. Pepper's Lonely Hearts Club Band*, stereo was still so peripheral that neither the band nor their producer thought it necessary to attend stereo mixing sessions. It was left to engineers Chris Thomas and Geoff Emerick to complete the stereo master for that record, in fact. However, only two years later, in 1969, when it came time to release *Abbey Road*, a mono mix was never even attempted. Once all that mattered to the band and their producer, mono had simply become irrelevant after only two short years.

In fact, mono now inheres most overtly in modern mixing as a safeguard, specifically, against a lack of balance in the stereo image that a mix presents, and to check how a mix will sound given a mono transduction. Recordists thus check the phase coherence of their mixes by switching the master output on their mixing consoles, whether they be virtual or analog, to mono. As Owsinski (2006: 77) explains:

> When you combine a stereo mix in mono, any elements that are out of phase drop in level or completely cancel out. This could be because the left and right outputs are wired out of phase (pin 2 and pin 3 of the XLR connector are reversed), which is the worst-case scenario, or perhaps because an out-of-phase effect causes the lead vocal or solo to disappear. In any event, it's prudent to listen in mono once in a while just to make sure that a mono disaster isn't lurking in the wings. In fact, many engineers listen to their mix in mono strictly to balance elements because they feel that they hear the balance better this way. Listening in mono is also a great way to

tell when an element is masking another . . . and it is a good way to achieve a level of precision not available in stereo.

Stereo mixes made during the mid-1960s document the abrupt and awkward transition from mono to stereo which occurred at the time. When stereo recording first became widespread:

> it was common for mixers to pan most of the music from the band to one side while the vocals were panned opposite. This was because stereo was so new that the recording and mixing techniques for the format hadn't been discovered or refined yet, so pan pots were not available on mixing consoles. Instead, a three-way switch was used to assign the track to the left output, right output, or both (the center) (Owsinski 2006: 20).

The "stereo-switching" which Owsinski describes is everywhere apparent on the Billboard charts throughout the middle and late 1960s. **Table 3.2** lists a number of clear examples.

As usual, it was The Beatles who made most daring use of stereo-switching initially. Throughout the stereo mix for "A Day In The Life," for instance, the final track on *Sgt. Pepper's Lonely Hearts Club Band*, John Lennon's and Paul McCartney's lead-vocal tracks are switched to every possible position along the horizontal plane. During the first two strophes, Lennon's vocals are switched to the right extreme. During the third strophe, however, Lennon's vocal track is switched to the center and, then, to the left; astute listeners may notice that, as Lennon's vocal track reaches center along the horizontal plane, it dips in volume. Meanwhile, during the bridge, McCartney's vocals are switched to the right. For the final strophe, Lennon's vocals are switched to the leftmost position along the horizontal plane.

Table 3.2   Stereo-switching on stereo releases by Jimi Hendrix, the Beatles and Pink Floyd. These tracks are notable in that the lead-vocal tracks are switched hard-left or hard-right.

Record	Clearly Switched Track
Jimi Hendrix, *Are You Experienced?*	1. Purple Haze 4. Love Or Confusion? 5. I Don't Live Today 7. The Wind Cries Mary 10. Foxey Lady
Jimi Hendrix, *Axis: Bold As Love*	2. Up From The Skies 4. Wait Until Tomorrow 7. If 6 Was 9 11. One Rainy Wish
The Beatles, *Revolver*	2. Eleanor Rigby 6. Yellow Submarine 9. And Your Bird Can Sing 12. I Want To Tell You
The Beatles, *Sgt. Pepper's Lonely Hearts Club Band*	1. Sgt. Pepper's Lonely Hearts Club Band 7. Being For The Benefit Of Mr. Kite 13. A Day In The Life
Pink Floyd, *Atom Heart Mother*	1. Atom Heart Mother 3. Summer '68 (verses) 4. Fat Old Sun

3.2 Panning

It has been decades since recordists situated tracks along the horizontal plane with the flick of a switch. Modern recordists now use 'pan pots', that is, panoramic potentiometers, usually located directly above the volume faders on hardware and software mixing consoles. Pan pots split audio signals into left and right channels, each equipped with its own discreet gain (volume) control. Signal passes through both channels at an equal volume while the pan pot points directly north. Twisting the pot to the left or to the right, however, attenuates the input signal as it passes through the opposite channel. Twisting a pan pot to the left, for instance, attenuates the input signal in the right channel, making it

Figure 3.4 A virtual mixing console, with pan pots noted. The pan pot on track 1 points hard-left; on track 2, it points to center; and the pan pot on track 3 points hard-right.

sound like the panned track is gradually moving to the left side of the stereo plane; while twisting a pan pot to the right does the opposite. Tracks thus seem to move in the direction that recordists point the pan pots on a mixer, even though recordists actually attenuate those tracks on the opposite side of the horizontal plane.

Mixers pan tracks for any number of reasons. Sometimes dynamic panning is done to add motion and interest to a dull and uninteresting mix. The slowly panning hi-hat tracks which introduce "Elephant Stone (re-mix)," track number three on Silvertone Records' twentieth-anniversary reissue of the Stone Roses' eponymous debut, provide a particularly clear example. The drummer Reni's hi-hat tracks slowly pan back-and-forth across the horizontal plane during the first minute of the track, for no apparent reason except to add some ear-catching excitement to an otherwise stagnant mix. Other times, tracks are panned to direct listeners to certain musical events in a mix which might otherwise pass by unnoticed. In these cases, soloing tracks are usually panned to the front-and-center, only to pan back to the horizontal periphery where they resume their accompaniment role once lead-vocals re-enter. This all said, the most common use for panning is simply to combat masking. Alexander Case (2007: 83) explains:

> Masking diminishes when the competing signals come from different locations. Use pan pots . . . to separate competing instruments left to right . . . The reduction in masking that this achieves is immediately noticeable, and can reveal great layers of complexity in a multi-track production. 'Co-located signals' fight each other for the listener's attention. Signals panned to perceptually different locations can be independently [heard] more easily.

Co-located signals, that is, signals distributed to the same position along the horizontal plane of a mix, always risk masking one another, especially when they share similar spectral profiles. A number of instruments involved in a typical pop production, for instance, present overlapping frequencies at various spectral regions; thus, when they perform simultaneously, and in the same horizontal regions, they compete for audible prominence there. Cymbals often mask vocals, for instance; rhythm guitars mask snare drum hits; kick drums mask the electric bass; et cetera. While some mixers have managed to use masking to their advantage — think of Phil Spector's notorious "Wall Of Sound" production aesthetic (the Ronettes "Be My Baby" should suffice to illustrate it) — masking is usually anathema to modern recordists, something to be avoided at all costs.

Example 3.1   Panning
Example 3.1a demonstrates panning hard-left and hard-right. Throughout the example, the comping electric guitar track, which strums chords on the downbeat of each bar, is panned hard-left, and hard-right, in turn. Headphones will help clarify the panning on this track. Example 3.1b demonstrates gradual panning, that is, the slow panning of tracks across the stereo spectrum. Throughout this example, the vibraphone track oscillates between, rather than leaps from, left and right extremes of the stereo spectrum.

3.3 Anchor Points

As noted, recordists usually reserve the center position in a stereo mix for only three or four crucial tracks: (i) lead tracks (i.e., vocals and soloing instruments); (ii) bass; (iii) kick drum; and (iv) snare drum. These centered tracks are colloquially called 'anchor points' and, disregarding a brief moment in the mid-1960s — the panning job on the stereo release of, say, the Beatles' "Strawberry Fields Forever" and Jimi Hendrix's "Purple Haze" clearly illustrate mixing without anchor points — most modern pop productions are, indeed, anchored by these tracks (i.e., (i)–(iv) above). **Table 3.3** lists a random selection of tracks culled from a variety of genres which very clearly follow this anchor point formula. Though there can be a wide degree of variance between where, exactly, the kick drum, snare drum and bass tracks are anchored in a mix, they almost always remain within a few degrees of center. When these tracks are not centered, mixers are aware that listeners expect them to be and, so, they situate them elsewhere in a mix to achieve some pyscho-acoustic or aesthetic effect. Lead vocal tracks, on the other hand, are almost without exception panned to the front-and-center, though, again, there are certainly a number of exceptions to this rule (as the tracks listed in **Table 3.2** aptly demonstrate).

Table 3.3   Tracks from a variety of subgenres that clearly follow the anchor-point formula.

Recordist	Tracks
Arctic Monkeys	My Propellor
Battles	Ddiamondd
Ben Folds Five	Fair
Black Moth Super Rainbow	Forever Heavy
The Breeders	Cannonball
The Cure	Catch
Frou Frou	Let Go
Ladytron	Black Car

(*continued*)

Recordist	Tracks
Lady Gaga	Just Dance
Lily Allen	The Fear
MGMT	Time To Pretend
The Streets	Fit But You Know It
Radiohead	Airbag
Robin Judge	Magnetic
Sia	Rewrite
St. Germain	Rose Rouge
Sqaurepusher	Star Time 2
Stone Roses	One Love
Tosca	My First
Weezer	My Name Is Jonas

3.4 The Haas Trick

To increase stereo separation, that is, to widen the horizontal plane of a mix, recordists sometimes use delay processing and panning in tandem. Roey Izhaki (2008: 168–169) calls this tandem technique "the Haas trick," because it builds on theoretical work on the psycho-acoustic basis of reverberation and delay done by the famous German theorist Helmut Haas:

> The Haas trick is, essentially, a demonstration of the Haas effect. Haas concluded . . . that the direction of sound is determined solely by the initial sound, providing that (a) the successive sounds arrive within 1–35 ms of the initial sound [and] (b) the successive sounds are less than 10 dB louder than the initial sound . . . The Haas trick is usually achieved in one of two ways. The first involves panning a mono track hard to one channel, duplicating it, panning the duplicate hard to the opposite channel and nudging the duplicate [ahead or behind] by a few milliseconds. The second way involves loading a stereo delay on a mono track, setting one channel to have no delay and the other to have short delays between 1 and 35 ms.

Examples of the Haas trick abound on modern rock, pop and electronica productions. I have already considered the technique at work on the Edge's electric guitar tracks for U2's "Stuck In A Moment You Can't Get Out Of" (see "Delay"). And indeed, it is rock guitarists in particular who have most readily embraced the Haas trick as a standard technique. Billy Corgan, for one, used the Haas trick extensively in the early and mid-1990s, albeit produced most often through manual doubling and mirrored equalization. Corgan and his co-producer Butch Vig deployed the Haas trick on a number of Smashing Pumpkins releases, including: "Today"; "Bullet With Butterfly Wings"; and "Zero." **Table 3.4** provides a number of illustrative examples from the Smashing Pumpkins' *Mellon Collie and The Infinite Sadness*.

Table 3.4   Clear instances of the Haas-Trick on Billy Corgan's electric-guitar tracks throughout *Mellon Collie and The Infinite Sadness*. Readers who have difficulty isolating the dry and delayed guitar lines should listen using only one headphone at a time.

Record	Track (Dominant Location of Haas'd Guitar)
The Smashing Pumpkins, *Mellon Collie and The Infinite Sadness*	Disc One: 7. To Forgive (left) 9. Love (right) 10. Cupid De Locke (left 0:00,1:05,1:50–2:50; right 0:35) 13. Procelina (left at 2:40 and 5:12) Disc Two: 6. Tales Of A Scorched Earth (left) 8. Stumbeleine (left) 12. Lily (My One And Only) (left)

4. PROXIMITY PLANE

The proximity plane runs from the front-and-center to the auditory horizon at the very back of a mix. Recordists use a number of techniques, often in tandem, to situate tracks along this proximity plane.

That said, proximity remains an entirely relational acoustic construct: tracks only sound closer and farther relative to other tracks in a mix. As Paul White (2009) explains:

> In real life we hear sound in three dimensions. Although a stereo production obviously places all the sound sources in front of the listener on a left-right soundstage, it can often seem harder to achieve a good sense of front-to-back depth . . . Nearby sounds obviously tend to be louder than distant ones, and that's easy enough to mimic, but there are many other factors, too. Consequently, there's a lot more you can do than simply rely on your level faders.

To push a track back in a mix, recordists attenuate its volume and its high-frequency content relative to the volume and equalization of tracks situated nearer to the fore. "Perspective is all about contrast," White (2009) continues, "so while sounds can be pushed back by making them less bright and more reverberant, they must be balanced by brighter, drier sounds at the front of the mix." Roey Izhaki (2008: 71) concurs:

> All depth considerations are relative. We never talk about how many meters away [a sound is] — we talk about in front or behind another instrument. The [proximity plane] of a mix starts with the closest sound and ends at the farthest sound. The depth field is an outsider when it comes to our standard mixing objectives. We rarely talk about a balanced depth field since we do not seek to have our instruments equally spaced in this domain. Coherent depth field is a much more likely objective . . . A classical concert with the musicians walking back and forth around the stage would be chaotic. Likewise, depth variations are uncommon, and usually instruments move back and forth in the mix as a creative effect, or in order to promote importance (just as a trumpet player would walk to the front of the stage during his solo).

4.1 Auditory Horizon

All proximity plane motion occurs along a front-to-back continuum. The furthest distance away which a track can be pushed before it slips out of earshot is called the "auditory horizon". Behind the auditory horizon of a mix is silence. If a track fades-in, for instance, it begins its trek toward the mix from behind the auditory horizon, that is, from a distance too far away to be heard by the aural perspective a mix construes. The amount of silence before the horizon is breached — and, then, before the track achieves full audibility — represents a certain distance the recorded performance must travel to be heard. If a track fades-out, on the other hand, it ends its trek past the auditory horizon, beyond earshot.

Fading-in and fading-out have become particularly popular devices in modern pop. In lieu of an introduction or some final cadence, recordists slowly push and pull tracks ever closer and farther along the proximity plane of a mix until they emerge into, or slip beyond, its earshot. In fact, the approach that recordists take to fading can play a crucial, if often unremarked, role in defining their style on record. Fading is extremely common in progressive and album-oriented rock, for instance. Bands like Pink Floyd, ELP and, more recently, Explosions In The Sky constantly fade tracks, pushing and pulling the component tracks on their records into, and out of, earshot. Meanwhile, garage rock bands like the Stooges, the Strokes, Wolfmother, the Hives and the White Stripes — and Top 40 acts like Fergie, Shania Twain and Céline Dion — rarely fade tracks, if at all.

Table 3.5   Fading and cross-fading on various Pink Floyd records from the early and mid-1970s. Cross-fades are indicated by "(cr)"; readers should note their increased prevalence as the band embraces the "concept album" format.

Album	Track	Fade-in	Fade-out
Atom Heart Mother	1. Atom Heart Mother	Yes	No
	2. If	No	No
	3. Fat Old Sun	Yes	Yes
	4. Alan's Psychedelic Breakfast	No	No
Meddle	1. One Of These Days	Yes	(cr)
	2. A Pillow Of Winds	(cr)	Yes
	3. Fearless	No	(cr)
	4. San Tropez	No	Yes
	5. Seamus	No	No
	6. Echoes	No	Yes
Dark Side Of The Moon	1. Speak To Me	Yes	(cr)
	2. Breathe	(cr)	(cr)
	3. On The Run	(cr)	(cr)
	4. The Great Gig In The Sky	(cr)	Yes
	5. Money	No	(cr)
	6. Us And Them	(cr)	(cr)
	7. Any Colour You Like	(cr)	(cr)
	8. Brain Damage	(cr)	(cr)
	9. Eclipse	(cr)	Yes
Wish You Were Here	1. Shine On You Crazy Diamond, 1–5	Yes	(cr)
	2. Welcome To The Machine	(cr)	(cr)
	3. Have A Cigar	(cr)	(cr)
	4. Wish You Were Here	(cr)	(cr)
	5. Shine On You Crazy Diamond, 6–9	(cr)	Yes
Animals	1. Pigs On The Wing, 1	No	No
	2. Dogs	Yes	No

(continued)

Album	Track	Fade-in	Fade-out
	3. Pigs (Three Different Ones)	No	(cr)
	4. Sheep	(cr)	(cr)
	5. Pigs On The Wing, 2	(cr)	No

4.2 Reverberation Processing

Recordists use a variety of tools to situate tracks along the proximity plane of a mix. However, 'reverb processing' remains the most common tool that mixers use to shape the proximity of sounds. As Roey Izhaki (2008: 405) explains:

> In nature, reverb is observed mostly within enclosed spaces, such as rooms. Reverbs are easier to understand if we imagine an impulse sound, like a handclap, emitted from a sound source in an empty room. Such a sound will propagate in a spherical fashion and for simplicity we should regard it as traveling in all directions. The emitted sound will travel in a direct path to a listener (or microphone) followed by reflections that bounced from the walls, floor and ceiling. These will be gradually followed by reflections that have bounced many times from many surfaces. As sound both diminishes when traveling through air, and being absorbed by surface materials, the reflections will slowly decay in amplitude. Reverb is the collective name given to the sound created by bounced reflections from room boundaries . . . In modern times, we use reverb emulators, either hardware or software plug-ins, to simulate this natural phenomenon.

Reverb processing has become a core technique in modern mixing. One of the foundational tenets of multi-track production mandates that component tracks be recorded in as dry (non-reverberant) a manner as possible; recordists later shape and refine reverberation profiles for tracks once the spatial and spectral needs of the production at large are fully evolved. Multi-track mixes seldom develop in a straightforward manner, after all. As Brian Eno (1979) so famously put it in 1979, multi-track recordists usually engage in:

> in-studio composition, where you no longer come to the studio with a conception of the finished piece. Instead you come with actually a rather bare skeleton of the piece, or perhaps with nothing at all. I often start working with no starting point. Once you become familiar with studio facilities, or even if you're not, actually, you can begin to compose in relation to those facilities. You can begin to think in terms of putting something on, putting something else on, trying this on top of it, and so on, and then taking some of the original things off, or taking a mixture of things off, and seeing what you're left with — actually constructing a piece in the studio. In a compositional sense, this takes the music away from any traditional way that composers worked, as far as I'm concerned, and one becomes empirical in a way that the classical composer never was.

Even if they pursue a complete and clear conception of the final mix from the very moment they enter a studio, recordists nonetheless refrain from making final decisions about reverb processing until that mix nears completion. Because it extends spectral timbres in time and in space, reverb processing is prone to induce unintended masking errors; the time it takes to correct these errors can prove costly, both financially and creatively. At the very least, errors of this sort impede the forward-momentum of the record-making process, stalling work at what amounts to a technical footnote. "Too much reverb can make your mix less defined and powerful, especially if you apply it to low-frequency instruments like kick drum and bass," cautions David Franz (2004: 214):

> Consider using low-pass and/or high-pass filters on your reverbs to tighten up the frequency range of the reverb output. Doing this will clarify your mix significantly, avoiding unwanted frequency buildups.

This said, reverberation processing can also be used to clarify a mix:

> As a long list of rebellious rock-and-roll musicians will testify, there
> are no rules in music. While the creation of a single unifying space
> may be a goal for many pieces of music, it is perfectly reasonable to
> pursue contrasting spatial qualities among various musical tracks in
> a multi-track production instead. The vocal might be made to sound
> as if it is in a warm symphony hall with one reverb, while the drums
> may appear, sonically, to be in a much smaller and brighter room,
> courtesy of another reverb, and the tambourine gets some high-
> frequency shimmer from yet another reverb. Applying different
> [reverb processing] to different elements of a multi-track production
> reduces masking, making each sound or group of sounds treated
> with a unique reverb easier to hear. This enables a broad range
> of spatialities, and effects, to coexist in a single, possibly crowded
> multi-track recording. In popular and rock music, this approach is
> the norm. Even simple productions commonly run three or four
> different reverb units at once . . . A globally applied, single space or
> effect is the exception. (Case 2007: 314)

Recordists now use a number of reverb processors to tailor the component facets of a track's reverberation profile with remarkable precision.
Recordists use these processors to adjust, among other parameters:
(i) pre-delay times; (ii) early-reflection and late-reflection levels; and
(iii) decay and diffusion rates. Each of these components is "tightly
related to the properties of the natural reverb produced in acoustic
spaces," as Roey Izhaki (2008: 421) explains. Adjusting even just one
of these parameters thus refines the reverberation profile of tracks,
precisely as it specifies a particular acoustic space for those tracks. In
other words, recordists use reverb processing to position tracks along
the proximity plane and, in so doing, to construct an idealized space
for those tracks to inhabit.

Example 3.2   Reverberation And Proximity

Example 3.2 demonstrates the role that reverb processing plays in assigning proximity to tracks. The primary drum-kit sample, in Example 3.2, is pushed back along the proximity plane, and pulled to the fore again, between 0:08 and 0:31. As the decay time, and the amount of reverb, on that track are increased, the sample pushes further back along the proximity plane, that is, it decreases in proximity. When the decay time, and amount of reverb, are decreased, the track pulls forward. Between 0:41 and 1:02, the sound FX track which enters at 0:38, is pulled towards the fore of the mix, and then pushed back again, using the same technique. Finally, the FX track is pulled to the fore once more, before Example 3.2 fades-out to silence.

PRE-DELAY

Every reverberation begins with a brief interlude of non-activity, known colloquially as the "pre-delay phase". This phase intervenes between the arrival of the "direct sound", that is, the soundwave which provokes the reverberation, and its first "reflection". In creating this buffer, the pre-delay phase provides listeners with important information about the size and dimensions of the physical space in which the direct sound reverberates. Specifically, pre-delay delineates the distance which direct soundwaves travel before reaching reflective surfaces in a room. Longer pre-delay times — say, more than 85 ms — demarcate larger spaces while shorter pre-delay times denote smaller spaces.

In fact, pre-delay times can be measured in feet. We know that sound travels at a rate of roughly 1,000 feet per second, "so a 50 millisecond pre-delay gives the effect of placing a sound source 50 feet away from the opposite wall of a room," explains Bruce Swedien (2009: 141):

> Pre-delay determines how far the sound source is from the walls in a room. This has the subjective effect of creating depth [in a mix], and long pre-delays of 50 to 65 ms are often used to wash vocals and make them fit better in a mix . . . This sounds pretty huge but it is not unusual for concerts to take place in large concert halls or

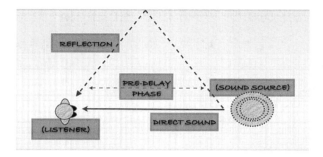

Figure 3.5 The pre-delay phase of a typical reverberation profile, separating the arrival of direct sound from its first reflection.

auditoriums that are considerably larger than 50 feet in length.

EARLY REFLECTIONS AND LATE REFLECTIONS

Following the pre-delay phase of a reverberation comes "early reflections". These "early reflections" arrive within 35 to 80 ms of the direct sound, and their onset delineates the definitive conclusion of the pre-delay phase of a reverberation profile. Early reflections are followed closely by another round of reflections called 'late reflections', which arrive roughly 35 ms after early reflections arrive. Both early reflections and late reflections provide important information about where the sound source — and, in turn, the listener — is situated in a room. According to William Moylan (2007: 30):

> Early reflections arrive at the listener within 50[—80]ms of the direct sound. These early reflections comprise the early sound field. The early sound field is composed of the first few reflections that reach the listener before the beginnings of the diffused, reverberant sound. Many of the characteristics of a host environment are disclosed during this initial portion of the sound. The early sound field contains information that provides clues as to the size of the environment, the type and angles of the reflective surfaces, even the

construction materials and coverings of the space.

Early reflections reflect off only one or two near surfaces in a room; they don't travel all the way to room boundaries before they bounce back to listeners, as late reflections must. Because they do not travel as far as late reflections, early reflections are usually significantly brighter, that is, they contain more high-frequency components, and their attack transients thus remain relatively intact. A preponderance of these bright early reflections thus encourages listeners to localize tracks closer along the proximity plane of a mix, especially when they are combined with tracks that feature a preponderance of late reflections instead. To achieve this effect, however, purists like Bruce Swedien (2009: 125) insist that the early reflections must be recorded live (amateur record-ists also tend to be particularly interested in what purists have to say on this matter: purists' "rules" offer the comforting illusion of objective standards which can be used to gauge work in the absence of profes-sional accolades):

> Early reflections are something that I have always considered "the forgotten factor" of acoustical support, when it comes to high qual-ity recording . . . The thing that is always apparent to my ear is that the quality of early reflections, when generated in a room, is quite different (and vastly superior) to the so-called early reflections that would be generated artificially. So, if we have well-recorded sound sources, with good early reflections, what you want to do is open up the pre-delay, or make the pre-delay larger in number, to accommo-date the early reflections. If you have done a good job of recording your sound source, if you don't have pre-delay in the reverb, you'll mask those beautiful early reflections. And those early reflections are a very important component of sound.

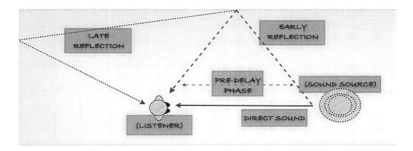

Figure 3.6   A reverberation profile, including pre-delay, early and late reflections.

DECAY AND DIFFUSION

The "decay phase" of a reverberation profile spans the onset of late reflections to the onset of silence. Decay rates are often expressed in terms of "RT60", in reference to the 60 decibels (SPL) of attenuation which is usually required for a sound to diminish to silence (RT refers to reverb time). A small acoustically tuned room may exhibit an RT60 of roughly 200 ms, say, while some cathedrals exhibit RT60 rates of more than 5,000 ms, that is, 5+ seconds. Only further complicating matters, decay rates vary according to wavelength and frequency: smaller wavelengths, which correspond to higher frequencies, tend to absorb and diffuse much faster than larger wavelengths (lower frequencies). As such, in Izhaki's (2008: 429) words:

> Longer decay also means a louder reverb that will cause more masking and possibly intelligibility issues. With vocals, there is a chance that the reverb of one word will overlap with the next word. This is more profound in busy-fast mixes where there are little time gaps between sounds. If too much reverb is applied in a mix and if decay [rates] are too long, we say that the mix is "washed" with reverb.

The decay rate of a reverberation profile offers important information about room size and furnishings. Reflective surfaces extend decay rates. More late reflections bounce back to the listener, and at greater amplitudes, from, say, concrete than from carpet. As such, when the late reflection phase is dynamically equivalent to the early reflection phase of a reverberation profile, listeners tend to infer a space furnished with highly reflective materials. The size of the room also plays a role, however. Larger rooms extend the decay phase of a reverberation profile while smaller rooms curtail it. In David Franz's (2004: 213) words:

> Reverberation actually occurs when a sound reflects off many surfaces and is mixed with other reflections, creating a denser blend of reflected sound. These reflections begin to fade away (decay) as they're absorbed into the material of the acoustic space. The longer a sound takes to decay, the larger and more hard-surfaced the acoustic environment is perceived to be, and the farther from the sound source the listener . . . seems to be.

Related to decay rates are "diffusion rates", which measure the amount of time that intervenes between the arrival of each subsequent reflection in a reverberation. As a reverberation profile reaches its decay phase, ever more time intervenes between the arrival of each late reflection; and then, as they decay to silence, reverberations become even more diffuse. Recordists can thus use this psycho-acoustic principle to their advantage, pushing tracks back along the proximity plane of a mix simply by increasing the decay and diffusion of their reverberation profiles. In Paul White's (2009) words:

> When applying reverb to distant sounds, choose a suitably diffuse reverb type . . . and also roll-off some high-end. Distant sounds tend to encounter a greater number of reflective surfaces than nearby sounds, so you can afford to add more reverb to sounds you wish to place at the back of the mix. Don't overdo it, though, unless your musical production has an artistic need for it.

4.3 Balancing Depth

Mixers typically follow conventions established in live performance when they balance tracks along the proximity plane of a mix. As I have already noted, lead tracks tend to occupy the front-and-centre of a modern pop mix (it is the kick drum, and electric bass, which usually occupy the fore of reggae, dub, electronica and hip hop productions). At the very back of a pop mix is the drum kit and, sometimes, synth pads and percussion; the kick drum and snare, however, are often pushed ahead of the rest of the drum kit, occupying roughly the same stratum as the rhythm guitar. Regardless of where they situate tracks along the proximity plane of a mix, recordists "layer depth" — they position tracks along the proximity plane — to prioritize the components of a multi-track production. Recordists balance the "depth dimension" of a mix to establish a pecking order between tracks, in other words. Paul White (2009) explains:

> In most pop mixes, the vocals need to be at the front, the guitars and main keyboard parts sit slightly behind, along with the drums, and then additional elements such as pads and backing vocals may be pushed further back still. Incidental percussion can also be pushed back and panned further from the center. Listen to the Who's production of "Won't Get Fooled Again" and you'll notice that those powerful guitar and drum sounds are a lot less bright than you might imagine, allowing the vocal to really come through.

Bob Dylan's *Time Out Of Mind* provides an interesting, and ever evolving, approach to the problem of vocal-track proximity. Over the course of the record's 11 tracks, producer Daniel Lanois presents a remarkably varied set of proximity planes; the mix for each track offers a totally different conception of where the component instruments in a typical folk-rock arrangement should be situated, at least in terms of their proximity to the fore. "Love Sick," for instance, which opens *Time Out*

Of Mind, positions Dylan's lead-vocal track far in front of its accompaniment, even as the next track on the album, "Dirt Road Blues," buries his vocals further back in the mix. "Not Dark Yet," "Standing In The Doorway" and "Make You Feel My Love" feature standard folk rock proximity planes, with vocals far in front and pads far behind, just as "Cold Irons Bound" and "Can't Wait" position Dylan's vocals somewhere between front-and-center and buried. This all said, an even more varied approach to vocal proximity can be heard on a number of Led Zeppelin records released between 1970 and 1975, as I detail in **Table 3.6** below.

Table 3.6   Vocal proximities on *Led Zeppelin II, IV, Physical Graffiti* and *Houses Of The Holy*.

Record	Track (Ranked Closest To Farthest Vocal-Proximity)
Led Zeppelin, *II*	9. Bring It On Home
	1. Whole Lotta Love
	3. The Lemon Song
	7. Ramble On
	6. Living Loving Maid (She's Just A Woman)
	2. What Is And What Should Never Be
	5. Heartbreaker
Led Zeppelin, *IV*	7. Going To California
	3. The Battle of Evermore
	4. Stairway To Heaven (acoustic portions)
	1. Black Dog
	2. Rock and Roll
	5. Misty Mountain Hop
	4. Stairway To Heaven (electric outtro)
	6. Four Sticks
	8. When The Levee Breaks
Led Zeppelin, *Houses Of The Holy*	4. The Crunge
	3. Over The Hills And Far Away
	6. D'yer Mak'er
	2. The Rain Song
	5. Dancing Days
	8. The Ocean
	7. No Quarter
	1. The Song Remains The Same

(continued)

Record	Track (Ranked Closest To Farthest Vocal-Proximity)
Led Zeppelin, *Physical Graffiti*	Disc One:
	2. The Rover
	4. Houses Of The Holy
	6. Kashmir
	3. In My Time Of Dying
	1. Custard Pie
	5. Trampled Under Foot
	Disc Two:
	8. Black Country Woman
	4. Ten Years Gone
	1. In The Light
	3. Down By The Seaside
	5. Night Flight
	9. Sick Again
	7. Boogie With Stu
	6. The Wanton Song

4.4 Buried Vocals

As with every convention in Recording Practice, exceptions to the vocals-at-the-fore convention abound. Loud, aggressive musical genres — like, say, thrash, black metal, death metal and speedcore — usually bury lead-vocals well behind accompaniment tracks, to reinforce the perceived loudness of productions (clear examples can be heard on the Smashing Pumpkins' "Tales Of A Scorched Earth" from *Mellon Collie And The Infinite Sadness* and on Tool's "Vicarious" from *10,000 Days*). Similarly, recordists will often convey the impression that a track has suddenly increased its volume by pumping accompaniment tracks to a level above the lead-vocals in a mix; this pushes the vocals back along the proximity plane precisely as it pulls accompaniment tracks closer to the fore (a clear example of this practice can be heard on the Smashing Pumpkins' "Bullet With Butterfly Wings"). Again, though, it is extremely rare that lead-vocal tracks are ever buried to the point that they become inaudible.

Recordists may also bury a lead-vocal track to buttress some broader aesthetic or thematic effect contained within a song. The Cure's "Secret," for instance, the third cut on the band's *Seventeen Seconds* LP, features an extremely quiet — if not whispered — lead-vocal track, albeit doubled an octave above. The distant placement for Robert Smith's vocals deftly reinforces the song's thematic content: ostensibly about unexpectedly meeting a long-forgotten love affair at a party, Robert Smith's hushed delivery neatly encapsulates the emotional turmoil the singer struggles to keep secret. Album producer Mike Hedges would push this technique to an extreme limit only two tracks later on the same album, by opting to bury Smith's lead-vocals on "Three" so far back in the mix that they remain, for-all-intents-and-purposes, completely inaudible (in fact, when I first heard the track I changed headphones, believing that a wire had come loose).

Some bands bury lead-vocal tracks as a matter of style. Records by Led Zeppelin, the Stone Roses, the Jesus and Mary Chain and the Strokes, among many others, provide clear illustrations of this. On numerous tracks by these bands, the lead-vocals sit much further back along the proximity plane than is the norm in the rock genre. Of all of the records listed in **Table 3.7** below, in fact, it is the Strokes' *Room On Fire* which, once again, provides the most extreme example, though some tracks on the Stone Roses' *Second Coming* give that record a run for its money in this respect. The proximal position which producer Gordon Raphael determines for Julian Casablancas' vocals throughout *Room On Fire* can only be described as far away; though, to be clear, Raphael deftly applies equalization and distortion to augment the vocal tracks with enough high-frequency edge that they remain coherent throughout.

Table 3.7   Tracks with obviously buried vocals on records by the Strokes, Julian Casablancas, the Stone Roses, the Jesus And Mary Chain, the Smashing Pumpkins and the Yeah Yeah Yeahs.

Record	Track
The Cure, *Seventeen Seconds*	3. Secrets 5. Three
The Jesus And Mary Chain, *Psychocandy*	1. Just Like Honey 2. The Living End 9. Inside Me
The Jesus And Mary Chain, *Honey's Dead*	1. Reverence 3. Far Gone And Out 6. Tumbledown 9. Rollercoaster
Julian Casablancas, *Phrazes For The Young*	1. Out Of The Blue 2. Left & Right In The Dark 5. Ludlow St.
The Stone Roses, *The Stone Roses*	1. I Wanna Be Adored 9. Shoot You Down
The Stone Roses, *Turns Into Stone*	8. Fool's Gold 11. Something's Burning
The Stone Roses, *Second Coming*	7. Begging You 10. Tears
Smashing Pumpkins, *Mellon Collie and The Infinite Sadness*	Disc II, 6. Tales Of A Scorched Earth
The Strokes, *Room On Fire*	4. 12:51 8. Under Control 10. The End Has No End 11. I Can't Win
Yeah Yeah Yeahs, *Show Your Bones*	3. Fancy

5. VERTICAL PLANE

The vertical plane runs top-to-bottom through a mix. Though the concept of a vertical plane may seem straightforward — sounds are located side-to-side and front-to-back in a mix, so why shouldn't they also be situated top-to-bottom? — the notion that acoustic phenomena possesses any kind of vertical nature remains scientifically controversial. There is no definitive measure of height for sound, after all; and one sound is not objectively taller than another, even if it emanates, or seems to emanate, from a higher elevation, and its waveform is, indeed, larger in mass. In fact, scientists who study the neurological basis of psycho-acoustic phenomena maintain that, when it comes to hearing, vertical connotations are entirely relative and, thus, subjective. Daniel J. Levitin (2006: 21) summarizes the scientific objection:

> The terms [i.e., high and low] are culturally relative. The Greeks talked about sounds in the opposite way because the string instruments they built tended to be oriented vertically. Shorter strings or pipe organ tubes had their tops closer to the ground, so these were called the low notes (as in low to the ground) and the longer strings and tubes — reaching up toward Zeus and Apollo — were called the high notes . . . Some writers have argued that high and low are intuitive labels, noting that what we call high-pitched sounds come from birds (who are up in trees or in the sky) and what we call low-pitched sounds often come from large, close-to-the-ground mammals such as bears or the low sounds of an earthquake. But this is not convincing. Low sounds also come from up high (think of thunder) and high sounds can come from down low (crickets and squirrels, leaves crushed under foot).

Despite Levitin's caveats, published accounts of the mixing process, especially those written by working recordists, universally posit a "vertical plane"; and practical experience making and listening to records bears out the existence of a top-to-bottom continuum in every mix. Whether it is a product of cultural or neurological conditioning, or a practical reality which simply confounds current scientific theory, the vertical plane plays a crucial role in modern mixing. "Humans hear in three dimensions," argues David Franz (2004: 186):

Try closing your eyes and listening to your environment. Right now I can hear my computers fan humming close to me on the right side and, through the window, I can hear a plane flying over my house. When mixing, we can simulate this three-dimensional sound using only two speakers . . . by [i] panning (width) . . . [ii] EQ positioning (height) . . . and [iii] using reverbs and delays (depth).

FREQUENCY BALANCING

Sound achieves height in a mix through relational — what I have elsewhere called mirrored — processing. When they discuss the vertical plane, or, the "tall dimension", of a mix, recordists actually discuss the practice of "frequency balancing". Within the context of each particular mix, tracks with abundant high-frequency content simply seem to occupy a position along the vertical plane located over-and-above tracks with a duller equalization. An electric bass which lacks energy above, say, 2 kHz, for instance, sounds like it emanates from an elevation under a synth pad with a high-pass filter set to shelve everything below 2 kHz — even if both tracks seem to emanate from similar elevations when they sound in isolation. Again, the vertical plane is an entirely relational construct which accrues through tandem equalizations. As Bobby Owinski (2006: 8–9) explains:

> The 'tall' dimension [of a mix], which is called 'frequency range', is the result of knowing what sounds right as a result of having a reference point . . . Essentially, you're trying to make sure that all the frequencies are properly represented. Usually that means that all the sparkly, tinkly highs and fat, powerful lows are there. Sometimes it means cutting some mids. Clarity is what you aim for.

However they situate sound along the vertical plane of a mix, the concept of balance guides recordists as they do so. Recordists may opt to stunt the vertical plane of a mix, filtering the high-frequency content from tracks, as is the norm in genres like trip hop and ambient-dub (Massive Attack's *Mezzanine* [1998] provides an obvious example). More often than not, though, recordists fashion a broad, and broadly expansive, vertical plane when they mix their records; that is, they shape a vertical plane which encompasses a broad array of frequencies across the audible spectrum. While almost any Top 40 production will demonstrate the sound of a broadly expansive vertical plane, Shania Twain's "Up" and Warren Zevon's "The Werewolves of London" have always struck me as particularly clear examples.

Example 3.3   Mixing: Putting It All Together
Example 3.3 demonstrates the more common mixing techniques and concepts elucidated in the preceding chapter of this field guide. Example 3.3 is an original mix, for an original composition, called "A Harlequin Romance." An analysis of the mix is provided in Table 3.8 below. Readers are again encouraged to audition the track using headphones, and at a moderate volume.

Table 3.8   Analysis of the mix for Example 3.3 ("A Harlequin Romance").

Time	Track	Horizontal	Proximity	Vertical
0:00	Acoustic piano	Center	Middle	Bottom-to-middle
0:17	Lead-vocal	Center	Fore	Middle-to-top
0:29	Cello	Right	Middle	Bottom
	Cello reverb	(Bussed) left	Background	Middle-to-top (high-pass filter applied)
0:42	Drum kit	Center	Background-to-middle	Full spectrum
	Snare reverb	(Bussed) right	Background	Top (high-pass filter applied)
	Dry DI guitar	Mirrored (spread left and right)	Middle	Middle-to-top (bass roll-off applied)

(*continued*)

Time	Track	Horizontal	Proximity	Vertical
1:02	String section	Spread left and right	Middle-to-fore	Bottom-to-middle
1:12	Distorted guitar	Center	Middle	Middle
1:13	Double vocal "and if I had . . ."	Center	Background-to-middle	Middle (high- and low-pass filters applied)
1:36	Dry DI guitar	Haasd to the right	Middle	Middle-to-top (bass roll-off applied)
2:42	DI violin solo	Center	Middle-to-fore	Middle-to-top (high-pass filter applied)

Chapter 4

Mastering

The Final Say

W hen they are done mixing, recordists are ready to master their productions. Mastering is, in fact, the final stage of record production. During mastering, recordists use a variety of specialized techniques to polish tracks so they sound optimal on a variety of playback machines and in a variety of different formats. Though modern freelance mastering engineers like Bob Ludwig and Bob Katz shaped the mastering process into an integral component of record-making at large, the process began life as a simple quality control measure. By the mid-1950s, most record labels had adopted analog tape as their primary medium for tracking. For the first time, then, record labels used different technology to make records (tape) than listeners used to hear them (disc). Transfer engineers were thus hired to ensure that, when tape masters were transferred onto disc, their dynamic, and frequency, balances weren't disfigured in the process.

The transfer process soon took on a life of its own, however. Once concerned with preserving what recordists made, transfer engineers — or, as they were soon called, "mastering" engineers — quickly saw fit to change the records they mastered, and in significant ways which recordists did not always appreciate. For instance, mastering engineers routinely attenuated the low-frequency content of the "masters" they produced. Tape will simply distort when it is confronted with an over-abundance of low-frequency content but, with vinyl disc technology, too much bass energy can force the needle (stylus) to literally "jump the groove", simultaneously damaging the record, the stylus and the record label's professional reputation. Labels were therefore only too happy to place the mastering engineer as a final gatekeeper between the recording studio and the record store. If mastering engineers judged a mix somehow insufficient, their verdict was final; and they could alter an insufficient mix however they saw fit, even if it meant introducing changes that mortified the original authors.

Even a band as successful as The Beatles, whose every artistic whim readers might expect their label to indulge, still had to defer to the final judgment of a mastering engineer before their records could make market. This circumstance proved increasingly difficult for the band to respect. Paul McCartney was especially annoyed, given that it was his bass tracks which mastering engineers routinely attenuated. In fact, the "low-end" was a constant bone of contention during mixing sessions with the band. "The main problem from EMI's perspective was the possibility of too much bass causing the stylus on the average record player to 'jump the groove'," explains Ryan and Kehew (2008: 399). "Being the conservative organization that they were, they compensated perhaps a bit too much, although it was still a valid concern." As engineer Norman Smith (cited in Ryan and Kehew 2008: 399) remembers:

> We were sort of restricted. The material had to be transferred from tape onto acetate, and therefore certain frequencies were very difficult for the cutter to get onto disc. I mean, if we did, for instance, slam on a lot of bass, it would only be a problem when it got up to the cutting room . . . Paul [McCartney] used to have a go at me for not getting enough bass on a record. During mixes he'd always say, "Norman, a bit more bass?" And I'd say, I can't give you more bass, Paul. You know why — I'll put it on there, but as soon as it gets

upstairs into the cutting room, they [read: EMI's salaried mastering engineers] will slash it . . . because they thought the needle would jump.

The duties of the mastering engineer have only expanded since the time of The Beatles. The mastering process no longer simply assures quality; rather, it contributes a quality all its own. Mastering engineers are routinely called on to perform myriad adjustments to the records they master, including:

> fine-tuning the equalization of the final master. In addition, the mastering engineer sets the spacing between songs, creates or corrects fade-ins and fade-outs for songs as required, adjusts the song sequence (order) and the relative volume levels of the songs so that the album flows smoothly from beginning to end, and often provides a final objective "ear" to give the recording an impartial listen before it goes to the plant for manufacture. The mastering engineer also plays an increasingly creative role now, both when dealing with the tasks [just listed] . . . and when applying EQ and compression to make the mix sound bigger, punchier and richer. The mastering engineer can add limiting to maximize the overall volume levels, fix mistakes made in the mixing process, edit songs, remove background noise and hiss, and adjust the overall sound and flow so that the album sounds like a cohesive whole instead of a bunch of unrelated songs. (Gallagher 2008: 5)

In the following section of this field guide, I survey and explain a number of musical concerns which usually underwrite the modern mastering process. As I explain above, mastering is a relatively recent development in Recording Practice; and it still remains mysterious to almost everyone but mastering engineers themselves. A spate of books authored by the likes of Bob Katz (2007), Bill Gibson (2001) and Mitch Gallagher (2008) have done much to rectify this situation. However, mastering remains a mystery for most modern listeners. This chapter

is ultimately designed to change this circumstance. Readers who familiarize themselves with the concepts and techniques elucidated below
should find themselves equipped with the critical listening skills
needed to hear mastering at work in the modern pop soundscape.[6]
Interestingly, the mastering process begins by analyzing and adjusting
(tuning) the acoustics of the mastering environment. As such, I begin
my investigation there.

1. TUNING

Mastering engineers routinely compensate for acoustic biases in the
environments that their clients use to track and mix their records.
Recordists often unwittingly exaggerate what sounds deficient, and
attenuate what sounds exaggerated, given the distorting influence of
room acoustics. When their productions are subsequently translated
to different environments, that is, when their records are played on
different machines in differently dimensioned and furnished spaces,
the spectral and dynamics profiles which they worked so hard to flatten
into a transparent and balanced shape can suddenly sound misshapen
and deformed. Bill Gibson (2001: 12–13) explains:

> one of the essential factors in successful mastering is a finely tuned,
> finely designed listening environment. If your control room has
> inherent acoustical problems everything you mix in it will have
> frequency problems. Acoustic problems are consistent so they can
> usually be repaired during mastering . . . One of the primary values
> of a mastering engineer lies in his or her ability to compensate for
> bad mixing rooms. No matter what gear you've amassed, if certain

---

6 This said, many of the techniques I consider are, in fact, tailored for transparency,
   which is to say, most modern mastering techniques are designed to be self-
   effacing (which makes me wonder if the entire mastering process might be best
   considered, on a metaphysical level, a musical palimpsest of sorts).

acoustic considerations haven't been addressed, you're going to have a rough time getting world-class sounds. When you make decisions about mastering — the final sonic molding of your valuable music — you must make those decisions based on an accurate listening environment.

The mastering engineer's first job is thus to 'tune' the mastering environment, that is, to dimension and furnish the mastering environment into an acoustically neutral configuration. Tuning is ultimately done to shape as neutral a response as possible across the audible spectrum. Engineers introduce "broadband" noise — noise which spans the audible spectrum — into the mastering environment and, using some kind of calibrating device, analyze its spectral profile in various regions throughout a room (e.g., by the door, by the wall, in the corner, at the back of the room, at the desk, etc.). To do this, engineers typically use 'pink' noise, which has equal energy per octave band, and a 'Real Time Analyzer' (RTA), which analyzes the amount of energy per octave that a sound contains. They then adjust their speakers, and alter the room dimensions and furnishings, until as flat a response across the audible spectrum as can be shaped emerges. Though the ultimate goal of tuning is to generate as neutral a response as possible throughout a room, the focus usually remains squarely fixed on the central listening position. Two-way corners, three-way axial junctions, windows, doors, and other typically biased spots in a room are important, to be sure, but only insofar as they influence what engineers ultimately hear while they master.

1.1 Acoustic Issues

Engineers confront a number of acoustic issues when they tune the mastering environment. Most crucial, however, are "first reflections", "flutter echoes" and "reverb time". First reflections bounce back to the primary listening position in a room within 20–35 milliseconds of the sound source. Given that sound travels at a rate of roughly 1.13 feet per millisecond, reflective surfaces situated within 10 feet of the central listening position in a room — including mixing consoles, computer monitors, equipment racks, speakers, keyboards, lamps, walls, floors, ceilings and so on — create first reflections. These first reflections are particularly distorting; given their rapid onset, first reflections can easily induce comb-filtering if they reach a sufficient amplitude.

Flutter echo is another concern. When sound reflects between parallel surfaces, a rapid fluttering echo, comprised of no more than 15 reflections per second, typically accrues (White and Louie 2005: 156). This creates "a distinctive ringing sound," according to Paul White (1998), especially "following a percussive sound such as a hand clap." Moreover, flutter echoes are usually only audible during the decay and release of a sound (Thompson 2005: 318). They are also usually restricted to the midrange and top of the audible spectrum.

Reverb time, that is, the time it takes for reverberations to decay to silence in a room, is another important concern in tuning. This characteristic — called RT60 by engineers, in reference to the 60 decibels (SPL) of attenuation needed for a sound to diminish to silence — is most often expressed in milliseconds. A tuned studio control room, for instance, might be said to have a RT60 of about 30 ms, while a carpeted living room might have a RT60 of, say, 50 ms (White 1998). To be clear, the goal of tuning the RT60 in a room is not to kill reverberations completely. Mastering engineers actually have little use for completely anechoic (non-reverberant) work spaces. Some amount of reverberation is unavoidable, and required, to judge how a record will sound in common listening environments. Mastering engineers thus require that decay rates simply remain as uniform as possible across the audible spectrum. Paul White (1998) explains:

> reverberation time [RT60] is frequency-specific and should be measured and given for one frequency band. Reverberation is created

whenever sound energy is fed into a room . . . When the source of energy is removed, the reverberation will decay at a rate determined by the geometry and absorbency of the room and its contents. Excessive low-frequency reverberation related to one dominating mode can cause serious problems for the engineer. The danger is that you may attempt to correct your mix using EQ to compensate for the apparent bass boost, but then when you play back your mix on a properly balanced hi-fi system, the results sound bass-light. Furthermore, excessive reverb time at one frequency can cause notes to hang on, generally blurring the sound and making it more difficult to concentrate on fine details.

1.2 Absorption and Diffusion

There are only two methods for counteracting the distorting effect of room acoustics: absorption and diffusion. Absorption is most effective for controlling high-frequency reflections; engineers use absorption primarily for tuning first reflections, flutter echoes and midrange/high-frequency reverberant decay (Gallagher 2008: 145). Soft and thin materials dissipate smaller waveforms into heat through friction, absorbing the reverberations which would otherwise follow. Engineers must be careful, though. Absorption can very easily distort more than it clarifies, as Mitch Gallagher (2008: 146) notes:

> Many types of absorptive materials only work well on higher frequencies, leaving mid-range sound bouncing around without much control. This can result in an odd dark-sounding room. Too much absorption, and the mids and the highs will be reduced, while the bass frequencies will be running around with abandon, resulting in a boomy, muddy room. Overdo the overall absorption and the room will be too dead — it will be uncomfortable to work in. Most rooms require less absorption than you think; the idea is to use just enough to . . . tame reverberant decay.

Diffusion is another common tuning technique. As absorption dissipates soundwaves into heat, so diffusion scatters (diffuses) them down to inaudible size. In so doing, diffusion can eliminate flutter echoes completely. Of course, any irregular surface will diffuse reflections. However, even diffusion across a broad frequency range, which is the goal of tuning, requires specialized materials and designs which are difficult to build. As such, commercially produced diffusers are rare in the modern project studio, given that they are usually prohibitively priced. And, in any event, both commercial and DIY diffusers remain basically powerless against bass frequencies below about 250 Hz.

1.3 The Lows

It is "the lows", that is, the low-frequency response of the mastering environment, which causes the most trouble during tuning. Bass frequencies correlate with long wavelengths, which flank through and bend around large objects and walls, making them impossible to absorb and diffuse

Figure 4.1   DIY insulation of walls in a tuned listening environment. Aside from the exposed wood and the mouth of the HVAC duct, all pictured materials are manufactured to be absorptive and, thus, will combine to significantly reduce the RT60 in the listening environment.

by regular means. "Even worse, bass response can vary dramatically in different locations in a room," explains Mitch Gallagher (2008: 148):

> Moving as little as a few inches may result in a completely different bass response. It's not unusual to have variations in low-frequency response that run to 15, 20 or even 30 dB[SPL] or more. Those variations can occur within just a few Hertz of one another . . . There are going to be a lot of places in a room where sound waves boost one another and where they cancel each other. Where your speakers are placed and where you're listening from will make a big difference in the low end you're hearing. It's easy to prove: just play low-frequency tones or even bass-heavy music and walk around; listen near walls; in the corners; and in front, middle, and back of the room. Unless you have an acoustically magical room you'll hear the amount of bass varying from place to place within the room. Low end tends to build up in corners and near walls. For this reason [engineers] avoid placing monitor speakers in or near a corner; it's best to place your monitors at least a few feet away from nearby walls if possible.

Variations in low-frequency response typically register as "room modes", that is, especially resonant (spiking) bass frequencies produced by standing waves. Daniel Thompson (2005: 315) provides the most lucid explanation of this sometimes confusing acoustic phenomenon:

> A 'standing wave' occurs when the wavelength of an acoustical sound component has an exact mathematical relationship with a particular room dimension. The soundwave, upon reaching the wall, is reflected and superimposed back onto itself following an exact pattern of compressions and rarefactions. This pattern repeats as the soundwave reflects back and forth between two opposite surfaces. The net result is that the points of zero excitation (nodes) and maximum excitation (antinodes) always occur at the same physical locations, as if the wave were standing still; hence the term 'standing' wave . . . Frequencies that correspond to standing waves in a given

room, also called room modes, will have an exaggerated response. This can be particularly noticeable at low frequencies, where standing waves are fewer and farther apart in frequency. Room resonances can lead to a noticeable boost in amplitude response at certain low frequencies, yielding a 'boomy' overall sound. At higher frequencies, multiple modes tend to blur the effect of any single standing wave and average out into a relatively even room response.

The exact frequency of room modes varies according to room dimensions. Room modes accrue when the wavelength of a frequency is twice the distance between two or more parallel surfaces in a room (White and Louie 2005: 132). A room with parallel walls spaced 9.5 feet apart, for instance, is prone to producing a standing wave at 60 Hz, given that the wavelength of a 60 Hz soundwave is exactly 19.00 feet. The 60 Hz soundwave overlaps its reflections precisely in the space between the parallel walls, "as if the sound wave were stationary" (White and Louie 2005: 373). "Additive phase" subsequently accrues, creating a spike in amplitude for the standing wave and its associated harmonics, which can be extremely difficult to detect during tracking and mixing. In fact, especially when they work with project recordists, modern engineers start the mastering process by seeking and destroying these problem frequencies, notching (attenuating) spiking bass frequencies down to a balanced volume wherever they find them. Ray Staff (cited in Flint 2005) explains:

> it is quite common to get recordings where one note is very dominant, especially on the bass around 50–70 Hz, but if you try filtering it out with EQ or compressing the bass end, the process affects everything else in that area. For example, taking the bass down sometimes affects the low end of the vocal, drum kit, or it can take the body out of the guitars. I can usually tidy up very low-end rumble at 20–35Hz, but loud bass notes force you to make bigger compromises.

To tune the low-frequency response of the mastering environment, engineers use a special kind of absorber called a "bass trap" (or, alternately, a "broadband absorber"). Bass traps are especially thick absorption panels designed to dissipate all frequencies across the audible spectrum, but especially those low frequencies which conventional absorption and diffusion cannot touch. Because bass frequencies accumulate most readily in corners and near walls, engineers typically situate bass traps in axial (three-way) corners around the mastering environment, specifically, in wall-to-wall-to-ceiling and wall-to-wall-to-floor junctures. These bass traps control and disperse standing waves in a room, and in so doing, unearth distortions occurring in the extreme bass register which would otherwise remain buried under the added resonance of its modes (i.e., vocal pops, hum from electrical mains outlets, subway rumbles).

2. MONITORING

No amount of tuning can compensate for poor monitoring practice. In Bob Katz's (2007: 83) words:

> The major goal of a professional mastering studio is to make subjective judgments as objectively as possible. What enables this to be done most successfully is the intelligent use of an accurate, high resolution monitoring system. A high resolution monitor system is the mastering engineer's audio microscope, the scientific tool which enables the subtle processing decisions required by [the] art.

Recordists thus use a number of established techniques when they construct and use their monitoring systems. In general though, most recordists opt for "calibrated" monitors, i.e., speakers adjusted to a known standard for gain and frequency response. And they connect all the various components in their studio which lead to those monitors using the highest quality audio cables available to them.

In fact, recordists will typically use a variety of monitors for mastering. Near-field monitors provide an accurate playback in close proximity, while far-field monitors provide the most accurate playback from greater distances. Many recordists will also use a number of "real-world" monitors, that is, affordable speakers used by the lay listener, to test the accuracy of their masters outside of the mastering context. Regardless of which monitors they use, though, the center of the listening position, and the center speaker-cones of each monitor pair, usually form an equilateral triangle, so the perceived stereo image accrues directly between all three points (White 2009). To be clear, different monitors are designed for different configurations — the particular configuration which a particular monitor system requires is usually designated in the accompanying documentation.

This all said, monitor selection is much more a question of personal preference and taste than the scientific marketing for mastering and recording technologies would seem to imply. Most engineers agree that clients are better served when they use monitors which they know intimately, even if those monitors are slightly biased in certain frequency regions. As Mitch Gallagher (2008: 97–98) explains:

> Monitors, as studio speakers are known, are possibly the most critical components in the mastering gear chain. After all, every bit of audio you hear will pass through those monitors. Every decision you make about processing and editing your audio will be based on what you hear from your monitors. The speakers you choose have to be as neutral as possible. They must not color the sound, or you won't be able to accurately judge the quality and balance of the tracks. They must have excellent detail and dynamic response. They must have wide response so you can hear every frequency in your music, from the lowest lows to the highest highs . . . Your monitors must also be easy to listen to, so you'll be comfortable scrutinizing your tracks for hours on end without ear fatigue setting in. The only way to determine this is to try the monitors yourself. You might think, since virtually all manufacturers claim their monitors have

flat frequency response, all monitors would sound pretty much the same. But this is far from true.

LEVELS

Even with calibrated speakers and a professionally tuned environment, a neutral response across the frequency spectrum is improbable, to say the least. Some troublesome regions will inevitably plague recordists for as long as they master in a particular space. In light of this, and to save a bit of money, some recordists forego tuning altogether. Instead, they learn as much as they can about the acoustic quirks of the environments they work in, and of the monitors they use for mastering, and they adjust the dynamic range and frequency balance of their masters accordingly. For instance, if they know that room acoustics make everything between 60 Hz and 120 Hz sound louder than it actually is, and that their monitors tend to under-emphasize everything at 1 kHz, recordists may attenuate the 60–120 Hz range and boost around 1 kHz to compensate. This said, recordists who follow this option must ensure that they test the resulting balances on different monitor systems, in different environments, when they are finished. While this is hardly an ideal solution for recordists, especially those reassured by the scientific approach laid-out in marketing and trade literature on mastering, it nonetheless represents a functional strategy which has been used by many recordists, with great success, over the years.

Regardless of the monitors they use, selecting an appropriate volume for mastering is a crucially important technical skill. If the mastering environment is flat (neutral) across the audible spectrum, most recordists recommend monitoring (listening) at 85 decibels (SPL), or, −12 dBFS, given that the human ear is most accurate in this range (Gibson 2003: 18). When they work in a difficult space, however, engineers usually opt for much quieter levels (volumes), boosting tracks only periodically to check for egregious imbalances. Some engineers use quieter levels as a rule, and then check their masters on headphones. "What works at higher levels doesn't necessarily work when played softer," notes Bobby Owsinski (2006: 75). "However, balances that are made at softer levels always work when played louder." "I believe in mastering at low levels using near-field monitors," and in "being in close proximity to the speakers," explains Craig Anderton (in Gallagher 2008: 180):

> [This] tends to minimize the effects of the room. I also use head-phones as sort of a reality test. One thing about headphones — although you can't really 'sign off' on a mix or a mastering job just with headphones — they are valuable for hearing little clicks and pops, ticks, and artifacts like that, which you might not hear over a set of speakers. Probably you will, but if you have any kind of back-ground noise or whatever, you might miss something. Headphones will give you that 'sound under a microscope' effect. So going back and forth between your headphones and nearfield monitors, and possibly switching to a set of 'lowest common denominator' speak-ers [i.e., 'real world' monitors] . . . you can get a pretty good idea of what's going on.

Of course, most recordists monitor at different levels to judge differ-ent facets of a record. Even if most mastering engineers advocate low levels in general for mastering, they also generally agree that there is, indeed, such thing as too low a level. "If you listen too soft, you'll add too much bass," Ed Seay (cited in Owsinski 2006: 75) explains. "If you listen too loud, though, you'll turn the lead vocals down too much." In light of this conundrum, George Massenburg (cited in Owsinski 2006: 75) offers the following advice:

> Monitor 'way loud' to see what rocks . . . Monitor at a nominal level to get sounds together. Then . . . monitor about 5dB over back-ground noise to hear all the elements in focus. If a mix works at 30 dB SPL, 25 dB SPL, it'll almost always work a lot louder. If you can

hear everything at that low a level, then when you turn it up, you'll have a very even balance.

PHASE COHERENCE

Aside from their dynamic output, engineers are also concerned about the integrity of the horizontal (stereo) image their speakers construe. A key component of the mastering process is ensuring the integrity of — and, when appropriate, widening — the stereo image of productions, after all. If the stereo balance presented by their monitors is imprecise, engineers will tailor width based on a distorted stereo image, which inevitably results in either too much or too little widening. To ward against this, engineers routinely begin each mastering session by switching their monitors to mono and checking that the center image remains "phase coherent", that is, unmoving (i.e., it does not drift to the left or right of center). Though there are a number of "stereo position indicators" on the market, most engineers consider these nothing more than eye candy. In fact, as Bob Katz (2007: 205) explains, most established engineers recommend that recordists always use their ears to judge the phase coherence of their monitor systems, especially given how easily visual information misleads judgments about sound:

> Music feels much better when the stereo balance is 'locked in', which can be as small as an 0.2 dB level adjustment in one channel. It is generally unhelpful to use meters to judge channel balance because at any moment in time, one channel will likely measure higher than the other. I've seen songs where one channel's meter (peak or VU) is consistently a dB or so higher than the other, but the balance sounds exactly correct. Since lead vocals are usually centered, this is a good guide, but there are always exceptions. Proper balance should be determined by ear.

3. SEQUENCING, SPACING AND FADING

When they are finished their tuning and monitoring routines, recordists are ready to begin work mastering recorded sounds. The first stage
in mastering, after tuning, is usually "sequencing". During sequencing,
recordists order the songs on an album according to either their own,
or the client's, specifications. As inconsequential as this process may
seem on first blush, sequencing is an extremely difficult and complex
procedure.

Everything in mastering proceeds from sequencing. Once they
decide on a sequence, engineers don a "bi-directional" micro/macro-
analytic lens, simultaneously evaluating tracks as singular entities and
components in a broader sequence. In other words, once a sequence
is made, every adjustment becomes an adjustment to both a specific
track and to the broader project. When they boost, say, the midrange
of even just a few seconds of a guitar solo somewhere on track six, for
instance, mastering engineers simultaneously boost the midrange of the
sequence as a whole. "You have to think about everything at the same
time," notes Chris Gehringer (in Robjohns 2003):

> I don't really treat different musical styles differently . . . I decide if
> there is enough top, if the bass is big enough, are the vocals loud
> enough, and just do what I think is needed. The challenge is to make
> the whole thing sound like a homogenous record . . . Generally what
> I do is put the whole album together and, as I'm working, I compare
> each song to each other. When I get to the end I listen right through
> the whole thing, and then hearing it as a whole I might decide that
> song five, say, needs a new approach. So I might go back and redo
> that track with the Sontec EQ instead of the Avalon, for example.

Though the particulars of sequencing vary from genre to genre — and,
even, from subgenre to subgenre, record to record and track to track
— a few large-scale patterns tend to dominate sequencing on modern

records. In the classical domain, for instance, the order of movements in large-scale compositions tends to prescribe sequencing. It makes little sense to start a record with the final movement of Beethoven's Ninth Symphony, for instance, only to end with its first movement. In most genres of popular music, however, 'set lists' change on a nightly basis and trial-and-error rules research-and-design. When they sequence a pop record then, mastering engineers struggle to finalize something which most often defies finalization.

The notion of a "concept album" complicates this dynamic some-what. Concept albums tend to be conceived with a final sequence already in mind; or, they are sequenced to elucidate some external program, whether that program be: (i) narrative (e.g., telling a story), (ii) thematic (e.g., elucidating a philosophical concept) or (iii) impressionistic (e.g., exploring a particular feeling). Celebrated examples of narrative sequences include:

The Beatles' *Sgt. Pepper's Lonely Hearts Club Band*, which, though it was sequenced long after each component track was completed, ostensibly documents a fantasy concert performance by the fictional Edwardian band 'Sgt. Pepper's Lonely Hearts Club Band';

Pink Floyd's *Dark Side of the Moon*, and *The Wall*, which both recount, in sometimes harrowing detail, the slow descent into madness which awaits any feeling human being born into Western advanced-industrial capitalism, or so the album's fantastically wealthy lyricist, Roger Waters, would have listeners believe;

Frank Zappa and the Mothers of Invention's *Freak Out!*, which recounts a 'bad trip', presumably inspired by LSD, suffered by GTO-groupie Suzy Creamcheese;

and The Streets' *A Grand Don't Come For Free*, which tells the story of a soccer hooligan trying to locate a large sum of lost money (one-thousand pounds, to be exact).

Examples of thematic sequences include:

> Iron Maiden's *Seventh Son Of A Seventh Son*, which explores a series of world mythologies surrounding the mystical powers of seventh-born males who, themselves, are children of seventh-born males;

> Marvin Gaye's *What's Goin' On?*, which explores the stark decay of American urban-industrial society during the early-1970s;

> Jethro Tull's *Thick As A Brick*, which parodies the high-art pretensions of English progressive rock bands working in the early- and mid-1970s, like ELP, Yes, Genesis and King Crimson; and

> Pink Floyd's *Animals*, which bleakly, and without direct reference to George Orwell, categorizes humans into archetypal animals, specifically, dogs, flying pigs and sheep.

Finally, examples of impressionistic sequences include:

> The Beach Boys' *Pet Sounds*, which elucidates the onset of adolescent fears and misgivings about life via strange musical timbres (and, in case listeners miss the point, the album begins with the words: "wouldn't it be nice if we were older");

> Joni Mitchell's *Blue*, which explores, in confessional detail, feelings of loss and home-sickness arising in the wake of a romantic break-up at Christmastime (the record reportedly chronicles the demise of Mitchell's relationship with Graham Nash);

> The Cure's *Faith*, which offers a number of different, often gothically bleak, perspectives on the vagaries of religious faith; and

> Radiohead's *Ok Computer*, which examines the paranoia and anxiety many in the post-industrial West felt during the mid- and late-

1990s,while the so-called digital revolution provoked a seemingly never-ending wave of cultural and industrial upheavals.

Non-programmatic sequences, on the other hand, usually follow a different logic than programmatic sequences. Most often, the logic of the non-programmatic sequence is steeped in the concert paradigm of musical exchange; the concert paradigm figures prominently in published accounts, in fact. Bob Katz (2007: 95–94), for one, likes to divide his sequences into discrete "concert sets", each with its own emotional design:

> Before ordering the album, it's important to have its *gestalt* in mind: its sound, its feel, its ups and downs. I like to think of an album in terms of a concert. Concerts are usually organized into sets, with pauses between the sets when the artist can catch her breath, talk briefly to the audience, and prepare the audience for the mood of the next set. On an album, a set typically consists of three or four songs, but can be as short as one . . . The opening track is the most important; it sets the tone for the whole album and must favourably prejudice the listener . . . If the first song was exciting, we usually try to extend the mood, keep things moving like a concert, with an up-tempo or mid-tempo follow-up. Then it's a matter of deciding when to take the audience down for a breather. Shall it be a three or four-song set? . . . Then I pick candidates for the second set, usually starting with another up-tempo in a similar "concert" pattern. This can be reversed; some sets may begin with a ballad and end with a rip-roaring number, largely depending on the ending mood from the previous set.

The Beatles' *Sgt. Pepper's Lonely Hearts Club Band* provides an invaluable opportunity to gauge the effect sequencing can have on record reception. The record also offers an interesting hybrid of programmatic and non-programmatic sequencing: though some critics still debate whether the album even has a concept at all, more agree that the record follows a programmatic sequence, specifically, a fantasy variety show complete with audience laughter and applause hosted by the fictional Sgt. Pepper's Lonely Hearts Club Band. Sequenced at a time when Recording Practice completely depended on A-side/B-side technology, competing sequences for the A-side of Sgt. Pepper's emerged during mono mixing sessions for the album. Initially, the album's A-side sequence ran as follows:

1. "Sgt. Pepper's Lonely Hearts Club Band"
2. "With A Little Help From My Friends"
3. "Being For The Benefit Of Mr. Kite"
4. "Fixing A Hole"
5. "Lucy In The Sky With Diamonds"
6. "Getting Better"
7. "She's Leaving Home"

At the very last moment, though, George Martin re-sequenced the album as follows:

1. "Sgt. Pepper's Lonely Hearts Club Band"
2. "With A Little Help From My Friends"
3. "Lucy In The Sky With Diamonds"
4. "Getting Better"
5. "Fixing A Hole"
6. "She's Leaving Home"
7. "Being For The Benefit Of Mr. Kite"

Readers are encouraged to test both sequences, to judge for themselves how sequencing (quietly) influences their reception of the album.

SPACING AND FADING

Recordists use "spacing", and "fading", to reinforce the basic emotional design of a sequence, much as authors use punctuation to reinforce the intended meaning of sentences. Spacing determines the length of gaps between tracks on a record, while fading determines how tracks move into, and out of, those gaps. To promote a sense of conceptual cohesion, for instance, recordists often cross-fade seamlessly from one track to the next, such that one track fades out as another fades in. This cross-fading characterizes the spacing on a number of celebrated concept albums, i.e., the Beatles' *Sgt. Pepper's Lonely Hearts Club Band*; Pink Floyd's *Dark Side Of The Moon, Wish You Were Here*, and *Animals*; and, more recently, Prefuse 73's *Everything She Touched Turned To Ampexian* and Nine Inch Nails' *The Fragile*.

Of course, the opposite is also true: longer gaps between tracks can easily suggest that, as an entity, a sequence should be received as a collection of distinct songs, rather than as a musical program of any sort. Compare, for instance, the sense of connectedness which accrues given the cross-fade from Lemon Jelly's "Elements" to "Space Walk," tracks one and two, respectively, on the duo's *Lost Horizons* LP; with the sense of distinctiveness arising from the extended fade-out, brief gap, and slow fade-in that separates tracks five and six on the same album, namely, "Nice Weather For Ducks" and "Experiment Number Six." Extended gaps which follow a series of cross-fades, on the other hand — like the minute-long fade-out and gap which separates Pink Floyd's "On The Run" from "Time" on *Dark Side of The Moon* — tend to invoke a sense of internal closure within a broader sequence. That is, extended gaps, especially when they occur after a series of cross-fades, usually suggest that some sort of internal cadence has been reached, which in turn prompts listeners to conceptually combine what precedes the gap into an aggregate musical statement.

Rarely are the gaps in a sequence standardized. They are certainly never random. In fact, spacing is a surprisingly complex and emotion- ally wrought procedure. "It's funny how gaps seem to vary depending on the mood you're in," notes Ray Staff (cited in Flint 2005):

> Normally, I prefer people to attend the session and listen to the
> gaps for themselves, because opinions can differ. I've had people

send me an unmastered CD saying that they've worked out all the gaps, so I've read their CD's Table of Contents to get their timings, and matched mine up exactly. After hearing the master they've then decided that the gaps didn't sound right. That's because they're hearing different detail, or because my fades are smoother, making [the album] sound different . . . It's not unusual for people to say 'Start the next one straight after the previous song has finished', and that's because they're not relaxed and are sitting there in anticipation. They often end up calling back later asking if we can add another second to every gap. If you have two energetic songs together you might place them straight after one another, but you might need a longer gap between a big lively song and a moody one. You have to listen on a musical and emotional level, and do what feels right.

4. EQUALIZATIONS: SURGICAL AND GLOBAL

After sequencing, spacing and fading, engineers turn their attention to equalization. It is during equalization that the bi-directional micro/macro-analytic lens that engineers don during mastering becomes most apparent. One of the first equalization tasks a mastering engineer must perform is de-noising. Using spectral analysis and their own finely tuned ears, engineers evaluate the microtic details of a track's frequency balance, looking for continuous (dynamically constant) and intermittent (dynamically impulsive) broadband (spectrally diffuse) and tonal (spectrally focused) noises. When necessary, recordists then apply "surgical" equalizations: selective boosts and cuts to sliver-thin frequency bands in an effort to contour the overall harmonic balance. This de-noising process has taken on a newfound prominence lately, given the recent onset of the project paradigm. Returning once more to Bob Katz (2007: 140) for an explanation:

> Project studio mixing rooms are not as quiet as professional studios. Air conditioner rumble, airflow noise, and fans in computers,

cover up noises in the mix. Regardless, the mix engineer should be concentrating on other things besides whether the singer produced a mouth tic. Consequently, when the mix arrives at the quiet mastering suite, we notice problems that escaped the mix engineer — click track leakage, electrical noises, guitar amp buzz, preamp hiss or noises made by the musicians during the decay of the song. We use our experience to decide if these are tolerable problems or if they need to be fixed.

Example 4.1   De-Noising

Example 4.1 provides an aural record of a de-noising process. The example begins with a "noisy" demonstration recording; tape hiss, and the thumping sound of the piano's sustain pedal depressing and releasing, occupy a distractingly loud portion of the output. A 'notch' filter is applied to the track, in the region of 4–6 kHz, to attenuate the hiss, and the track fades-out. The 'de-noising' reveals too much low-frequency energy once the track is faded-in again, however, particularly in the 60–80 Hz region; and, consequently, the sound of the sustain pedal depressing and releasing is too obvious (i.e., at 0:27, 0:30, 0:32, and 0:36). Another notch filter is thus applied to the 68 Hz region, when the vocals enter, de-noising the pedal sounds. For the sake of comparison, the offending region is pumped back to its original level for the second time through the verse ("a late night, long ago . . ."), before being attenuated again. The track sounds for another 10 seconds and then fades-out to silence.

Sometimes notching is simply not an option, however. Frequency bands often contain noise and crucial musical information. In such cases, a downward expander may be the more viable de-noising option.[7] Expanders are dynamics processors which follow the same threshold-ratio principle as compressors, even as they function like a gate. When

---

7   Bob Katz (2007: 142) explains: "Compression techniques used in mixing and mastering can bring up noise in original material from tape, preamps, guitar and synth amplifiers, all of which could be perceived as problematic. Since compression aggravated the noise, expanders are its solution. As little as 1 to 4 dB of reduction in a narrow band centered around 3–5 kHz can be very effective . . . Too much expansion, however, and you will hear artifacts such as pumping or ambience reduction."

the input amplitude registers below its threshold, an expander will attenuate the signal by however many decibels as the selected ratio dictates. Thus the expander expands the dynamic range of tracks, making the quieter sections even quieter. "Many times I prefer using downward expanders to gates in most noise-reducing applications," summarizes David Franz (2004: 209). "The level changes aren't as drastic, making the level changes sound more musical." Expanders are also used to broaden the dynamic range of extremely compressed tracks.

When the offending frequencies are situated in an extremely narrow frequency band, as is usually the case with overly sibilant vocal tracks, engineers may also opt for a "de-esser". As Bobby Owsinski (2006: 55) summarizes:

> one of the major problems when tracking vocals is a predominance of Ss that come from a combination of mic techniques, the mic used (usually a condenser) and mostly from the use of severe compression or limiting. Sometimes this isn't much of an issue until [later], when a compressor is put on the vocal to even out the level and all of the sudden every S from the singer is so loud that it takes your head off. This effect is what's known as sibilance. As you can imagine, it's undesirable.

De-essers work like compressors, but only within a focused band of the input spectrum. Setting the de-esser to detect signal in only a very limited frequency range — sibilance is located in the 4–9 kHz range — the de-esser attenuates the input signal when it registers above the selected threshold like a compressor, but only within the specified region of the input spectrum. Thus the de-esser leaves all but the offending regions of the input spectrum untouched.

GLOBAL EQUALIZATIONS

While they de-noise, engineers also equalize the broader tonal balance (spectral profile) of tracks. Most commercial masters, regardless of the markets they have been mastered for, tend to exhibit a remarkably similar spectral profile. Specifically, most commercial records feature a flat, or almost flat, midrange from about 60 Hz to 2–8 kHz, which can be flanked on either side by surprisingly steep roll-offs. Rock, pop, jazz and folk records, for instance, almost always feature what engineers call a "symphonic tonal balance". Tracks mastered for these markets typically present a more-or-less neutral (flat) midrange, flanked, on either side, by steep roll-offs, beginning at about 40–60 Hz and 3–7 kHz, respectively.

Records made for different markets diverge on where their bass and treble roll-offs should be situated, and on how steep those roll-offs should be. Thus, masters produced for different markets prioritize the midrange differently. Punk albums, for instance, tend to emphasize the midrange, creating a more aggressively loud frequency balance than is the norm, while trip hop and reggae productions usually emphasize the bass region and, at the same time, roll-off high-frequency content starting as low as 2 kHz. And, of course, electronic dance music and hip hop records typically bump bass frequencies to the point that their "global" frequency balance looks more like a downward ski-slope than anything else. However, even in these extreme cases, excessive deviation from neutral in the midrange is almost pathologically minimized by

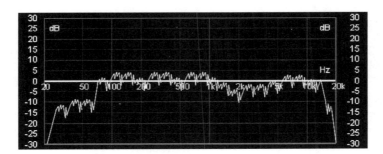

Figure 4.2   The symphonic balance on a parametric equalizer. The frequency balance presented in this figure constitutes what John Andrew Fisher (1998) would call an "ideal-type", that is, an archetype more than a specific example.

engineers. After all, regardless of which markets they ultimately master for, the mastering engineer's first job is to ensure widespread translatability for tracks. As Mitch Gallagher (2008: 13) explains:

> Probably the biggest thing a mastering engineer strives for with regard to equalization is even frequency balance. This enables the music to sound good on small or large speakers, over headphones, on the radio, or wherever it might be played. The idea is to make the mix . . . sound good on any system. Achieving this [translatability] may require different approaches for each song on an album. Certain songs, or even sections of songs, are going to have different needs than others. Yet, in the end, the collection of songs has to sound like a tonally cohesive collection rather than a mishmash of bright and dark songs, some with booming bass, some with punchy mid-range.

Example 4.2   Prioritizing The Midrange

Example 4.2a plays the same original track, called "Trying To Fit In," with four different global frequency curves applied. Each curve prioritizes the midrange differently, locating the flanking roll-offs variously higher, and lower, in the audible spectrum. For the sake of comparison, all four variations feature an entirely flat midrange. All that changes, from variation to variation, is where, specifically, their flanking roll-offs begin and end. Version 1, which begins its roll-offs at 40 Hz and 8 kHz, respectively, cross-fades into Version 2, which rolls-off beginning at 53 Hz and 3 kHz, between 0:17 and 0:21. From 0:36 to 0:42, Version 2 then cross-fades into Version 3, which begins both roll-offs at 80 Hz and 16 kHz; and, then, between 0:56 and 0:59, Version 3 cross-fades into Version 4, which rolls-off beginning at 30 Hz and 12 kHz. Example 4.2a then fades-out. Examples 4.2b through 4.2e follow the same protocol as Example 4.2a, but applied to tracks from different genres.

High frequency energy produces more subjective loudness — that is, it sounds louder — than low frequency energy. "Brightness", then, is a crucially important facet of intrinsically loud masters. If tracks do not sound as bright as they should, recordists have two options at their disposal, namely, "harmonic exciters" and "upward expanders". Of these, the harmonic exciter is easiest to understand. While equalizers can only boost the amplitude of frequencies which are already contained in a particular band, a harmonic exciter boosts the harmonics of fundamental tones in the input spectrum, adding emphasis to only consonant high-frequencies. Upward expanders, on the other hand, boost amplitude according to a selected ratio whenever a signal registers above their threshold. In doing this, the upward expander emphasizes the attack transients in the input signal, which brightens the track significantly. Both harmonic excitation and upward expansion are extremely perilous procedures, however, as attack transients easily become painfully — or, at the very least, distractingly — loud given only a slight boost.

SMILE CURVE

Tracks are also equalized for effect during mastering, that is, tracks are sometimes 'hyped'. A common hyping technique involves boosting the perceived loudness of tracks by, seemingly paradoxically, minimizing their midrange. The human ear tends to emphasize the midrange of sound even when that range is not objectively predominant. However, this psycho-acoustic phenomenon reverses itself as sound becomes louder: the midrange becomes progressively less dominant the louder a sound grows. "Our perceptual frequency curve changes at different levels," explains Paul White (2003). "Low and high frequencies predominate over the midrange at higher SPLs." Recordists thus attenuate the midrange of tracks to make them sound louder, applying a "smile EQ curve" spanning the midrange (i.e., roughly 200 Hz to about 2 kHz). This smile curve replicates the human frequency response to the same music heard at a louder volume.

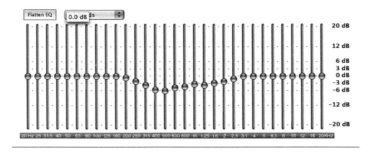

Figure 4.3 A smile curve applied across a 31-band graphic equalizer.

5. THE LOUDNESS RACE

When they are done equalizing, recordists turn their attention to dynamics processing. Mastering engineers unanimously condemn the "loudness race", which is what critics call the current impetus to make commercially released records as loud as possible — even as they participate fully in it. The upshot of this loudness race has been a dramatic flattening of dynamic range on records, spanning the musical genres from classical to rap. As Bob Katz (2007: 113) explains:

> At the dawn of the 20th century, when making Edison cylinders, everyone had to play loudly to overcome the background noise of the medium. Musicians playing soft instruments had to move in close to the recording horn or they wouldn't be heard and there was very little dynamic range as musicians were taught to never play soft. By 1927, although the electrical recording era had arrived, a vast improvement on the crude mechanicals of the wax cylinder, the low signal-to-noise ratio of the 78 RPM shellac record still kept us from hearing the full impact of big bands. But by 1950, with the arrival of the Long Playing vinyl record, the noise of the recording medium had been sufficiently reduced so that engineers could achieve an impressive amount of dynamic range and impact. Just ask any record collector to demonstrate some of the best-sounding pop LPs of the

60s through the 80s — you'll be impressed! Ironically, in the 21st century, we have come full circle. While the medium's noise floor is inaudible, we're making popular music recordings that have no more dynamic range than a 1909 Edison Cylinder!

What Katz condemns is, on some level, as old as Recording Practice itself: engineers have ever used loudness to distinguish their records. "Even when two identical programs are presented at slightly different loudnesses," Katz (2007: 168) elsewhere argues, "the louder of the two appears to sound better." This basic psycho-acoustic principle has guided dynamics processing in mastering since the practice first emerged in the middle-1950s, when jukeboxes were common in bars and diners. Because the volume of a jukebox was typically fixed, recordists pumped the loudness of their records to distinguish them from their competitors. Recognizing the "psychoacoustic bump" this increased loudness gave to records, some labels went so far as to make it a policy that records bearing their imprint should sound especially loud, that is, that their record should be the "hottest" (loudest) around. Motown, for instance, was once famous for its hot masters, as were bands like The Beatles and the Rolling Stones (Ryan and Kehew 2008: 131–149). As longtime Motown producer (and songwriter) Brian Holland remembers:

> [Loudness] was a big part of the Motown sound. We used ten, even twenty equalizers on a tune — sometimes two on one instrument to give it just the right treble sound, a higher intensity. So you could hear the backbeat, 'cling!' We used equalization to make records clear and clean. We also used a lot of compressors and limiters, so we could pack the songs full and make them jump out of the radio. We were interested in keeping the levels 'hot' on a record — so that our records were louder than everyone else's. It helped establish the Motown sound. I was very impressed with the English way of recording. Their records really jumped out. (cited in Wadhams: 2001)

Digital loudness is different than analog loudness, however. Whereas engineers and producers, like Brian Holland, once used VU meters and their own finely-tuned ears to establish and refine the impression of loudness, digital technology allows for peak normalization, that is, algorithmic expansion of digital-audio tracks such that they always peak at precisely "full scale", or, 0 dBFS (deciBels Full Scale). Bob Katz (2007: 168–169) explains:

> Digital recording allow us [read: mastering engineers] to 'peak normalize'. If we compress and peak normalize this recording, its average level goes up as we decrease dynamic range . . . In the days of the LP, variation in intrinsic loudness of pop recordings was much more consistent, perhaps as little as 4 dB. Even at the peak of the vinyl loudness race, I could put on a Simon and Garfunkel LP, or even a Led Zeppelin, and follow that with an audiophilic direct-to-disc recording, barely having to adjust the monitor control to satisfy my ears. In the earliest days of the compact disc, before the digital loudness race began, many mastering engineers would dub analog tapes with 0 VU set to —20 dBFS . . . It was not thought necessary to peak to full scale. Listeners would raise the volume on their home systems if they wanted things louder. However, the inventors of the digital system abandoned the VU meter, which opened Pandora's box.

The maximum amplitude of a digital recording is fixed at full scale, or, 0 dBFS. The peak amplitude of digital-audio information is always 0 dBFS. To increase loudness, then, mastering engineers must increase the average amplitude of tracks. To do this, they compress what they master, and then apply a generous amount of "make-up" gain. If engineers want to boost a track which already peaks at full scale (0 dBFS) for three more decibels of loudness, for instance, they must first compress its dynamic range by —3 dBFS. Only then can they apply +3 dBFS of make-up gain and, in the process, raise its average amplitude by +3 dBFS. This dual impetus may go a long way in explaining why it is that, since 1980, records have become louder by +17 dBFS of average amplitude even as their average dynamic range — the difference from base to peak amplitude — has decreased by the same (i.e., —17 dBFS) (Katz 2007: 168).

Moreover, what constitutes an acceptable dynamic range varies from genre to genre. Pop and rock records, for instance, tend to feature a very narrow dynamic range, usually between 6 to 10 dBFS (Katz 2007: 113). Even then, passages on pop records which register 6 dBFS or more under peak amplitude usually do so only for very brief periods (less than 3 to 5 seconds on average); engineers simply understand that pop, hip hop, electronica and rock records are most often heard in noisy environments, so they must be made as loud as possible to compete with other sounds in the playback environment. Classical, jazz and other primarily acoustic — what Travis Elborough (2009) calls "wooden instrument" — genres, on the other hand, spend much longer at base amplitudes. Digital and analog recordings of, say, a string quartet usually peak at about —8 dBFS, for instance, while recordings of solo harpsichord performances can peak as low as —12 dBFs (Katz 2007: 171). Still, the tendency to boost tracks and, in turn, to compress their dynamic range, is everywhere apparent now. Digitally mastered records of symphonic orchestra music, for instance, routinely peak at "full scale" now, whereas analog masters peaked, on average, —4 dBFS lower (Gibson 2003).

Example 4.3   Peak-Normalizing For Loudness

Example 4.2 demonstrates the sound of "peak-normalization" used to pump the loudness of an original folk-rock track titled "I Miss You All." The original mix sounds for the first 45 seconds at an unprocessed level. Then, at exactly 45 seconds into the track, "I Miss You All" is peak-normalized, compressed by —4 dBFS, and boosted with +4 dBFS of make-up gain. This increases the average amplitude of the track by +4 dBFS. After 30 seconds, at 1:15, the track cross-fades to its original unprocessed state; and, then, after another 30 seconds, at 1:45, it cross-fades back to its peak-normalized state. For best results, readers should use headphones, and a moderate volume, for playback.

CLIPPING

Recordists will sometimes introduce brief bursts of distortion to boost the perceived loudness of tracks, especially recordists who master for electronica and hip hop markets. Though the conventional wisdom on distortion says that all manner of "clipping" — which is what recordists call the peculiar clicking noise that digital-audio tracks make when pushed beyond full scale — should be eliminated before duplication, some recordists have taken to thumbing their nose at that particular convention. In fact, select application of "good old-fashioned clipping" is now essential for mastering electronica tracks, advises Paul White (2003):

> The final weapon in the guerilla mastering arsenal is that of good old-fashioned clipping . . . As a very general rule of even more general thumb, periods of clipping should be kept to under one millisecond (around 44 samples maximum at a 44.1 kHz sample rate) and if two or more periods of clipping follow each other in quick succession then the maximum period of clipping needs to be made shorter to prevent audible side effects . . . If you are recording acoustic music then using clipping as a means of squeezing a decibel or two of extra gain out of it may not be a good idea, but when it comes to high-energy dance music, clipping is frequently employed either at the mixing or mastering stage (possibly both!) and, as with most things in audio, if you can't hear it working (or if it makes something sound subjectively better), it's fair game.

Mastering engineers must proceed with extreme caution should they decide to follow White's (2003) advice, though. Recordists who push "the clipping barrier," as Greg Milner (2009: 280) calls it, risk deforming their productions beyond all musicality. By 1999, in fact, Milner (2009: 280–281) continues:

everybody had a favorite example of loudness gone wild. Was it Ricky Martin's 'Livin' La Vida Loca'? Cher's 'Believe'? Rage Against The Machine's *Battle of Los Angeles*? Santana's *Supernatural*? . . . After 1994, there was no turning back. With each passing year, CDs got more compressed. More waveforms slammed up against that 0 dBFS barrier. In 1999, the Loudness War reached a crisis point. They called it 'the year of the square wave,' in tribute to the flat-topped waves that had donated their transients to the cause of loudness.

It was during the "year of the square wave" — 1999 — that the most notoriously clipped record to reach market was released, specifically, the Red Hot Chili Peppers' *Californication*. Partially inspired by the fact that audience-opinion prompted Rush's record label, Warner Brothers, to fund re-mastering of the band's obviously clipped and hyper-compressed *Vapor Trails* LP, Simon Howson, an Australian film studies student, published an online petition to have *Californication* re-mastered. According to the petition:

> The main objective is to release new versions of the album that do not contain excessive compression, and are free of digital distortion (clipping) that is sadly prevalent on the current CD, and even LP, copies. The music should not be mastered simply to make all of the songs as loud as possible when broadcast on the radio (cited in Milner 2009: 282).

Though *Californication* has yet to be re-mastered, Howson's online petition generated more than 7,000 signatures within its first few months of publication. And, according to Greg Milner (2009: 283), many audio-engineering professors still find it useful to have their students "rip . . . the CD digitally, and count the number of places they find clipping."

If readers have difficulty hearing clipping in *Californication*, they should consult the iTunes version of Harold Budd's *Pavillion of Dreams*, which features clear and abundant clipping throughout.

PARALLEL COMPRESSION TECHNIQUES

While peak limiting and digital clipping are effective tools for boosting the loudness of masters, they are hardly transparent. Engineers usually caution against their use, in fact, given how little of each is required before the dynamic and tonal balance of tracks becomes completely deformed. As an alternative, many engineers deploy the so-called "parallel compression" technique. This dynamics processing technique capitalizes on a very simple psychoacoustic principle: the human ear is much more forgiving of upward boosts to quiet musical passages than it is of downward cuts to loud passages. "The latter, downward attenuation, sometimes feels like an artificial loss," notes Bob Katz (2007: 133), "while upward [boosts] usually feel very natural."

Unlike peak limiting, which normalizes and compresses the dynamic range of tracks in order to boost average amplitude, and unlike digital clipping, which augments tracks with rapid-fire bursts of digital distortion, parallel compression leaves the dynamic range of tracks more-or-less intact. Engineers simply compress a "split" copy of the input signal, and mix it in with the original at output. Thus recordists boost the volume during quieter passages, even while louder passages remain untouched. Bob Katz (2007: 134–135) calls this particular approach to parallel compression "transparent parallel compression", and to achieve its desired effect he suggests very specific settings: (i) threshold: —50 dBFS; (ii) attack: 1 ms or less; (iii) ratio: 2 or 2.5:1; (iv) release: 250–350 ms, "though with a capella music as much as 500 ms may be needed to avoid overemphasis of reverb tails"; (v) crest factor: peak; and, finally, (vi) make-up gain: to taste.

When transparent parallel compression proves insufficient, recordists may opt for "attitude parallel compression". "This second approach to parallel compression is a way of achieving attitude or punch without damaging the loud peaks," Katz (2007: 135) explains:

or to warm or clarify the low to mid levels of the music. The attitude parallel compressor effectively brings up the mid levels, where the meat of the music lives, which can help achieve that desirable epic quality in rock and roll. This parallel technique can often fatten up sound better than a normal compressor because it concentrates on the mid-levels without harming the highest levels.

To achieve the distinctive sound of attitude parallel compression, Katz recommends a slightly looser approach to settings: (i) threshold set to produce anywhere between 1–3 and 5–7 dBFS of gain reduction; (ii) attack: 125+ ms; (iii) ratio: to taste; (iv) release: to taste, but "set to work in tandem with the attack time to obtain maximum rhythm and punch"; (v) crest factor: RMS; and, finally, (vi) make-up gain: to taste, though "since the gain reduction is much less than in the [transparent parallel compression] technique" recordists should "expect to mix the compressor at a higher level but rarely past —6 dBFS."

Whichever technique they choose, if recordists use analog means to parallel compress tracks, they must ensure that both tracks are synchronized. To do this, recordists capitalize on the psychoacoustic principle of "phase cancellation". Lowering the ratio on the parallel compressor to 1:1, recordists adjust its output volume to match the input volume and they invert its polarity (phase). Then they place a simple delay on the dry signal, and adjust its delay time until complete null (no sound) obtains between both tracks, which indicates that both signals are in phase. Should this process prove too arduous, engineers may simply opt to deploy digital technologies: DAWs and hard-disk recorders now come with built-in latency compensation, which automatically corrects for potential discrepancies in phase between input and processed tracks.

6. EVOLVING FORMATS

Engineers usually conclude the mastering process by formatting their masters to meet the 16 bit/44.1 kHz requirements of a compact disc, even if they do not master specifically for physical release. Sometimes this requires "dithering", and some form of "noise-shaping". As Merton and Gunn (2007: 321) explain:

> If you have been recording your audio at 16-bit, you will not need to dither. However, if you have been recording 24-bit files, when you save 24-bit audio into a 16-bit file for CD, the 8 bits that don't make it to the 16-bit file are simply those that happen to be filling the lowest bits of the audio stream. Unfortunately, sometimes you have desired audio in those bits. This is called truncating the audio, and this "truncation" can end up sounding harsh. Dithering adds imperceptible amounts and frequencies of noise to your file so that the noise 'pushes' all the desired audio into the 16-bits that are saved, and only the noise is eliminated . . . 'Noise shaping' tailor[s] the dither even more to your audio material . . . The 'industry standard' [is] the POW-r dithering algorithms. These are three algorithms — the first is plain, and the second and third have various amounts of 'noise shaping' to tailor the dither even more to [the] audio material . . . 'Type 3' is the most appropriate for modern pop and rock music.

After dithering and noise-shaping, mastering engineers who still master for compact disc code their masters to meet 'Red Book standards'. 'Red Book' is the colloquial name given to a set of international standards that SONY and Philips established in 1980 — compiled and sold (for roughly $5,000) in the form of a binder with a red coloured cover and spine — to ensure that all compliant compact discs are compatible with all commercially available compact disc players.[8] Among other

---

8 A number of other colour-coded books exist alongside the Red Book. The Scarlet Book, for instance, delineates the standard for all Super Audio CDs; the

specifications, Red Book standards require that:

(i) all tracks on a compact disc be at least 4 seconds long;

(ii) all track numbers and timings be unique and organized in ascending order (i.e., 1, 2, 3, 4, and so on);

(iii) compact discs have no more than 99 tracks;

(iv) "index 0" on all compact discs corresponds with 0 seconds;

(v) "index 1" on all compact discs occurs within 2 or 3 seconds of "index 0"; and

(vi) all compact discs are written (inscribed) using 'disc-at-once' mode, that is, the entire disc is written in one continuous pass so reading lasers can scan it from beginning to end without interruption (Gibson 2001: 64–66).

Of course, the Red Book standard is becoming increasingly unimportant now. The internet now dominates legal distribution and — as is easily demonstrated by taking a quick stroll through the rows of DVDs and gaming gear which sit where compact discs once were in surviving "big box" record stores — a majority of North American and European listeners, especially those younger than 25 years old, acquire their music by downloading it. In fact, most listeners younger than 21 years old do not even own a dedicated compact disc player anymore except, maybe, in their cars (Gerd and Leonhard: 2008). Younger listeners tend to use the compact-disc drives on their computers to listen to compact discs but, even then, they usually use the drive to "rip" the music onto their hard-drives. From there, this music makes its way onto iPods, Rios, Zunes and other MP3 players. Not surprisingly then, a number of bands have begun to abandon physical formats altogether as a financially

---

Yellow Book provides the standard for all CD-ROMs; the Green Book defines the format for CD-Interactive technology; the Orange Book, Parts I and II, elucidate requirements for write-once CDs of audio and CD-ROM data; the White Book explains standards for compact discs encoded with MPEG format data; while the Blue Book/CD-Extra standard elucidates requirements for CDs encoded with Red Book audio and Yellow Book data (Gibson 2003: 67–71).

cumbersome residue from pre-digital times.

Radiohead generated a tsunami of publicity when they decided to release their sixth full-length record, *In Rainbows*, exclusively online, charging a fee determined by downloaders. Six million listeners downloaded the album within its first three months of release, setting an average price of $3.00 per download. This made *In Rainbows* the most profitable release in the band's entire catalogue. Without record labels, duplicators, distributors and other "middle-men" to pay, and using only their own project equipment to make the record in various mobile locations — always under the watchful eye of producer Nigel Godrich, of course — the band could pocket all of the proceeds from *In Rainbows* for themselves. Demand for a compact disc release of *In Rainbows* soon peaked, however. The band was thus compelled to license *In Rainbows* for physical distribution but doing so was clearly an afterthought, and it remains entirely unclear whether or not they will bother to do so again in the future. More than likely, physical releases will continue for as long as they remain profitable.

The trending of the record industry away from physical formats continues unabated. One much ballyhooed trend, namely, distribution through social networking and online streaming websites, has spawned a new generation of recording artist who operates almost entirely outside the traditional parameters of the record industry. Bands like the White T-Shirts and Arcade Fire, for instance, famously parlayed early success on Myspace, Youtube and Pitchfork into global chart success. That said, these bands clearly create and promote tracks much more than albums. The album itself — or, at the very least, the compact disc album — looks more like a relic with each passing day, something that only "old people", collectors and stodgy purists bother with anymore.

Just as the concept of A-sides and B-sides quickly became outmoded once the compact disc emerged, so the concept of a compact disc is fading fast into the mists of history. Album-length records are still made, of course; and compact discs still sell. But when downloaders can purchase just one track from any album online, and when peer-to-peer (p2p) networking theoretically makes the entire history of recorded sound available to downloaders at only the click of a button (and criminally free-of-charge), the notion that productions should be mastered to serve the internal logic of a fixed sequence — the notion that anything about the listening experience can, and should, be fixed — simply seems laughably outdated now.

This dissolution does not represent the-end-of-recording-practice-as-we-know-it, as some commentators have suggested. Mastering engineers have already begun to adjust their thinking to suit the new iPod epoch. Even if computers and handheld MP3 players have compelled recordists to "emphasize the lowest common denominator" by making "disposable singles" tailored for success on the internet, as Bob Katz (2007: 19) opines, recordists nonetheless continue to make the highest quality masters they can muster. To do this, they follow a time-honored technique: they arm themselves with as much information as they can gather about how best to master for a variety of formats, including distribution on the internet. Bobby Owsinski (2006: 97) advises the following when mastering for MP3 encoding, for instance:

1. Filter out the top end at whatever frequency works best (judge by listening). MP3 has the most difficulty with high frequencies. Cutting these frequencies liberates lots of bits (literally) for encoding the lower and mid frequencies. You trade some top end for better quality in the rest of the spectrum.

2. Don't squander bandwidth. Your song might compress a lot better at 32 kHz than at 44.1 kHz because the encoding algorithm can concentrate on the more critical midrange.

3. Use multi-band compression or other dynamic spectral effects sparingly. They just confuse the algorithm.

4. Remember: MP3 encoding almost always results in the post-encoded material being hotter than the original material. Limit the output of the material intended for MP3 to —1 dB instead of the commonly used —.1 or —.2 dB.

Despite the cranky protests of some engineers, who find themselves on the losing-end of industrial momentum, frenzied scrambles to suit evolving formats is an ever-recurring if not characteristic trend in mastering. Engineers once had to change tack completely and learn to master for audio-cassette and compact disc, after all; just like they had to learn to transfer tape to disc when tape technology first became widespread and mastering took its first wobbly steps as a musical enterprise. Evolving formats are at the very core of mastering: the intrinsic variability and impermanence of formats in popular music is the very reason that mastering exists. If one thing is certain for the record industry in this entirely uncertain age, it is that the craft and practice of mastering — and of Recording Practice at large — will continue to evolve well into the twenty-first century, when current aesthetic and technological trends have long since played themselves out and the-next-big-thing, whatever that thing may be, has once again seized the record industry and re-shaped it completely.

Example 4.4 Mastering: Putting It All Together

Example 4.4 demonstrates the most obvious mastering techniques elucidated in the preceding chapter of this field guide, in the context of an original folk rock mix called "Trying To Fit In." An analysis of the mastering techniques used to create the final track is provided in Table 4.1 below. It is once more recommended that readers use headphones, and a moderate volume, to audition the track.

Table 4.1 Obvious mastering events occurring in Example 4.4

Time	Mastering Event	Explanation
0:20–0:21	Peak-normalization	Track was deemed too quiet; peak-normalization was thus used to pump the average amplitude by +4 dB FS

(continued)

Time	Mastering Event	Explanation
0:32–0:35	Surgical equalization/ de-noising	Increase in average amplitude revealed over-abundant energy at 5 kHz (exaggerated sibilance and cymbal hits); notch filter attenuates region by —4 dBFS
0:46	Global equalization	Previous surgical equalization revealed over-abundant energy between 31 and 100 Hz; Graphic EQ attenuates that region by —3 dBFS
0:59	Midrange prioritization	Sound still too boomy in bottom end; roll-off introduced at 50 Hz
2:30–2:37	Global equalization	To increase dynamic contrast implied in original mix, a roll-off at 150 Hz is introduced for guitar/vocal solo

CODA

This field guide is by no means exhaustive. In many respects, I have only been able to scratch the surface of Recording Practice — and just barely at that! As I noted at the very outset of this study, Recording Practice is an immense, and immensely complicated, topic which requires volumes of encyclopedic exposition to comprehensively elucidate. That said, this field guide has provided a comprehensive survey of the most fundamental terms that recordists now use to communicate, in a way that practitioners and analysts alike should find useful.

Clearly this field guide represents an experimental form of academic research. My ultimate goal in writing this field guide was to marry practice and analysis in the service of creating an improved pedagogy for popular music Recording Practice. As I worked, I continuously sought new ways to allow practice to inform my research and exposition. As a researcher who consciously maintains both analytic and practical engagements with the musics that I study and teach, I can think of nothing to substitute for practice when it comes to generating analytic insights. In fact, I would recommend that those of us who consider ourselves to be scholars of popular music continue to find a central position for practice in our research and pedagogy. Despite the prevailing view in many university music departments, theory and practice aren't inherently exclusive. To recognize this, we simply need to rethink those "armchair" academic paradigms that put a taboo on studying popular musics in the first place.

"By now, there is a widespread consensus that pop records are constructed artworks, which has begun to suggest a growing slate of questions about compositional techniques and criteria," notes Zak (2007):

> Scholars have their own traditions and it is reasonable to seek help in answering such questions from older compositional practices with long histories of thought and articulated principles. But since such traditions developed in a pre-electric era where the enabling technology was limited to musical notation, we must also imagine new approaches to criticism and analysis that move beyond the customary concerns of musicologists and music theorists ... Among the problems inherent in establishing an academic discipline aimed at illuminating record production, then, is the need for a fundamental aesthetic reorientation as well as new modes of analytic description.

Whatever form this aesthetic reorientation finally takes, if analysts are to recognize and make sense of the particulars of recorded musical communications, Recording Practice *per se* will have to become an even more central analytic concern than it is today. "Records are both artworks and historical witnesses," Zak (2001: 23) elsewhere explains. "In short, they are all that they appear to be." It is my ultimate hope that this field guide has helped readers of all disciplinary backgrounds and expertises to hear recordists shape those appearances — even if only a little more clearly.

APPENDIX: POST-PRODUCTION

This appendix explains some of the more common 'post-production' techniques currently at work in the modern pop soundscape. Though post-production is integral to tracking, it also relies on concepts which I do not introduce until Chapter 2 of this field guide. Including a section on post-production prior to any explicit consideration of signal processing struck me as overly confusing. I hope readers will agree with this assessment.

The title 'post-production' is something of a misnomer. Recordists often deploy post-production and tracking in tandem to prepare audio signals for 'later stage' procedures like signal processing, mixing and mastering. Other times they post-produce 'for effect'; or, they post-produce to correct marginal errors which do not warrant re-recording an entire take. The list of motivations for post-production is vast. In any event, what ultimately matters for a field guide like this is that we simply recognize post-production — which is non-linear, nonveridic (even if done to produce veridic sounds), and aimed at reshaping tracked performances to suit 'control room' evaluations — as a collection of musical techniques which are, for the most part, wholly unique to Recording Practice.

In fact, many post-production techniques allow recordists to transform performances they capture during tracking into an ideal state, in order to make those performances amenable to the needs of the production at hand. The simplest example is likely 'comping'. When they comp, recordists assemble (comp) the best portions of multiple takes into a superior composite take, that is, recordists include only the most interesting, or musically superior, bits of each take while they discard those portions that do not pass muster. Post-production is also often done to correct timing errors. Recordists have a number of options available to them for this. Beat Detective's "audio-quantize" function, for instance, allows users to automatically align audio tracks with an algorithmically or manually detected tempo, while LogicPro's Flex algorithm, to name an equally popular alternative, allows recordists to manually re-position transients and, in so doing, to align tracks which would otherwise remain ahead of, or behind, the beat.

Recordists may also post-produce to fix pitch issues, that is, they may engage in so-called 'pitch correction' work. Through records by the likes of Cher, T. Pain and Kanye West, for instance, Antares Auto-Tune has achieved widespread notoriety as a commonly used pitch correction device. In fact, the Auto-Tune algorithm is most often used as a signal processing, rather than a post-production, device now; when it is emphasized in a mix, pitch-correction most often works to create a novelty 'sound effect' more than an idealized composite performance. Nonetheless, the device has come to characterize the sound of vocal performance in numerous genres of record production (according to Tom Lord-Alge [cited in Milner 2009: 343], the device is used on "pretty much every fucking record out there!"). As Greg Milner (2009: 343) writes:

> While working with Cher on the song 'Believe' in 1998, producers Mark Taylor and Brian Rawling discovered that if they set *AutoTune* on its most aggressive setting, so that it corrected the pitch at the exact moment it received the signal, the result was an unsettlingly robotic tone. When 'Believe' became a huge worldwide hit, Taylor and Rawling initially tried to keep their *AutoTune* trick a secret, although word soon got out and the 'Cher effect' became a ubiquitous production tool over the next few years…. For obvious reasons, producers and musicians don't often admit that they use *AutoTune* to fix voices that are out of tune, but it's obviously used to make singers out of people who cannot actually sing. The Spice Girls, who broke out around the same time, were clearly Auto-Tuned to the gills. Since then *AutoTune* has done as much as ProTools itself to change the sound of pop music.

Aside from Auto-Tune, recordists may also use other pitch-correction algorithms, set for instantaneous or near-instantaneous attack times, to achieve the same effect; or, with polyphonic signal, they may turn to Celemony's Direct Note Access algorithm, which allows users to adjust the pitch of individual notes in polyphonic audio signal.

POST-PRODUCTION CASE STUDY: TEO MACERO AND MILES DAVIS' BITCHES BREW

Of course, post-production is by no means exclusively digital, and it is not even particularly modern. Recordists have post-produced tracks for decades now. Though it is certainly not the first example, Teo Macero's production — or, perhaps better, Macero's post-production — of Miles Davis' *Bitches Brew* offers a widely-celebrated, and widely-scorned, example. Tape-splicing and looping play the central role on the record; post-production itself is given center stage.

Bitches Brew is nonveridic in its entirety, that is, the record does not sound like it could be, or like it was, achieved through live performance. Nonetheless, and despite the controversy that has dogged it since its release, *Bitches Brew* remains one of the best-selling and critically celebrated offerings in Davis' recorded repertoire. The record earned Davis a Grammy nomination, an unexpected placing on the Billboard Top 40 record chart, the first gold record of Davis' career and, as noted, the contempt of many critics who saw the record as, in one anonymous reviewer's words, "a nearly fatal commercial dive." Those who valued *Bitches Brew*, however, considered it a paradigm shift in jazz Recording Practice. Davis' and Macero's embrace of post-production techniques on the record, like tape-splicing and looping, struck many as 'game-changers' for the jazz genre at large (these techniques were already de rigeur in the rock genre).

Though listeners hear a composite of ensemble performances on *Bitches Brew*, the post-production techniques that characterize the record create a different musical focus than can be heard on more traditional jazz fare. "Pharaoh's Dance", the first track on *Bitches Brew*, is typical of the album. It is, according to critic Bob Belden, in his liner notes for Columbia's recent re-release of the album, "a composite composition" — no more, no less. A look at the edit-slate for "Pharaoh's Dance" explains why (the edit-slate can also be seen in Belden's liner notes for the re-release). Post-production techniques like tape-splicing and looping play the crucial role on the track, and they remain clearly audible throughout. Whereas other jazz producers had typically used post-production to perfect the performances they mixed their records to convey, Macero aggressively spliced, looped and post-produced "Pharaoh's Dance" into an entirely nonveridic state. A composite of thirty-five edits of material culled from three days of jamming in Columbia Studio B, "Pharaoh's Dance" was, in fact, completed by Macero two days after tracking had concluded and the very last note had already reached tape.

"Pharaoh's Dance" obviously progresses according to the peculiar logic of post-production. The traditional chronology of a jazz performance (i.e., melody, improvisations, melody) is refigured each time Macero introduces another tape-splice or loop. Fourteen obvious tape-splices can be heard in the first 3 minutes alone; and, as each splice rudely interrupts the performance preceding it *in medias res*, attention is drawn from the traditionally valued instrumental prowess and complexities of Davis', and his crew's, performance practice, to the way that Macero constantly assembles and re-assembles their performances into a seemingly never-ending sequence of composite musical permutations. In this respect, the record looks decades ahead, to what Greg Milner (2009: 346) recently dubbed "the ProTooled world," insofar as the record is "all about the arrangement, orchestrations, the mix. . . . not so much about playing and recording."

Works Consulted And Cited

Aiken, Jim. 2004. *Power Tools For Synthesizer Programming: The Ultimate Reference For Sound Design*. San Francisco: Backbeat Books.

Anderson, Ian. 2007. *Accidental Revolution: The Story of Grunge*. New York: St Martin's Griffin.

Anderton, Craig. April 2009. "EQ Curves and Musical Style." *Harmony Central*. Available online at: www.harmony-central.com/articles/tips/ tech_eq_curves

Bartlett, Bruce and Henny. 2005. *Practical Recording Techniques: The Step-By-Step Approach To Professional Audio Recording, 4e*. Boston: Focal Press.

Benni, Luna. 2002. "Steve Albini: An Interview With A Wizard Of Sound." *Luna Kafé Interviews*. Available online at: www.lunakafe.com/moon73/ usil73.php

Boudreau, John and Frank, Rick. 2006. *Studio Recording: Mic Techniques*. New York: Shure Incorporated.

Brackett, David. 1995. *Interpreting Popular Music*. Cambridge: Cambridge University Press.

Brown, Jake. 2009. *Rick Rubin: In The Studio*. Toronto: ECW Press.

Buskin, Richard. April 2002. "Different Strokes: Interview With Gordon Raphael On Producing The Strokes." *Sound On Sound*, available online at: www.soundonsound.com

Buskin, Richard. December 2003. "Classic Tracks: 'Strange Days.'" *Sound On Sound*, available online at: www.soundonsound.com

Buskin, Richard. March 2004. "Classic Tracks: The Police's 'Every Breath You Take.'" *Sound On Sound*, available online at: www.soundonsound.com

Buskin, Richard. May 2004. "Classic Tracks: 'What's Love Got To Do With It?'" *Sound On Sound*, available online at: www.soundonsound.com

Buskin, Richard. June 2004. "Classic Tracks: 'Wuthering Heights.'" *Sound On Sound*, available online at: www.soundonsound.com

Buskin, Richard. July 2004. "Classic Tracks: 'The Reflex.'" *Sound On Sound*, available online at: www.soundonsound.com

Buskin, Richard. October 2004. "Classic Tracks: 'Heroes.'" *Sound On Sound*, available online at: www.soundonsound.com

Buskin, Richard. September 2004. "Classic Tracks: 'Anarchy In The UK.'" *Sound On Sound*, available online at: www.soundonsound.com

Buskin, Richard. December 2004. "Classic Tracks: The Cure 'A Forest.'" *Sound On Sound*, available online at: www.soundonsound.com

Buskin, Richard. January 2005. "Classic Tracks: The Smiths 'The Queen Is Dead.'" *Sound On Sound*, available online at: www.soundonsound.com

Buskin, Richard. February 2005. "Classic Tracks: The Stone Roses 'Fools Gold.'" *Sound On Sound*, available online at: www.soundonsound.com

Buskin, Richard. April 2005. "Classic Tracks: Chic 'Le Freak.'" *Sound On Sound*, available online at: www.soundonsound.com

Buskin, Richard. May 2005. "Classic Tracks: The Who 'Who Are You?'" *Sound On Sound*, available online at: www.soundonsound.com

Buskin, Richard. December 2005. "Classic Tracks: The Pixies 'Monkey Gone To Heaven.'" *Sound On Sound*, available online at: www.soundonsound. com

Buskin, Richard. January 2006. "Classic Tracks: The Staple Singers 'I'll Take You There.'" *Sound On Sound*, available online at: www.soundonsound. com

Buskin, Richard. May 2006. "Classic Tracks: Dire Straits 'Money For Nothing.'" *Sound On Sound*, available online at: www.soundonsound.com

Buskin, Richard. June 2006. "Classic Tracks: 'Our House' by Madness." *Sound On Sound*, available online at: www.soundonsound.com

Buskin, Richard. July 2006. "Classic Tracks: Bryan Adams 'Run To You." *Sound On Sound*, available online at: www.soundonsound.com

Buskin, Richard. August 2006. "Classic Tracks: The Knack 'My Sharona." *Sound On Sound*, available online at: www.soundonsound.com

Buskin, Richard. September 2006. "Classic Tracks: Derek & The Dominos 'Layla." *Sound On Sound*, available online at: www.soundonsound.com

Buskin, Richard. November 2006. "Classic Tracks: The Future Sound Of London 'Papua New Guinea." *Sound On Sound*, available online at: www.soundonsound.com

Buskin, Richard. December 2006. "Classic Tracks: Orbital 'Chime." *Sound On Sound*, available online at: www.soundonsound.com

Buskin, Richard. January 2007. "Classic Tracks: Les Paul and Mary Ford 'How High The Moon." *Sound On Sound*, available online at: www.soundonsound.com

Buskin, Richard. February 2007. "Classic Tracks: Depeche Mode's 'People Are People." *Sound On Sound*, available online at: www.soundonsound.com

Buskin, Richard. April 2007. "Classic Tracks: The Ronettes 'Be My Baby." *Sound On Sound*, available online at: www.soundonsound.com

Buskin, Richard. September 2007. "Classic Tracks: Madonna 'Like A Virgin." *Sound On Sound*, available online at: www.soundonsound.com

Buskin, Richard. April 2008. "Classic Tracks: Frankie Goes To Hollywood 'Relax." *Sound On Sound*, available online at: www.soundonsound.com

Buskin, Richard. July 2008. "Classic Tracks: Devo 'Whip It." *Sound On Sound*, available online at: www.soundonsound.com

Buskin, Richard. November 2008. "Classic Tracks: Afrika Bambaataa & The Soulsonic Force 'Planet Rock." *Sound On Sound*, available online at: www.soundonsound.com

Buskin, Richard. March 2009. "Classic Tracks: The Flamingos 'I Only Have Eyes For You." *Sound On Sound*, available online at: www.soundonsound.com

Case, Alex. 2007. *Sound FX: Unlocking The Creative Potential Of Recording Studio Effects*. Boston: Focal Press.

Chanan, Michael. 1995. *Repeated Takes: A Short History Of Recording and Its Effects On Music*. New York: Verso.

Clarke, Robert. 2005. "What Causes Feedback In A Guitar Or Microphone?." *Scientific American Online*. Available online at: www.scientificamerican. com/article.cfm?id=what-causes-feedback-in-a

Coleman, Mark. 2003. *Playback: From The Victrola To The MP3, 100 Years of Music, Machines, And Money*. New York: Da Capo.

Cunningham, Mark. 1998. *Good Vibrations*. London. Sanctuary Press.

Doyle, Peter. 2005. *Echo And Reverb: Fabricating Space In Popular Music Recording, 1900–1960*. Middletown: Wesleyan University Press.

Doyle, Tom. October 2006. "Interview: John Cale." *Sound On Sound*, available online at: www.soundonsound.com

Droney, Maureen. 2003. *Mix Masters: Platinum Engineers Reveal Their Secrets For Success*. Boston: Berklee Press.

Eisenberg, Evan. 1987. *The Recording Angel: Music, Records And Culture From Aristotle To Zappa*. New Haven: Yale University Press.

Eisengrein, Doug. August 2007. "Do The Dip: Sidechains." *Remix Magazine*. Available online at: www.remixmag.com/production/tips_techniques/ columns/sidechaining_signal_ swapping

Elborough, Travis. 2009. *The Vinyl Countdown: The Album From LP To iPod And Back Again*. Brooklyn. Soft Skull Press.

Emerick, Geoff and Hornsby, Jeremy. 2006. *Here There And Everywhere: My Life Recording The Music Of The Beatles*. New York: Gotham.

Eno, Brian. 1979. "Pro Session: The Studio As Compositional Tool." *Downbeat Magazine*. Available online: http://music.hyperreal.org/artists/brian_eno/ interviews/downbeat79.htm

Everest, F. Alton. 2006. *Critical Listening Skills For Audio Professionals*. New York: Cengage.

Fisher, John Andrew. 1998. "Rock and Recording: The Ontological Complexity of Rock Music", in *Musical Worlds: New Directions In The Philosophy Of Music*, ed. P. Alperson. Pennsylvania: University of Pennsylvania Press, pp. 109–123.

Flint, David. September 2005. "Preparing Your Music For Mastering." *Sound On Sound*, available online at: www.soundonsound.com

Franz, David. 2004. *Recording And Producing In The Home Studio*. Boston: Berklee Press.

Fukuda, Masaki. 2001. *The Boss Book: The Ultimate Guide To The World's Most Popular Compact Effects For Guitar*. New York: Hal Leonard.

Gallagher, Mitch. 2007. *Acoustic Design For The Home Studio*. New Jersey: Thomson Course Technology.

Gallagher, Mitch. 2008. *Mastering Music At Home: How To Master Your Recordings For CD And Web Distribution*. New Jersey: Thomson Course Technology.

George, Bob. February 2000. "Grand Master: Mastering Engineer Dave Mitson." *Sound On Sound*, available online at: www.soundonsound.com

Gerd, David and Leonhard, Kusek. 2008. *The Future Of Music: Manifesto For The Digital Music Revolution*. Boston: Berklee Press.

Gracyk, Theodore. 1996. *Rhythm And Noise: An Aesthetics Of Rock*. Durham, Duke University Press.

Greene, P. and Porcello, T. (eds.) 2005. *Wired For Sound: Engineering And Technologies In Sonic Cultures*. Middletown: Wesleyan University Press.

Gibson, Bill. 2001. *Sound Advice On Mastering*. Michigan: ProAudio.

Gibson, Bill. 2002a. *Equalizers, Reverbs And Delays*. Michigan: ProAudio.

Gibson, Bill. 2002b. *Microphone Techniques*. Michigan: ProAudio.

Gibson, Bill. 2003. *Recording And Mixing Vocals*. Michigan: ProAudio.

Gibson, Bill. 2004. *Recording And Mixing Guitars*. Michigan: ProAudio.

Gibson, Bill. 2005. *Compressors, Limiters, Expanders And Gates*. Michigan: ProAudio.

Gibson, Bill. 2006. *Mixing*. Michigan: ProAudio.

Hodgson, J., Starr, L. and Waterman, C. 2009. *Rock: A Canadian Perspective*. Canada: Oxford University Press.

Hunter, Dave. January 1999. "Voxes, Vees and Razorblades: The Kinks Guitar Sound." *The Guitar Magazine*. Available online at: www.davedavies.com/articles/tgm_0199–01.htm

Hunter, Dave. June 2008. "Effects Explained: Overdrive." *Gibson Online*

Magazine. Available online at: www.gibson.com/en-us/Lifestyle/effects-explained-overdrive

Irwin, Mark. 2007. "Take The Last Train From Meeksville: Joe Meek's Royal Holloway Road Recording Studio, 163–7", *Journal Of The Art Of Record Production*, 1/2, available online: www.artofrecordproduction.com

Izhaki, Roey. 2008. *Mixing Audio: Concepts, Practices And Tools.* Boston: Focal Press.

Jones, Steve. 1992. *Rock Formation: Music, Technology And Mass Communication.* London: Sage.

Katainen, Riku. 2008. "Dauntless Studio Diary 2008." Available online at: http://dauntlessdiary.blogspot.com

Katz, Bob. 2007. *Mastering Audio: The Art And The Science.* Boston: Focal Press.

Kyttala, Teemu. 2009. *Solid State Guitar Amplifiers.* Available online at: www.thatraymond.com/downloads/solidstate_guitar_amplifiers_teemu_kyttala_v1.0.pdf

Lacasse, Serge. 2007. "Intertextuality And Hypertextuality In Recorded Popular Music", in *Critical Essays In Popular Musicology*, ed. A. Moore. Aldershot: Ashgate, pp. 147–170.

Lehman, Scott. 2009. "Chorus." *Harmony Central.* Available online at: www.harmony-central.com/Effects/Articles/Chorus

Levitin, Daniel. 2006. *This Is Your Brain On Music: The Science Of A Human Obsession.* New York: Plume.

Lockwood, Dave. January 2002. "The Master's Voice: Jon Astley." *Sound On Sound*, available online at: www.soundonsound.com

McDermott, John with Cox, Billy and Kramer, Eddie. 2009. *Ultimate Hendrix: An Illustrated Encyclopedia Of Live Concerts And Sessions.* New York: Backbeat Books.

Martin, George and Horsnby, Jeremy. 1994. *All You Need Is Ears: The Inside Personal Story Of The Genius Who Created The Beatles.* London: St. Martin's Griffin Press.

Meiners, Larry. July 2001. "Gibson Gets Satisfcation With Maestro Fuzz-Tone." *Flying Vintage Magazine.* Available online at: www.flyingvintage.com/gcmag/fuzztone.html

Merton, Oreen and Gunn, Don. 2007. *Logic 7 Ignite!* New Jersey: Thomson Course Technology.

Millard, Andre. 2005. *America On Record: A History Of Recorded Sound.* Cambridge: Cambridge University Press.

Milner, Greg. 2009. *Perfecting Sound Forever: An Aural History Of Recorded Music.* New York: Faber and Faber.

Moore, Allan. 1993. *Rock: The Primary Text.* Philadelphia: Open University Press.

Moorefield, Virgil. 2005. *The Producer As Composer: Shaping The Sounds Of Popular Music.* Cambridge: MIT University Press.

Morley, Neil. 2009. "Phasing." *Harmony Central.* Available online at: www. harmony-central.com/Effects/Articles/Phase_Shifting

Morton, David. 2004. *Sound Recording: The Life Story Of A Technology.* Baltimore: John Hopkins University Press.

Moylan, William. 2007. *Understanding And Crafting The Mix: The Art Of Recording,* 2nd Edition. Boston: Focal Press.

O'Brien, Glenn. June 1978. "Eno at the Edge of Rock." Andy Warhol's *Interview* 8/6, pp. 31–3.

Owsinski, Bobby. 2006. *The Mixing Engineer's Handbook,* 2nd Edition. New York: Cengage.

PBS. 2009. *Les Paul: Career Timeline.* Available online at: www.pbs.org/wnet/ americanmasters/episodes/les-paul/career-timeline/101/

Pedersen, Greg. April 2007. "Bob Ezrin: I Was A Teenage Record Producer." *Electronic Musicians Magazine.* Available online at: http://emusician.com/ em_spotlight/bob_ezrin_interview/index.html

Peters, Michael. 2008. *The Birth Of Loop: A Short History Of Looping Music.* Available from: http:www.loopers-delight.com/history/Loophist.html

Petersen, Greg. October 2005. "Ampex Sel-Sync, 1955: When The Roots Of Multitrack Took Hold." *Mix Online Magazine.* Available online at: www. mixonline.com/mag/audio_ampex_selsync

Prendergast, Mark. 2003. *The Ambient Century: From Mahler to Moby — The Evolution of Sound in the Electronic Age.* New York: Bloomsbury.

Preve, Francis. 2006. *The Remixer's Bible: Build Better Beats*. San Francisco: Backbeat Books.

Ramone, Phil. 2002. "Foreword." In *Mix Masters: Platinum Engineers Reveal Their Secrets For Success*. Boston: Berklee Press, pp. 4–5.

Reich, Steve. 1974. *Writings About Music*. New York: New York University Press.

Robjohns, Hugh. June 2003. "Chris Gehringer Of Sterling Sound: Mastering Engineer." *Sound On Sound*, available online at: www.soundonsound.com

Rosen, Steven. May 1977. "Interview With Jimmy Page." *Modern Guitars Magazine*. Available online at: www.modernguitars.com/archives/003340.html

Rudolph, Thomas E. and Leonard, Vincent A. 2001. *Recording In The Digital World: Complete Guide To Studio Gear and Software*. Boston: Berklee Press.

Ryan, Kevin and Kehew, Brian. 2008. *Recording The Beatles: The Studio Equipment And Techniques Used To Create Their Classic Albums*. Houston: Curvebender.

Schmidt-Horning, Susan. 2004. "Engineering The Performance", *Social Studies of Science*, 34/5, pp. 703–31.

Simons, David. 2004. *Studio Stories: How The Great New York Records Were Made*. San Francisco: Backbeat Books.

Stark, Scott Hunter. 2005. *Live Sound Reinforcement: A Comprehensive Guide To P.A. And Music Reinforcement Systems And Technology*. New Jersey: Thomson Course Technology.

Sterne, Jonathan. 2003. *The Audible Past: Cultural Origins Of Sound Reproduction*. Durham: Duke University Press.

Swedien, Bruce. 2009. *In The Studio With Michael Jackson*. New York: Hal Leonard.

Tamm, Eric. 1990. *Robert Fripp: From King Crimson To Guitar Craft*. New York: Faber and Faber.

Tamm, Eric. 1995. *Brian Eno: His Music And The Vertical Color Of Sound*. New York: Faber and Faber.

Taylor, Timothy. 2001. *Strange Sounds: Music, Technology, And Culture*. Berkeley: University of California Press.

Théberge, Paul. 1995. "What's That Sound? Listening To Popular Music, Revisited", in *Popular Music: Style And Identity*, eds. W. Straw, S. Johnson, R. Sullivan and P. Friedlander. Montreal: Centre for Research on Canadian Cultural Industries and Institutions, pp. 275–84.

Théberge, Paul. 1997. *Any Sound You Can Imagine: Making Music/Consuming Technology*. Middletown: Wesleyan University Press.

Thompson, Daniel. 2005. *Understanding Audio: Getting The Most Out Of Your Project Or Professional Recording Studio*. Boston: Berklee Press.

Toulson, Robert and Ruskin, Angelina. 2008. "Can We Fix It? — The Consequences Of 'Fixing It In The Mix' With Common Equalization Techniques Scientifically Evaluated", *Journal Of The Art Of Record Production*, 3/3, available online: www.artofrecordproduction.com.

Toynbee, Jason. 2000. *Making Popular Music: Musicians, Creativity And Institutions*. London: Arnold.

Vdovin, Marsha. November 2005. "Artist Interview: Philip Glass Producer Kurt Mankacsi." *Universal Audio Webzine*, available online at: www.uaudio.com/webzine/2005/november/text/content3.html

Wadhams, Wayne. 2001. *Inside The Hits: The Seduction Of A Rock And Roll Generation*. Boston: Berklee Press.

Walser, Robert. 1993. *Running With The Devil: Power, Gender And Madness In Heavy Metal*. Middletown: Wesleyan University Press.

Warner, Timothy. 2003. *Pop Music Technology And Creativity: Trevor Horn And The Digital Revolution*. Aldershot: Ashgate.

White, Glenn and Louie, Gary. 2005. *The Audio Dictionary*, 3rd Edition. Seattle: University of Washington Press.

White, Paul. 1998. *Music Technology: A Survivor's Guide*. London: Sanctuary Publishing Ltd.

White, Paul. March 2003. "More Of Everything! Maximizing The Loudness Of Your Masters." *Sound On Sound*, available online at: www.soundonsound.com

White, Paul. February 2009. "Creating A Sense Of Depth In Your Mix: Mix Processing Techniques." *Sound On Sound*, available online at: www.soundonsound.com

Williams, Alan. 2007. "Divide And Conquer: Power, Role Formation and Conflict in Recording Studio Architecture", *Journal Of The Art Of Record Production*, 1/1, available online: www.artofrecordproduction.com.

Zagorski-Thomas, Simon. 2005. "The US vs. The UK Sound." *Proceedings of The Art Of Record Production Conference*, London: 2005. Available online at: www.artofrecordproduction.com

Zak, Albin. 2001. *The Poetics Of Rock: Cutting Tracks, Making Music*. Berkeley: University of California Press.

Zak, Albin. 2007. "Editorial", *Journal Of The Art Of Record Production*, 2/2, available online: www.artofrecordproduction.com.

Index